First Edition 1935
Second Edition 1949
Reprinted 1958
Reprinted 1961
Reprinted 1965
Reprinted with additions 1979
Reprinted 1991

ISBN 7198 0062 5

Dedicated to my fellow members of the
Worshipful Company of Goldsmiths,
present and future, who are striving to
maintain the standard of good design and
workmanship in the precious metals

Printed and bound in Great Britain
by BPCC Wheatons Ltd, Exeter.

CONTENTS

PREFACE

THIS book, to which some additions of matter and illustrations have been made, is substantially identical with the first edition of 1935.

It should appeal to everyone in any way connected with, or interested in, silver in any shape or form. It attempts to explain the basic processes which are used by all workers in silver, from the individual artist craftsman to the trade employee in a factory where things are made by the hundred. Though no exhaustive account of machine and mass production methods is attempted, the principles underlying them are clearly given.

Craftsmen have always made use of appliances that will ease and speed their work. The introduction of mechanisms, first hand-operated and later power driven, has relieved them of much merely laborious and dull manual work. These helps must be used intelligently. Their powers and limitations must be understood thoroughly.

Certain methods of the handicraftsman do, undoubtedly, give better results, even on the purely utilitarian side; e.g., the superior strength of a hand raised vessel over one produced by spinning or stamping. But it is on the æsthetic side that the great superiority lies.

Under present-day social and economic conditions hand work can provide but a small part of the industry's output. Mechanical aids and processes are a necessity.

The improvement of commercial manufactures is our most urgent and immediate task. To reach any success a clear understanding of what may be called the idioms of the two methods, hand and machine, is essential. This book deals with the first named, but the writer trusts that in doing so he will have helped his readers to work out a solution of the problem of the second for themselves.

Trade workers of all ranks will find something to interest them. The young beginner may realize something of what he has to learn. The silversmith who has to specialize unduly may get a wider view of the industry than is possible within the restricted field in which he works. Though the fortunate, highly skilled, versatile silversmith, who is employed only on individual pieces, may find the book rudimentary on the technical side, he will be interested in its treatment of the problem of design.

The designer will be helped to understand the oneness of craftsmanship and design. He will be able to learn from the book the limits of drawn design, and to realize how many problems arise that cannot be solved until the designer can visualize, not only a drawing on paper, but the actual, concrete reality in three dimensions. He will often find great help from the knowledge of construction and of the functioning of various parts that the book gives.

The seller of silver wares will gain much understanding of the making and the designing of the wares he handles. He will be able to talk far more intelligently and convincingly about the things he sells. Is it too much to hope that the book will do something to raise the standard of design and craftsmanship? If the real worth of a piece of silver can be brought home to a buyer, he will be more ready to choose the right thing. The retailer and his whole staff will find themselves well repaid for time spent in study of the book. The purchaser of silver goods, if he can be induced to read certain parts, will be better able to sort out his likes and dislikes into some kind of order, and eventually to work out for himself a standard of taste.

The connoisseur and collector of, and the dealer in, old silver will find the book explains how the old silversmiths fashioned their wares. In consequence, they will be able to appreciate points that have hitherto escaped their notice. It cannot be too widely known that the silversmith's craft has, save for the introduction of gas for soldering, of mechanically operated rolls for producing sheet, and of power-driven polishing appliances, changed but little since the craft developed in the ancient world. The lathe for turning, and even spinning, was in use in days of the Pharaohs. Die-stamping is coeval with the craft itself.

The writer would assure his readers that all he advocates in the book has been thoroughly well tested in his actual teaching practice in the schools. He offers it to his fellow teachers and students in the hope that they will find many fruitful suggestions therein.

The book, though it treats of design, does so indirectly. The illustrations of actual pieces are suggestions only, intended to point out ways of approach to the problems presented. They should not be regarded as designs to be copied.

Short sections have been added on the two decorative processes of CHASING and SAW-PIERCING that can be attempted in their elementary stages with a degree of success. ENGRAVING and ENAMELLING call for many long hours of practice before any worth-while results can be achieved. It has been decided that these processes need separate treatment. It is hoped to issue books dealing with them at a later date.

BERNARD CUZNER
LONDON, 1948

A SILVERSMITH'S MANUAL

CHAPTER I

THE METAL—THE SILVERSMITH'S APPLIANCES

FOR more than thirty years the writer taught in the schools of art in Birmingham—the College of Art in Margaret Street and the School for Jewellers and Silversmiths in Vittoria Street—students of all ages, conditions, and capabilities along the lines laid down; so that he is able to claim that his methods and principles have been tested severely.

To those who are intimate with the craft as practised in trade workshops, much will seem extremely (perhaps even absurdly) simple. Of these instructed and initiated people the writer asks indulgence and sympathy for their less fortunate brethren.

The writer is well aware that there are many slight, and some considerable, differences between the practices of silversmiths in different centres. The Birmingham practice modified to the needs of a school is here taken.

I.—THE METAL

The following table gives the essential facts about silver:

Specific gravity of Silver:		
Fine (pure)	... ...	... 10·47
Standard	... ...	... 10·312
Melting point of Silver:		
Fine (pure)	... ...	962 deg. C.
Standard	... ...	890 deg. C.
Weight of cubic inch of Silver:		
Fine (pure)	... ...	5·52 oz. Troy
Standard	... ...	5·5 nearly
Composition of Standard Silver:		
Fine Silver	... ...	925 parts
Copper ...	... ...	75 parts
		1,000 *

Silver is weighed by troy weight. The old sub-division of the ounce is now discarded, and a decimal system, 0·1 oz. (2 dwt.) is in general use.

Pure silver is intensely white in colour, does not oxidize under any conditions, but when melted in air it occludes oxygen on solidification—the "spitting" of silver.

Except for a very few purposes, pure silver is little used, being far too soft. To make a useful alloy it is mixed with copper; it then becomes an ideal metal to work, and has a finer, richer colour than when pure. Hence comes the superiority of rolled "Sheffield" plate over modern electro-plate.

---

* "Britannia" silver 230 parts silver and 10 parts copper is used occasionally. It is softer and raises more easily than ·925 standard.

Silver may be bought from the refiner in sheet and wire. It may also be had as slitting—sheet $\frac{1}{8}$ inch or more in thickness, slit into long strips roughly square in section. It is usually convenient to have it in this form and to draw it down oneself into whatever kind of wire one needs.

Refiners, as a rule, will undertake to cast in silver from any pattern one may send them.

It is not wise practice to melt up, and use, scrap—snippings and cuttings—and lemel—filings—oneself. One never knows what impurities may creep in. Even if the standard of the metal remains untouched so that the work will pass unscathed through the Assay Office test, its working qualities will suffer.

From the refiner, too, one buys the solder, in sheet, and filed. Three grades of sheet solder are useful:

	SILVER per cent.	COPPER per cent.	ZINC per cent.
Hardest	82	14	4 *
Enamelling	77	17	6
Ordinary	67	24	9

These are most useful in long strips of sheet of about 8 metal gauge in thickness.

Filed solder is very occasionally needed.

The qualities to be sought in good solder are strength and malleability; a soldered seam should stand much hammering. Solder should not fret; that is, become pitted with tiny holes when raised to a heat near its melting-point. Lastly (this applies especially to the more fusible solder), it should flow cleanly, leaving no lumps.

The melting-points of silver solders, while so high as to take things made with it far beyond any reach of harm from anything that can happen to them in common use, are not so high that they need temperatures beyond the reach of simple appliances.

When properly handled, standard silver has almost every conceivable good quality that a non-ferrous metal can have.

It combines strength, malleability, and ductility to an extreme degree.

Its colour is far, far richer than that of any other white metal; and its associations are so beautiful that one feels it something like sacrilege to force it into unworthy forms, or to put it to base uses.

There is but one flaw in standard silver. In working it is difficult to prevent the oxide of the alloyed copper from forming patches of duller colour. These are known as fire marks. With care they can be avoided, or reduced to such a minimum as to be practically unnoticeable, but they cannot be avoided entirely without considerable trouble. This point is dealt with later.

* These proportions are often varied. Some makers' hardest solder is 80 per cent. silver 20 per cent. copper. Very occasionally an easily fusible solder, containing a little tin, is useful in completing a work which has already many solderings.

II.—THE SILVERSMITH'S APPLIANCES

Illustrations of appliances and tools not shown in line drawings can be found in any good tool dealer's catalogue.

What is here specified is an equipment that would allow of the production of the pieces commonly made by the silversmith.

However, no one need wait until he can have everything shown, neither

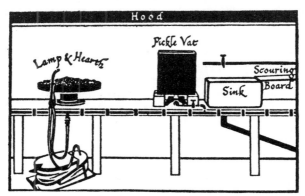

FIG. I.—*Layout of a silversmith's bench for soldering, annealing, pickling, etc.*

need one hesitate to use such makeshifts as common sense suggests. A glazed earthenware pan and cold pickle will be slower but just as efficient as the more convenient gas-heated lead vat. A piece of stout iron gas- or water-pipe filed smooth and polished with emery cloth will serve as a side stake. From an engineer's scrap-heap all sorts of useful stakes and such like can be got at a trifling cost. So one might go on.

Fig. 1.—The "lamp,"* or blowpipe, shown is the type usual in Birmingham. A convenient size for general work has a gas supply of ⅜ inch. A tap to regulate the air supply is an advantage, though not essential. Good soft rubber flex-pipe is better than metallic. The flame is regulated by gripping the lever more or less tightly. The hearth or annealing pan should be from 15 inches to 20 inches in diameter. It should revolve easily, but should be rigid and free from wobble. That shown in the drawing is of cast iron, but very efficient ones are made of thick sheet iron. The pan is filled with coke breeze, well burned, about the size of a walnut. Firebrick slabs about 12 inches by 12 inches by 2 inches with one side corrugated are most useful for work needing support on a flat surface. The foot bellows should be amply large, thus avoiding too much exertion to keep a steady air blast.† The top of the annealing pan should be about 3 feet 6 inches above floor level.

---

* "Lamp" would seem to have survived from the time when the smaller solderings were actually done with the flame of a lamp.

† Very efficient small simple blowers electrically driven are obtainable. These are, in many ways, better than bellows.

The pickle vat should be of stout lead, the corners well burned, not soldered, of a convenient size for the work undertaken. It is heated by a gas-ring, which should have a gentle flame. The pickle itself is diluted sulphuric acid—about 20 parts water to 1 of acid. (*Caution:* In mixing acid and water, add acid to water. It is dangerous to add water to acid.) As the pickle evaporates it is filled up with water. Acid is added when the pickle weakens.

It is well to have a sink with water supply fixed close to the pickle vat so that all traces of acid may be washed quickly away. The board for scouring is convenient.

If possible, all hearths and pickle vats should be fixed under a hood so that fumes shall be carried off. Provision should also be made under the hood for a gas-ring for melting pitch, etc.

If there are but one or two workers, the hood may be dispensed with.

A silversmith's bench should be at least 2 inches thick, preferably of beech or some hard wood. It should be very rigidly fixed, and be fitted with provision for a jeweller's peg and skin.* To it must be fixed a strong and heavy smith's *Leg Vice;* 56 lb. is the lightest that will stand the strain of work of any size. The bench should afford at one point a clear length of 3 feet so that bench work may be carried out in comfort. The height of the bench may vary according to personal convenience; 3 feet is a standard. The lighting of the benches needs careful arrangement.

Stools of a suitable height: low for use when filing on the peg; high when assembling work.

A small pair of rolls, and a draw bench (Fig. 2), though not absolutely

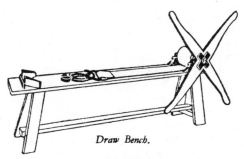

Draw Bench.

FIG. 2.—*For wire drawing.*

necessary, are of the greatest convenience, especially when working far away from a bullion dealer's warehouse.

A plain lathe of from $4\frac{1}{2}$ inches to 6 inches centre is also a great help, especially if power-driven.

These are fixed appliances.

There are also a number of movable appliances in common use. The most important of these are the following: *Steadies,* sections of tree trunks,

---

* A tray of tin plate, or thin wood, to catch filings, etc., may be used instead of the leather skin.

almost any wood will serve, about 2 feet to 2 feet 6 inches high and from 1 foot 6 inches diameter to any convenient size; with holes and depressions cut in them in which stakes may be fixed and metal may be shaped. *Sandbags*, round cushions of stout leather filled with dry sand.

The novice silversmith will find that there are certain materials so important that he must always have them on hand for use at any time. Indeed, suitable materials are as important as suitable tools. The number enumerated below is a minimum, and it will be realized that other metals may also prove useful for work of special kinds.

Scrap Lead, about 14 lb., and an iron ladle to melt it in. This is run into blocks about 5 inches square by 1 inch thick. A smaller quantity of tin cast into a similar block is also useful.

Sheet Metal for various purposes is needed. A few pounds of 8, 10, and 12 metal gauge, 12 inches wide, brass or gilding metal sheet, will be ample.

Soft Iron "Binding Wire" for securing parts to be soldered together. .048 inch, .036 inch, and .028 inch are useful sizes. 1 lb. of each S.W.G. equivalents 18, 20, 22.

Metal Wire from $\frac{3}{16}$ inch to $\frac{1}{16}$ inch diameter in brass and nickel silver—a few feet of, say, six sizes. Included should be some $\frac{1}{16}$ inch 50 per cent. copper 50 per cent. spelter wire for brazing.

Cast Steel Rod, square and round, from $\frac{1}{2}$ inch to $\frac{1}{8}$ inch, say 1 lb. of six different sizes, and about 2 feet 6 inches of oblong section $\frac{5}{8}$ inch by $\frac{1}{2}$ inch for tool making should be provided. Bright "silver steel" rods for drills, etc., are also most useful.

FIG. 3.—*Heads, of malleable cast iron. Three useful shapes, each about* 2¼ *inches across.*

Usual shop tools are: *Flat Dies*, one cast iron 12 inches by 12 inches or larger, about 1 inch thick, planed flat and true on one face and four edges, and a smaller one steel-faced about 3 inches square. An ordinary domestic flat iron is an excellent makeshift. *Mandrels* or *Ring Stakes* of cast iron, turned true and smooth, tapering from 10 inches or 12 inches at the larger to 2 inches or so at the smaller end. Smaller ones, often known as *Triblets*, from 2¼ inches to 1 inch, and from 1¼ inches to $\frac{3}{8}$ inch, are also needed.

Draw Plates for wire of different sizes and sections. A range of round holes from 0·25 inch to 0·01 inch is advisable. Other shapes need not range so widely.

A *Swage Block* (Fig. 36), with several dies giving wires and mouldings of complicated sections is most useful. An old set of stock and dies, if large, can be easily adapted to this purpose.

Heads.—Fig. 3 (*a*), (*b*), and (*c*) show three extremely useful shapes which are very conveniently made of malleable cast iron. Where expense is no object, or where the heads are to be in very constant use, wrought steel is better. The shanks are ¾ inch square by about 1 inch long.

Bottom stakes, so called because they have long shanks or stems enabling their faces to reach the bottoms of deep vessels.

FIG. 4.—*Bottom Stakes, to reach the bottom of deep vessels. Three standard shapes.*

Fig. 4 shows three standard shapes. Two sizes of (*a*) are needed, a small one with a 1½-inch face and a larger one with a 3-inch face. A piece of old shafting filed true on the end serves admirably for the smaller size. Mushroom-shaped heads, as (*b*), of different sizes and degrees of convexity, and cushion-shaped heads, with sides somewhat flattened, as (*c*), are essential. The length of bottom stakes should exceed 7 inches. Heads such as are shown in Fig. 3 are fixed in upright holders (a piece of iron pipe hammered square does quite well) and used as bottom stakes.

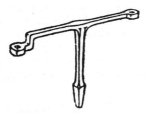

FIG. 5.—*A horse used in a steady block to hold heads. About 21 inches across.*

FIG. 6.—*A crank, fastened in a vice, and used to hold heads. Each arm is about 8 inches long.*

A Horse (Fig. 5), having a tapered square end to its shaft, which fits into a square hole cut in a steady block, and a *Crank* (Fig. 6), which is fastened in a vice, are used to hold heads. The ends with the double bend are used when raising and hammering vessels with mouths much smaller than their greatest diameters.

Cranked Stakes, two types of which are shown in Figs. 7 and 8, are extremely useful. A stake of the form of A Fig. 7, is known as a *Side Stake.**

---

* D Fig. 14 shows a more generally useful form of curved side stake.

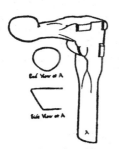

FIG. 7.—*A side stake. The arms are about 8 to 10 inches long.*

FIG. 8.—*Another type of cranked stake. The end A is known as a cow's tongue.*

Stakes of the form of A, Fig. 8, are known as *Cow's Tongues*. The arms of the cranks are about 8 inches or 10 inches long. These stakes are easily and conveniently made by filing up a pattern in wood and having them cast in

FIG. 9.—*Another stake, known as throw-back tool.*

malleable iron. The working surfaces should, of course, be filed and polished smooth.

Fig. 9 shows a stake, sometimes known as *Throw-back Tool*. This is used for shaping the necks of vessels. It should be about 2½ inches wide. If to the stakes already named are added a jeweller's *Sparrow-hawk* and its larger relative, a tinman's *Beck-iron*, the workshop will be adequately equipped for simple work. In actual practice all manner of unlikely pieces of iron and steel will be made to serve. Indeed, in every silversmith's workshop will be found numbers of things looking as if they were only scrap iron. For some time

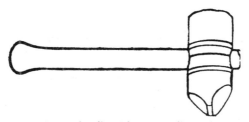

FIG. 10.—*Boxwood mallet with corners well rasped and filed.*

it may be necessary to make cast-iron heads of the type shown in Fig. 3 for each fresh type of form one raises and hammers. These are cast in malleable iron from plaster or wooden pattern.

A Tinman's Boxwood Mallet,* as shown in Fig. 10, about 2½ inches diameter, and a smaller one about 1¾ inches diameter cut and filed as drawn. Before using a mallet, care should be taken to rasp and file off corners to an obtuse angle. If this is not done, pieces will soon split off and spoil the tool. Mallets of buffalo horn are also extremely useful.

Although the mallet is the best tool for a beginner to use in raising, a hammer, such as that shown in Fig. 11*a*, about 4 inches long and weighing about 5 to 7 oz., is superior in practised hands. Beyond a *Raising Hammer*,

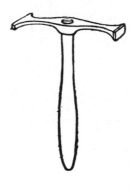

Fig. 11*a* (above).—*Hammer for raising,
shown in side and top view.*
Fig. 11*b* (below).—*Planishing hammer.
Heads about 3½ inches long.*

Fig. 11*c*.—*A neck or collet hammer
about one quarter actual size. The head is
from 4 inches to 7 inches long.*

are needed *Planishing Hammers*, Fig. 11*b*, weighing 3 to 5 or 6 oz., and *Neck* or *Collet Hammers*, of the type shown in Fig. 11*c*, will be wanted. These are needed in varying sizes and shapes. Some will have thicker and some thinner faces. Some will have their curves flatter and some rounder. Hammers of similar shape with heads more or less hemispherical are desirable.

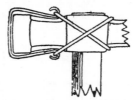

Fig. 11*d*.—*Side view of a "packed" or "spring-faced" hammer. The actual packings of Italian
cloth, next the hammer, and paper between hammer and spring are not shown.*

Trade workers make much use of "spring-faced," "steeled" or "packed" hammers. These are ordinary hammers on which steel springs, about ·035 inches thick, with a packing of a soft, closely-woven cotton, "Italian" cloth and paper, between the actual hammer face and the inner side of the spring. These are fastened firmly with strong binding wire, Fig. 11*d*.

* Lignum-vitæ is often used. It is not quite as good as boxwood.

These hammers enable us to strike a strong blow without leaving the slightest trace. They are used where a perfectly smooth surface is desired, or where it is necessary to rectify the form of a previously hammered surface.

In the early exercises to be given in this primer the only hammer needed will be an ordinary "Warrington" pattern hammer of about 3 oz., such as can be bought anywhere. If the cross pane, as the end opposite to the face is called, should be too thin, it can easily be ground away till a sufficient thickness is reached. Ball-pane engineer's hammers are also most useful. A larger one, about 12 oz., or even heavier, is needed for forging, striking big punches and chisels. Hammers for planishing should never be used for any other purpose.

If one finds a hammer with a convex face is needed, take a Warrington or ball-pane hammer, and grind the face to the required curve.*

An intelligent blacksmith will make any special hammer one needs, if one first makes a wooden model to guide him.

Large, long-handled *Draw Pliers* for drawing wire, and *Pliers* of the usual Lancashire type are needed. Flat square nose, flat snipe nose, half-round snipe nose, and round nose, all 4½ inches to 5 inches, should be provided. Light *Iron Tongs* for use in soldering, and a pair of *Copper Tongs* for use in pickling are very desirable. *Corn Tongs*, or large tweezers, are indispensable when soldering.

Hand Vices and *Slide Pliers* are needed. A small parallel *Bench Vice* is also useful.

A *Joint Leveller* for use in making hinge joints.

Shears.—A pair of 10-inch straight, a pair of 8-inch crooked, and a pair of *Dentist's Shears* are needed.

Files.—Those in most general use are: 6-inch three-square and half-round smooth; 6-inch three-square and half-round super; 6-inch flat, hand or pillar, second cut; and for use on larger work, filing stakes, punches, chisels, and such like, 10-inch flat, hand, smooth; 12-inch three-square, rough; for shaping mallets and any wood, 12-inch half-round rasp; 8-inch half-round cabinet rasp. All should be suitably handled.

Scorpers or *gravers* for cutting away surplus solder.

Saws.—A *Hack Saw* of the usual kind; use fine rather than coarse-toothed blades. A *Back Saw*, rather larger and coarser than a jeweller would use.

A *Saw Frame* for piercing saws; one deeper than 6 inches is rarely needed. The most useful saws for the silversmith are Nos. 1 to 4.

Needle Files.—All shapes are useful. 14 cm. is a standard length. Fine and coarse cuts of each shape should be provided.

Drill Stocks.—A jeweller's upright drill stock with a fairly heavy bob and a split chuck and a "Millers Falls" side-wheel drill stock are needed.

Drills.—Diamond or spear-pointed drills are best made as they are wanted. Ready-made ones are usually too fragile. For holes larger than about $\frac{3}{32}$ inch, twist drills are best.

Oil Stone.—Arkansas stones are excellent.

Stock and Dies.—Whitworth thread from $\frac{1}{16}$ inch to $\frac{1}{4}$ inch are more suitable for silver than the finer B.A. and B.S.F.

---

* Long-headed ball-faced hammers [see Figs. 3 and 17 (11)] are very useful. Most good tool shops stock them.

Measuring Tools needed are:

A 12-inch *Steel Rule* divided on both edges to $\frac{1}{8}$ inch and $\frac{1}{16}$ inch with some inches further divided to $\frac{1}{64}$ inch. An *L Square;* those made by "Stanley" for carpenters' use are excellent.

Starrett Dividers, a pair about 8 inches long, and a smaller pair 3 inches to 4 inches long.

Callipers, inside and outside.

Pencil Compasses.—These should be heavy brass.

A *Scribing Block.*—The simplest kinds are very serviceable.

A *Metal Gauge Plate.*—The gauges are based on the weights of copper sheets 10 mg., a usual gauge of silver for ordinary purposes is ·028 inch thick; ·030 inch and ·035 inch are useful gauges. The 4 feet by 2 feet by ·028 inch copper sheet weighs 10 lb.

A *Spindle*, preferably power-driven; the labour of polishing work of any size on a foot lathe is excessive. The writer prefers a slower speed than the ordinary electric spindle gives. From 1,000 to 1,500 revolutions per minute would seem to be less drastic than the usual 2,500. The power spindle, used wisely, is a most useful appliance, but the silversmith must not rely on it to obliterate marks of unskilful workmanship.

On the spindle are used *Bristle Brushes* of various shapes; the most useful are ordinary two-row circular of 4 inches to 6 inches diameter, and end brushes with a tuft of bristles about $1\frac{1}{2}$ inches long and 1 inch diameter. A good material to use with these is levigated powdered pumice and oil. Compositions of a stiff grease mixed with fine emery powder, crocus—a form of iron oxide—or sand moulded into bars are all good. Felt and leather bobs are indispensable for certain purposes. These vary in shape from thin discs to cones and spheres, and in size from $\frac{1}{2}$ to 6 or more inches in diameter.

The trade polisher uses bobs with Trent sand for most work, but they are not recommended for the all-round craftsman.

Polishing materials used by hand are *Emery Cloth, Glass Paper, Pumice Stone* of fine grain, *"Water of Ayr" Stone,** Leather Buffs.*

For finishing, that is, putting the final sheen on silver, we need *Mops* of chamois leather, calico, swansdown, and wool of various shapes and sizes. On these we shall use *Tripoli Composition, Chalk,* and *Rouge.*

Brushes, for scouring work in progress, and for washing finished work with soap and hot water.

The following must be provided: *Sulphuric Acid; Powdered Pumice; Sodium Pyroborate,* or *Borax* in lump and powder, is the almost universal flux or reducing agent used in hard soldering—when fused it dissolves metallic oxides A piece of *Smooth Slate* for rubbing; a *Glass Pot* for mixing; *"Pencils", Camel Hair Brushes*, for applying borax and water; *Charcoal*, for small soldering, blocks of willow charcoal are best; *Loam,†* a fine earth used by metal founders; *Tallow; Oil*, any good machine oil; *Paraffin*, for removing grease (also to clean the oil stone); *Emery sticks*, and strips of wood for covering with emery cloth; *Soap* and *Soda*, for washing greasy work; *Sawdust*, for drying work; *Rag*, the more absorbent the better; *Cotton Waste; Liver of Sulphur*, in $\frac{1}{4}$-lb. tins, for darkening silver; *Modelling Wax*, $\frac{1}{2}$ lb.

* A kind of slate, easily filed to shape, used with water. The slime, as it forms, is easily wiped away with a damp rag.
† To keep solder from running into places that must be free, paint with a thin mixture of loam and water.

CHAPTER 2

MALLEABILITY

EXERCISE 1 : A SIMPLE BOWL

THE ACTUAL WORKMANSHIP

LET us look for a moment at a few familiar instances of craftsmen in action, so that we may learn a little of the mental and physical state that is essential to the production of fine work. Think of a violinist, with his whole being concentrated on the action of fingers, hands, and body on his fiddle, with ears tense to tell him that his instrument is no longer a thing of wood and gut, but is a very part of his inmost soul. Think of a fine player of any game of skill. Of how his bat or club or racquet or cue, or whatever he may use, makes the ball obey his will. Or of how all the members of a group of well-trained dancers will make every fibre of their being move in perfect rhythm, so that their dance becomes a part of the eternal order of Nature.

Metals have three outstanding properties that distinguish them from all other substances. They are malleable, fusible, ductile. Metals are crystalline in structure. When subjected to strain as in cold working, the silversmiths' normal practise, the crystals are distorted, the metal hardens and becomes difficult to work. To restore its softness it is annealed, *i.e.*, heated to about 600 deg. centigrade, a dull red, when the strain is relieved and the crystals revert to their original shapes.

In working this exercise we learn that metals are malleable.

Any of the exercises given may be worked out in gilding metal, if it should be thought that silver is too costly for first attempts.

A Bowl.—Let us begin by making a simple bowl. That shown is a good model for a learner to follow; but if after studying the following instructions it is felt that an easier exercise is advisable, we may aim at making a simple hemisphere.

Begin by making a rough full-size sketch. This will help to get the idea of what one would like to make more clearly defined in one's mind. We shall not at first attempt to follow what we put down on paper at all closely, for two reasons: (*a*) the effort to beat up the bowl from a flat sheet of metal will tax us sufficiently, without the added trouble of working rigidly to size and shape; and (*b*) it is most important that we should understand how small a part the mere drawing on paper plays in the fashioning of a piece of silver-work. In the early stages we ask little more of a drawing than that it should help us to determine the size and general proportion—diameter in relation to height, and such like.

A bowl of 5 inches diameter and 2¼ inches high is a suitable size.

To determine the diameter of the blank, the theoretically accurate way is to calculate the surface area of our bowl and take a circular disc of the same area. In actual practice we take the average diameter of the vessel to be made, add to it the height, and thus find the diameter of the blank. For almost all purposes this is sufficiently accurate. Sometimes one has to use one's judgment as to whether to increase or decrease the diameter thus determined. In our case $7\frac{1}{2}$ inches is right. Take a piece of metal size 10 in the metal gauge. Scour bright so that any defects shall be clearly visible. If it is blistered, or shows signs of having been rolled from a faulty ingot,

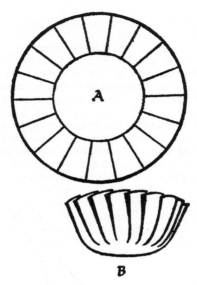

FIG. 12.—(A) *Disc with radial slits cut for making a bowl.*
(B) *Strips bent to overlap.*

discard it. Upon this metal describe a circle with the dividers with a radius of $3\frac{3}{4}$ inches. Cut this out with the shears, using extreme care to ensure accuracy and to avoid leaving any jags or spikes. Remove the sharp arris, or edge, left from the shears with a smooth file. (If this is not done, the fingers will suffer.) Strike a circle of $1\frac{5}{8}$ inches radius from the centre of the disc with the dividers, and all is ready. Great care must be taken when using dividers on metal that is to be raised. The points of dividers must not be too sharp, and must be applied lightly. Deep scratching will injure the work.

To understand what happens in raising, the beginner should take a disc of metal, A in Fig. 12, mark a circle for a base, and cut a series of radial slits from the edge to this circle. We shall then be able to bend each piece between the cuts upwards. This gives us something like a bowl, but instead of its sides being all of a piece, they are formed of overlapping strips (B in Fig. 12). By raising, we can change a flat disc of metal *into a bowl without cutting these slits.*

To understand still more clearly what has to be done in raising, cut a strip of metal $\frac{1}{4}$ inch wide and about 4 inches long. Mark it across its width at intervals of $\frac{3}{8}$ inch. Put a head (choose one not too rounded) into the vice. Hold the strip, with the lowest mark resting over the corner of the head, at an angle of about 45 degrees. Tap the strip with a mallet. Repeat this again, lowering the strip by $\frac{3}{8}$ inch, striking it at a point $\frac{1}{4}$ inch or so in front of the point where it rests on the head, and so on until the straight strip has become curved. When the strip and the slotted disc were bent, they yielded to a slight touch; but when we try the disc without cutting we find that we have to use very considerable force. Not only have we to hit quite hard, but we shall find it hard to hold the disc against the blows of the mallet. What we do then in raising is to make the metal change its shape. It flows under the rain of blows from a flat sheet to a hollow bowl.

To begin the actual raising. Take the disc, hold it on a wooden steady or a sandbag at the angle shown in Fig. 13, and with a round-headed hammer, or a mallet with a rounded end, striking evenly around the edge of the disc, and aiming blows at about $\frac{1}{2}$ inch within the edge; turn up the edge as shown in the figure. The object of this slight working on the inner side of the disc (a reversal of the principle involved in raising) is to hold the rim stiff while being raised.

For the beginner, it is perhaps as well to anneal* the disc at this stage. Here a caution is needed. The constituents of a metallic alloy, such as gilding metal or standard silver, have differing coefficients of expansion, so that the application of heat sets up strains within the metal itself. If, therefore, we heat our disc too quickly, we run some risk of weakening or even cracking the metal.

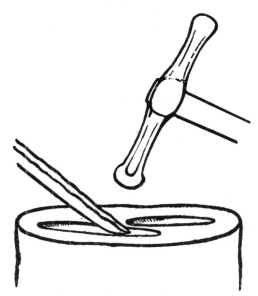

FIG. 13.—*Turning up edge of disc.*

Place the disc with the upturned edge downwards on the hearth,† either on the breeze or the flat firebrick; then turn on the gas fully and play it for

* Do not overheat. After 600° C.—a dull red heat—has been reached, no further softening takes place.
† This position avoids any risk of borax or any dirt that may get on the hearth adhering to the raising when heated. Time that may have to be spent in removing these is thus saved.

a few seconds on the disc without any air blast, turning the hearth slowly round. As the metal gets hot, blow gently with a large soft flame (that is, much gas and little air), taking care that the heat is distributed evenly. Take it to a dull red heat, keep it at this temperature for, say, half a minute, then plunge into a vessel of cold water big enough to ensure instant and complete immersion. This is "quenching." It gives a maximum degree of softness. Dry the raising carefully; if made just hot enough to avoid burned fingers any remaining moisture is easily wiped off; or we may put the raising in a box of dry sawdust, preferably warm. If the large vessel of water is not available gradually decrease the heat. Do not take the flame away until all traces of red have disappeared. Even beyond that, it is well to apply a small flame with little or no air blast until the disc is comparatively cool. When annealing silver, especially in a strong light, great care is needed. Silver shows little change of colour until it reaches a temperature but little below the melting-point.

For the beginner working in gilding metal, the disc should be pickled clean. If silver is used, there is no need to do this.

With a pair of pencil compasses strike a series of circles from the centre of the disc, the first one $\frac{1}{2}$ inch outside the circle marked for the base, the others increasing in radius by $\frac{1}{2}$ inch.

Look carefully at Fig. 14 (A). Note where the disc rests on the head. The base circle marks the point of contact. Aiming a blow with the mallet at the point indicated, the metal will crease in. Turn the metal slowly round, taking care that the point of contact with the head follows the circle exactly, and as it turns strike with steady strokes along the circle on which we started. When the first circle has been completed our raising will look like B. Now give it another course around, this time striking about $\frac{1}{2}$ inch farther from the centre. Repeat this until the edge is reached, and we shall have something like C. The raising will need to be annealed each time the rim is reached. It will be apparent that for each circle of mallet blows the raising is drawn backwards from the head, thus bringing the point at which the mallet falls nearer the edge or rim of our raising.

One difficulty for the beginner is the sensing of the position of the head. It cannot be seen through the metal, and to strike the metal wrongly will do nothing but jar our left hand as it holds the raising. Another is to realize the correct angle at which to hold the metal. If the raising be tilted too much we jar our hand, if too little we waste our mallet blow.

However, a little practice will teach us how to hold and how to strike, and we shall soon have the pleasure of watching the crease travel outwards under our steady blows and our flat disc change to a bowl deepening and narrowing with each course. We must remember that the outer edge contains very much the greater part of the metal, so that progress will seem slower. Also, by the time we approach the rim the metal will have grown much harder, and we shall find that our blows have to be delivered at closer intervals. When we start we can take $\frac{1}{2}$ inch courses. At the edge they will be less than $\frac{1}{4}$ inch.

A point of great importance is that the raising should be done with the centre of the mallet face. Beginners are very apt to strike with the corner. This is very obviously the weakest part of the mallet, consequently it wears away very rapidly, thus needing constant rasping and filing up.

Another most important point is that the handle of the mallet be kept, as it rises and falls, in a line with the centre of the head; and in the case of a side-stake, or other long stake, in a line with the long axis.

Caution.—The writer has found that students are very likely, once they find that they can raise a piece of metal, to go too fast. They attempt to take

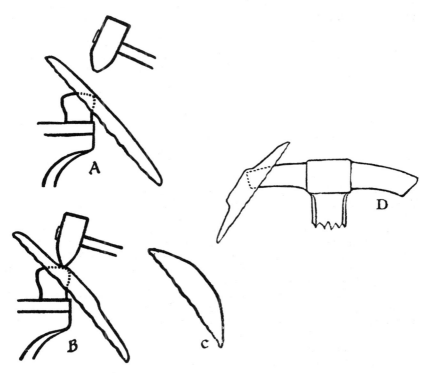

FIG. 14.—(A) *shows disc resting on bead.* (B) *shows raising after completing first circle.* (C) *shows the shape attained after several courses.* (D) *Raising on a side stake, the usual and best head for starting a raising.*

the metal in too quickly, and as a result the rim of the raising develops deep folds and crinkles. Often they are so deep as to overlap. An expert can sometimes remove them, but if a student, working alone, finds this happening he will be well advised to scrap his raising and begin again.

Our raising having taken a shape as at C (Fig. 14), we look at it carefully to find out if it is the shape of the lower part of the bowl we set out to make. If the angle the sides make with the flat bottom is too obtuse, we repeat the process again—as a silversmith says, we give it another course.

When we are satisfied that the form is right, we test our raising for accuracy. To do this, flatten the base, as shown in VI (Fig. 17), but use a flat-faced mallet in place of the hammer there shown. It may help if we flatten our base from the inside, standing it on the flat surface plate and using either a large boxwood punch or a mallet with a long head that will reach to the bottom of the raising. Do not hit too hard, or the base will stretch and refuse to lie flat. The raising should now rest evenly when put on the flat surface plate or die. If it does not, tap lightly with a mallet or a rounded hammer on those parts that protrude. These irregularities can be located easily by rubbing the bowl to and fro on the iron plate, when the bumps will show bright. With a scribing block we now mark a series of lines at about ½-inch

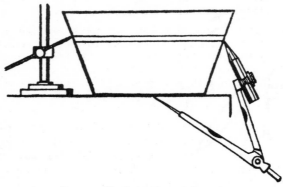

FIG. 15.—*Testing accuracy of the raising.*

intervals. For a beginner, it is perhaps as well to bind a pencil to the needle of the scribing block so as to avoid any risk of scratching.

Now, with a pair of pencil compasses, strike a series of circles on the bowl. If we have raised truly, these circles will run exactly parallel to those made by the scribing block (Fig. 15).

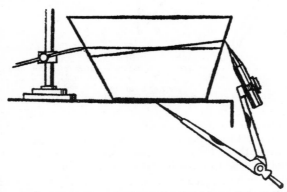

FIG. 16.— *Faulty Raising shown by difference between compass line and scribed line.*

If, however, our raising has not been done evenly, we shall see that where we have taken in the metal too far, the compass line will come above the scribed line; and where we have failed to raise our metal to the right angle, the compass line will come below (Fig. 16).

We shall find it a quite simple matter to remedy this error. Notice very carefully where the angle made by the sides of the bowl with the base is too obtuse. Here the compass line will be lowest.

If we now begin to raise at this point, where the error is greatest, and instead of going all around the bowl as usual we raise gently, first towards one side and then towards the other, the angle will come right. We shall, of course, be careful to decrease the strength of our blows as we get farther away from the error point. We shall also be careful to mete out exactly the same measure of blows on the right-hand side of the error point that we gave to the metal on the left-hand side of that point.

Here one must, of course, use some common sense. Sometimes one will find that the courses of raising have not been concentric with the original circle struck for the base. Sometimes a vigorous malleting with the flat end of the boxwood mallet with the raising held on a stake, as the unlettered arm of Fig. 8, will bring it right. Sometimes what is wrong can be put right by bending certain parts of the raising with thumbs and fingers, or a judicious squeezing between both hands, using one's knees if extra force is needed.

For the final shaping of the bowl, turn to Fig. 17 (I).

Here we see the shape of the raising at the end of the first stage.

Put a side-stake in the vice. (Note that the corner is very distinctly rounded.) Mark clearly with a pencil a line at the point where the mouth of the bowl is to begin to curve inwards.

Now with the mallet begin to raise inwards until the bowl assumes the shape shown by the lower of the two dotted lines.

The bowl is now like that shown in the continuous outline in Fig. 17 (II); here it rests on a sandbag. The bulge is caused by jarring action of edge of stake.

II shows how this bulge is removed by tapping from the inside. It could be removed equally well by malleting from the outside on a stake of the right form, but the method shown is better for a beginner.

At this stage any irregularities of form should be remedied with a perfectly smooth flat-ended mallet, using it exactly as the hammer in III and IV. Do not attempt to make any sharp angles. Be careful to use stakes with rounded edges. Now anneal your raising and pickle it until it is perfectly clean; if of silver, it should be quite white. Dry it carefully in sawdust or with a clean towel. See that no particle of dust, dirt, or grit is left on it.

The extreme edge, or rim, of our bowl must now be made level and true, parallel with the base.

Stand the bowl on the flat surface plate, see that it rests evenly without rocking, set the needle of the scribing block at the lowest point of the rim, and mark a clear line around it. Then, holding the bowl with its mouth towards us, we cut the ragged surplus edge away. For vessels whose rims make an angle of 90 degrees or less with their bases, straight shears will serve perfectly; but for vessels with incurving rims we may find crooked shears better, especially if the incurve is very great.

The rim may now be levelled. If very uneven, the projections may need a file to remove them—use a smooth one. If cut accurately, all that will be needed is rubbing on a sheet of emery cloth (No. 2 is a useful grade) laid on

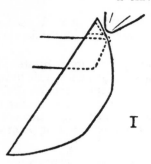

FIG. 17.—(I).

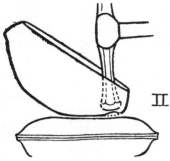

FIG. 17.—(II) *Removing bulge in the bowl from inside.*

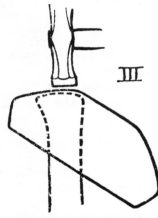

FIG. 17.—(III) *Planishing or smoothing the surface with flat-faced hammer.*

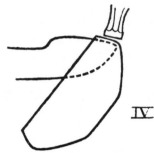

FIG. 17.—(IV) *Planishing the mouth of bowl.*

FIG. 17.—(V) *Outward contour of lip of bowl is made with help of groove in boxwood block.*

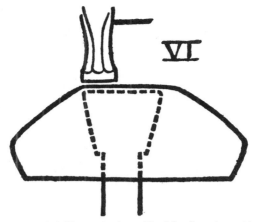

FIG. 17.—(VI) *Hammering base of bowl flat from the outside.*

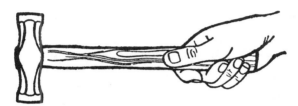

FIG. 17.—(VII) *The right grip when planishing.*

the flat surface plate; or, better still, the emery cloth, blue back for choice, can be glued on a perfectly flat board.

We are now ready to *planish* the bowl. Before starting this, study Fig. 17 (VII) carefully, noting the right grip to adopt for the sensitive blows needed for planishing.

Hammer blows of the accuracy needed by the silversmith are delivered from the wrist only. The upper arm should be pressed tightly against the body. The elbow should not move at all. It will be seen at once that a steady stance is necessary, and that the height of the work is a matter of great importance.

Before beginning on the bowl it is well to put a flat stake, like that shown in Fig. 4 (A), in the vice at such a height that when one stands naturally and rests a flat-faced hammer on it the stail, or handle, is horizontal.

Take a bit of scrap metal and strike it with the hammer until you can do it with precision without pecking it, *i.e.*, leaving the imprint of the corner of the hammer face.* As soon as you can use a hammer with some confidence you can go on with the bowl itself.

* The term "flat-faced," when applied to hammers, needs qualifying. Actually the face has a very distinct fullness, and the corners are rounded off.

First polish the face of the hammer as bright as possible. OO emery paper, or crocus powder on a leather buff stick, is good for this.

Now draw a clear pencil line with the compasses on the base. Beyond this, at intervals of $\frac{1}{2}$ inch, draw other circles up to the rim.

Put a head, or bottom stake, such as is shown in Fig. 17 (III), in the vice, hold the bowl upon it, give it a gentle tap with the bright hammer face. One will soon find one's place, as it were—that is, the point which is in actual contact with the stake, where the hammer will give a sound of falling on solid metal, and where it will produce the characteristic facet of hammered work.

Move both work and hammer about, still tapping gently, until one finds the hammer makes its proper facet as nearly as possible on the corner which has already been marked by the compass line

We now have to make our right and left hands work together. While the hammer is covering the lowest segment of the bowl with even facets as it falls, the left hand must be turning the bowl steadily round. Aim at leaving a truly circular ring of bright hammer marks just touching our compass line. This done, we aim our blows a little higher up. Fig. 17 (III) shows exactly the position for the second course—in the first, the hammer would be a little nearer the base and its face would be tilted slightly. Thus we go on, letting the hammer move up and down a little so that the rows of hammer blows overlap and merge into each other, until we reach the upper corner or point where the incurving of the mouth of the bowl begins. This again should be marked with a clear pencil compass line.

By this time we shall find ourselves wondering how, with such seemingly simple and mechanically inefficient tools we can make an accurately circular vessel, and how this vessel can be so smooth and even in surface. *Given an even strength of hammer blows and a head that approaches very nearly the curve of the vessel, such a result is inevitable.* If we are in any doubt as to the rightness of our tool, we look inside the bowl after our first course or two of hammering. If the inside is smooth we know that we have chosen wisely, if it shows too clearly the imprint of the head we know that our stake is too curved, or full, as the silversmith says.

If we detect any irregularities with our eyes, we go over the depressions with our hammer until the expansion of the metal lifts them up. Should the bumps or bulges caused by too vigorous hammering be obviously too high, the bowl must be annealed and the whole thing reshaped by raising with the mallet. This is, of course, done quite gently; a far, far smaller amount of force is needed than in ordinary raising. Beyond the defects apparent to the eye, our sense of touch will detect the slightest deviation from accurate and pleasant curvature. A well-raised and hammered bowl should be as pleasant to feel as it is to look upon.

Until we begin to hammer the incurving rim, the strength of our hammer blows is not a matter of the utmost nicety; but from the outset it is well to realize that really hard blows are rarely needed for planishing unless the work is very large and the metal very thick. In teaching young boys, the writer, exaggerating somewhat as one so often has to do in enforcing a point, tells them that if they are afraid to put their finger under the hammer they will know they are hitting too hard. Just as in raising we shall find that some considerable amount of practice is needed to hold whatever we are making while we planish it. Sometimes one finds that the fore-finger held against the side of the stake is of the greatest help.

Another useful way of holding a vessel on the head is to place one's thumb and forefinger (or second finger at times) at points about 2 inches on either side of the spot upon which the hammer will fall. This is an excellent way of "finding one's place" on a raising. One can turn the work some little way without moving the finger and thumb. For an advance, press the raising down on to the head with the hammer while moving the fingers. Common sense, freely applied, will soon solve the problem of the best hold for the work in hand.

The planishing of the incurve is done exactly as was the lower part of the bowl (see Fig. 17, IV), but we must be careful to diminish the strength of our blows as we approach the actual rim, that should hardly be touched. If struck with any force, the metal will stretch and the incurve, to which we have given so much work and care, will become more vertical. Then our shape will be lost.

The planishing done, the rim will probably need rubbing down again on the emery cloth.

We now come to the final shaping of the rim. When we have had some considerable practice we may find that iron or steel is better than wood; but for our first venture it will be best to take a piece of boxwood, usually a worn-down mallet, and rasp it to fit as exactly as possible the rim of our bowl. Then rasp and file a groove of the contour of the outward turn we want to give the lip of our bowl, Fig. 17 (V).

We shall now find that with a well-polished neck hammer we can tap the rim into the groove in the wood and leave a perfectly smooth surface. We may, if we think it necessary, give the lip a little more turn outwards by tapping it with a smooth mallet with a rounded face over the edge of a "throw back" (Fig. 9). This done, we may planish it gently on the "throw back," using a full-faced hammer.

Lastly, we have to finish the flat base on which the bowl rests.

To make it perfectly flat and even will need much skill, more than any beginner can hope to possess. However, if we have been careful to touch the metal within the base circle as little as possible, we shall find it not too difficult to make it quite satisfactory. The figure, Fig. 17 (VI), shows that the hammering is done from the outside. The stake is like the large one in Fig. 4. Note that one portion of the circumference of the head is rounded, while another is more angular.

Draw a clear pencilled circle at the point where base and sides meet. Put the bowl on the head, and, using a hammer with a slightly rounded face, strike it gently until one finds the point where the hammer facet comes exactly to the pencil line. Then turn the bowl, giving it the most accurately circular motion possible, and, as it turns, strike it evenly with the hammer until one has a circular row of facets, or hammer marks, touching the circle. Do this at first on the rounder side of the bottom stake. Afterwards, if the corner is not sharp enough, do it again on a more angular part. Great care is needed lest the mark of the edge of the stake should show inside the bowl. Now draw smaller circles decreasing each by $\frac{1}{2}$ inch in radius. Then, using the same hammer, and striking more and more gently as one approaches the centre, go over the whole of the base. Under the hammer the metal can be made to lie evenly, but care must be taken not to stretch it. If this happens, the base will bulge. However, if the outer circles of planishing are done by much harder blows than the inner ones it should come nearly flat. If a slight bulge should come, it can be transferred to the inside by rubbing the hammer-face lightly across the base, altering the direction of the motion constantly, until every part has had the same treatment. A professional hammerman can use his hammer in such a way that the metal is actually thickened in the slightest degree around the outer edge of the base; all within is thus pulled taut and level. Ability and skill to do this can be reached only by long and constant practice.

We should now examine our bowl even more closely, and ask ourselves if we can in any way improve its form or surface. As we have planished it in circles concentric with the base, we may find slight traces of each circle of hammer blows. We can get rid of these by using our hammer very gently, perhaps giving it a slight sliding motion, along radial lines.

When the bowl is finished it will be interesting to gauge the thickness of its rim and compare with the gauge of the disc from which it was raised.

In the case of such a shallow bowl as our first exercise there will be but little or no increase. But if we have raised something deeper, with its depth equal to, or exceeding, its diameter, the rim will be found to have thickened considerably, perhaps by 100 per cent.

With increasing skill this happening can be turned to good account; but if a beginner should find it taking place in his raising, he should hammer the work vigorously, thus keeping it nearer its original gauge. If allowed to thicken too much, the metal will become brittle, hard, and unmanageable.

The bowl is now complete save for the mounting of a wire in the rim. In a first exercise this can be omitted, or left until the student has had some practice in soldering.

Finally, we may polish it with pumice and oil. This done, it should be washed clean and finished with a calico mop, using tripoli composition and a little chalk. A vigorous rubbing with a chamois leather should give it all the polish needed.

By the time we have finished our first piece we shall have learned, as we can learn in no other way, something of the rightness and beauty of form that every piece of hand-made silverwork should have. We shall find our appreciation of fine work increased immeasurably, and we shall have experienced the craftsman's birthright of joy in the work of his own hands.

Possibly the shape of the bowl given, or the simple hemisphere suggested, will not appeal to everyone. Even at this early stage many will wish to make something more personal. First ideas will, no doubt, be vague. The following will help to put them into definite form.

If we consider the possible forms of hollow vessels we find that there are three basic types only.

Fig. 17 (1).—Contours of straight lines. They may be vertical or taper upwards or downwards.

Fig. 17 (2).—Contours all convex, rounded outwards.

Fig. 17 (3).—Contours concave, curved inwards.

All vessels that ever have been, or ever will be, made, must be of one of these types or of a combination of two or three of them. The three types are capable of infinite variation. Curves or contours may be contrasted or harmonized.

The test of our mastery of our art and craft is to use contours and surfaces as a painter uses colours, a sculptor forms, a writer words, or a musician sounds, to express their own ideals.

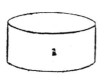 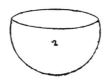 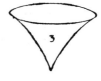

FIG. 17.—1 — 2 — 3.

CHAPTER 3

FUSIBILITY AND SOLDERING

OUR second exercise will teach us something about fusibility. At some place and at some time in the most remote recesses of the past it was noted that when metallic ores were smelted they, on occasion, yielded a different substance from what was expected. Searching for an explanation, it would be found that, somehow, ores of two metals had been in the furnace. Soon it would be perceived that an alloy, or mixture of metals, could be made which, while differing little in its properties and strength from its principal constituent, was much more easily fusible. Experiment would quickly establish the fact that with the precious metals these more easily fusible alloys differed but little, or not at all, in colour from gold or silver.

It was wholly natural that, at the very beginning of metal working, men should find out that pieces of metal could be joined securely together by the fusing of one of these alloys along and into the joints.

This process we know as soldering. The discovery of the smelting of metals from their ores involved the discovery of the need for a flux—a something that would dissolve the oxides formed by the action of the air on heated metal. With a flux, what must often have been a difficult and uncertain process became an easy and certain one. Sodium pyroborate, better known as borax, was probably known in very early times.

A solvent for the hard, glassy substance of the fused flux, and for the oxides that form on the metal, would be needed. Is it possible that the first acid "pickles" were vegetable in origin? That is a question to which we, to-day, can give no definite answer.

Metals, with very few exceptions, expand when heated and contract on cooling. Hence arise many of the difficulties of the process. Some parts of the work in hand will need to be heated to a greater degree than others; and so the unequal expansion sets up strains that tend to twist and warp. Speaking broadly, the one safeguard is the heating of the whole piece. We need to use our common sense and judgment to ensure this. If, for instance, we find it impossible to heat the flat bottom of the piece we are working on while it rests on a flat brick, we may do it much more easily if we use the grooved side. If the even heating still proves difficult, we may use a piece of stout wire gauze, or a tangled mat of soft iron wire, like a jeweller's wig, or boss, so that the flame can get underneath the bottom of our work.

Often thick heavy pieces have to be soldered to light thin vessels. Here care is needed to apply the greater part of the heat to the heavier and more solid portions.

Some of the harder solders tend to be viscous. When fused they will run over closely fitted joints rather than into them. When the surplus solder is filed off, the joints break. Experience is needed in judging the right degree of closeness in fitting that should be aimed at. We must remember that solder fills up interstices. The problem is to leave these of exactly the right size, and to fill them completely without overflowing.

Capillary attraction plays a great part in soldering. The molten solder exerts much force, drawing the pieces together vigorously, and running up long narrow spaces. This property often makes difficulties which can only be avoided by making sure that there are no crevices up which the solder will run, and so get drawn away from those places where it is needed most. Thus, in joining the two ends of a strip together to form a circular band it is better that these ends should be concave rather than convex, so that the extreme corners shall be in contact. If the ends are convex, the point of contact will be in the centre. There the solder will run, leaving a gap on either side.

Metals like copper and silver, and their alloys, have a higher coefficient of expansion than iron, the metal we use in wire to bind our work together. If we make a thin copper or silver bowl, and tie its foot on with thick iron wire, we shall find that the bowl will be grooved, showing where the iron had resisted the expansion of the thin sheet metal. Even if we take a thick bar of silver, say $\frac{1}{4}$ inch square, wind a thick iron wire around it and anneal it, we shall see distinct traces. We must be careful to use binding wire of such a strength that it will stretch as our work expands.

Silver solders, often even the very hardest, contain some zinc—a metal that not only melts but volatilizes at a comparatively low temperature. It is, moreover, a metal more easily attacked by acid than silver or copper. Care must always be taken not to overheat our work, otherwise the solder will "fret," i.e., become porous and spongy.

It will be found that if all soldered parts likely to be subjected to any considerable heat are painted thinly with borax and water, this tendency will be to a great extent prevented. Another cause of the "fretting" of solder is to be found in the greater susceptibility of copper and zinc to the action of acid when compared with silver. The base metals tend to be dissolved, leaving the solder in a spongy state. For this reason it is well to pickle one's work as seldom as possible.

The action of acid on alloys makes the surface slightly porous. Solder will run over this freely enough, but it not infrequently happens that it fails to attach itself to the actual substance of the metal. Although to the eye the joint looks perfectly sound, it may break away at a slight jar. Where strength is a consideration, we must take care to file or scrape the joints so that the solder can reach actual clean metallic surfaces.

The need for scrupulous cleanliness cannot be too strongly stressed. Hearths, tools, fire bricks, breeze, slates, and receptacles for borax and solder, and lastly the solder itself, must be kept clean and free from dirt and grease, and above all from metal dust or filings. This caution applies with especial force to such metals as lead, tin, and zinc. All these, when fused, have a powerful affinity for silver. Try the experiment of putting a tiny snipping of lead on a piece of thin silver and heating them to redness. The result will show very forcibly the need for the greatest care. The lead will eat a hole right through the silver. It is always well to scrape or clean sheet solder with emery cloth before using it. This removes any trace of grease which may cling to it from the rolling, as well as the film of tarnish which forms on solder after it has been exposed to the air for any length of time.

Solder tends to run to the hottest place on the work. It will, in small quantities, defy the force of gravity. Skilful use of this property will often enable solderings to be done easily which would be extremely difficult if molten solder would only flow downwards.

Hard solders—those which melt at high temperatures—are applied in three ways: in strip, in panels or pallions (little snippets varying from $\frac{3}{16}$ inch by $\frac{1}{8}$ inch to tiny bits less than $\frac{1}{32}$ inch in any dimension), and in grain or filings.

The flux, borax, is rarely used dry except when brazing, *i.e.*, soldering iron, copper, gilding metal, and brass with a high copper content, with brass made of 50 per cent. copper and 50 per cent. zinc. For silver work the best method of preparation for the novice is to take a lump of borax (jeweller's or octahedral borax or specially prepared borax compressed into cones), and rub it on a slate with water until it forms a creamy liquid. This is applied with a camel-hair brush, called a pencil in Birmingham. Another method is to take lumps of borax, put them into a saucepan with water, and boil them, stirring all the while until cold. This gives a stiffer cream, admirable for larger work, and which obviates the need for constant rubbing on the slate. For soldering base metals, ordinary commercial powdered borax mixed with water will be found admirable; if great care is taken that no lumps remain in the paste, it may be used for silver, too. If for any reason it is found necessary to apply borax freely to work that is still very hot, a lump of borax may be stroked swiftly over the place where it is needed.

While soldering the blowpipe is never still. Often, indeed, it is moved rapidly so that an intense heat may be applied locally. A flame of such fierceness that would melt a hole in silver of 8 or 9 m.g. if it played on one spot continuously and steadily, even for a few seconds, can be used with safety if kept in constant motion. The rapidly moving flame is an essential in soldering silver of a light gauge.

The flow of solder is often helped by stroking it along the seam, sometimes with the solder itself and sometimes with a piece of steel wire, such as a knitting-needle of about 18 B.W.G.

It is always well to adopt a system of marking solder—thus the ordinary grade may be scratched with diagonal lines, criss-crossing each other. The hardest solder might be marked with centre punch dots at $\frac{1}{4}$ inch intervals. The medium-grade enamelling might be lightly marked with a chisel. We should then obviate any risk of using a harder solder when an easier one is needed, and vice versa.

We must, of course, aim at close and careful fitting in all work to be soldered; but there are occasions when crevices have to be filled up with solder. With practice it is possible to regulate the flow of solder by sudden removal of the heat in such a way that a crevice can be filled up without adding appreciably to the solder already used.

Soft solder—66$\frac{2}{3}$ per cent. tin and 33$\frac{1}{3}$ per cent. lead, melting at about 300° C. has its uses for the silversmith, see page 97. The flux is zinc chloride, "killed spirit" or resin in some form. See caution on page 35.

CHAPTER 4

EXERCISE 2 : MOUNTING A BOWL

THE exercise in soldering the writer would first suggest is the mounting of a hemispherical bowl such as was given as an alternative to that shown in the illustrations to Exercise 1.

Let us begin by making a ring foot like that shown in Fig. 18. Cut a strip of sheet metal, or silver, as the case may be, three times the length of the smallest diameter of the foot and about ⅛ inch wider. See that it is quite parallel, and that the ends are filed bright and clean and straight and at right angles.

It is always desirable that the hardest solder should be used for the seams of such things as feet or wires which have to be soldered again; "mounted," as the trade silversmith would say, on to a larger piece. This practice will

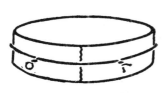

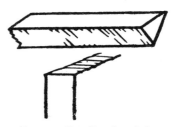

FIG. 18.—*Strip of sheet metal for making ring foot.*

FIG. 19.—*Roughing the ends by striking with three-square file.*

prevent the solder from running out of the seams, or places where the wires are joined, during subsequent solderings.

We have already noted the tendency of the harder solders, with high melting-points, to be viscous and to flow less freely than the easier kinds. Hence comes the advisability of roughening the ends of wires, etc., that have to be turned up into rings.

Rough each end by striking with a three-square file as shown in Fig. 19. Then bend it up into a ring and fasten it with binding wire (about 20 S.W.G. will be right). Tighten this wire by twisting the ends with pliers, taking care to pull the wire with some force before twisting. Leave a length of at least ¼ inch between the ends of pliers and the surface of the metal ring. If the pliers are too close the wire will not stand the strain of twisting. It is well to form the habit of twisting binding wire always towards the right when tightening. This will often save much time when it becomes necessary to tighten or slacken the binding wires. The action becomes automatic, like tightening or slackening screws.

If this be our first attempt at using hard solder, we will use panels. Take a piece of hardest sheet solder, cut a series of slits with the shears about 1/16 inch apart for a short distance, say ½ inch lengthwise down the strip. Then shear off transversely at intervals of ⅛ inch or so a number of panels.

If our strip of solder is narrow, $\frac{1}{2}$ inch or less, and we hold it and the ends of the blades of the shears on the tip of the middle finger of the left hand, we shall find it quite an easy matter to catch with the other fingers the panels as they come away. Otherwise we shall find they will fly in all directions, and so get lost.

Put the wired ring, having first painted the seam with borax and water,* on the hearth with the seam at the bottom, and so arranged that it cannot roll or fall out of position. It should lean against a piece of fire brick or coke at an angle of about 25 degrees from the perpendicular. Now play a fairly large gas flame all over the ring, using the gentlest possible blast, until the bubbling of the borax has subsided. The panels of solder should be ready on the borax slate; see that they are covered with borax water on both sides. Take them up either on the tip of the brush or with the corn tongs, and place them carefully on the seam. Three $\frac{1}{8}$-inch panels in a space of $\frac{1}{2}$ inch will be about right. Again heat the whole with a gentle flame. Any haste will make the panels move from their right position, perhaps violently. It will soon be seen that the borax has fused and so held the panels in their place. The blast is now increased. Apply the heat first to that part of the ring exactly opposite to the seam. This counteracts the effects of expansion. Then the heat is, as it were, led down towards the seam, the blowpipe is kept in constant motion until the ends of the strip are seen to be reaching a red heat. The greatest care must be taken that the ends of the strip on both sides of the joint get hot together. If we heat one, and leave the other comparatively cold, the solder will flow towards the hottest side and the joint will not be sound.

As the heat increases the solder will be seen to show signs of melting. When this happens the gas supply is lessened and the blast increased, thus making an intense heat. Move this smaller, fiercer flame rapidly from one side of the seam to the other, and the solder will suddenly flush in a glistening stream along and into the join. It will be found that different parts of the blowpipe flame have different actions on melting solder. The tip of the middle zone should be used for the final flushing. (Fig. 19a.) As described,

FIG. 19a.—*The three distinct zones of a blowpipe flame.* 1 *Unburned gas.* *The tip of* 2 *is the hottest part.* 3 *is the oxydising part.*

the solder has been put inside the band; but it may often prove to be better to put it outside. The slanting position was advised so that the flame could get between the brick and the metal.

When the solder has flushed, it is well to apply heat all around the ring so that no undue strains are set up in cooling.

* The writer has found that if a trace of a detergent is mixed with the borax and water the surfaces to be painted will be wetted all over. This is especially useful when parts that have been polished are to be soldered, or when one is working with greasy hands. If nothing else be at hand, soap will serve.

When cold remove the iron binding wire and pickle the ring clean and free from any trace of fused borax.

Iron should never be put in the pickle vat. The action of the acid upon it liberates hydrogen, smells unpleasantly, and deposits a film of copper upon any silver or metal work which may be in the vat. This is sometimes difficult to remove.

All surplus solder is now filed off, both inside and outside the ring, and it is ready for shaping. Mallet the ring on the mandrel, or ring stake, until it fits closely and is perfectly round. It is then hollowed. This may be done by putting the ring on a stake which has a groove in it—a convenient stake is shown in Fig. 7. Here the curve that joins the rounded knob to the straighter part gives us what is needed. Choose a suitable neck hammer and tap the flat band into the groove with it. Anneal and planish, using as a stake either the same stake or a mandrel. If the straight-sided mandrel is used, it is obvious that the ring will have to be tilted constantly so that every part is brought between the hammer and the stake.

The exact shape of the foot is a matter of taste, but probably we shall find that the lower edge will need to have a quicker curve than the upper one. If, however, we have a shallow foot, say $\frac{3}{8}$ inch deep only, we shall find a slight even curve satisfactory. This, if made from stout metal, 14 or 16 m.g., will need no wire to strengthen it and may be soldered on the bowl as it is. We now leave the foot for a while.

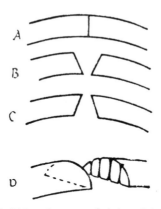

FIG. 20.—*Right method* (A), *and wrong methods* (B *and* C) *of filing ends of wire.*
(D) *Shows notching of ends.*

We have now to mount the wire around the rim of the bowl. This may be of any section—the simplest and most usual is half round; for a bowl of 5 inches diameter a reasonable size would be one measuring a fraction more than $\frac{1}{8}$ inch across the flat face. Having drawn the wire, coil it up neatly and closely, anneal it, and putting one end in the vice pull it with the draw pliers until it stretches slightly and remains quite straight. Then, very carefully, bend it around the rim. Mark across the two ends of the wire where they overlap. Cut the wire about $\frac{1}{4}$ inch shorter than this to allow for the stretching of the wire when rounding finally. File the ends of the wire until they meet rightly as at A, Fig. 20. Avoid the errors shown at B and C, and notch the ends slightly as at D. By holding the wire in a groove filed in the peg one may file the ends, even of soft, thin, pliable wires quite flat and true with ease.

For a beginner, the easiest way of holding the ends of a wire ring together for soldering is to make an iron plate, roughly like that shown in black

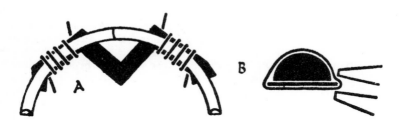

FIG. 21.—(A) *An iron plate for holding the ends of wire in readiness for soldering.*
(B) *Tightening the wires by a pinch with the pliers.*

in Fig. 21 (A), and with binding wire to cramp the two ends in position. Added security is given by pinching the wires gently with the pliers as shown at B. Some care is needed lest the pressure should break the binding wire. The use of a well-worn pair of pliers with rounded edges will help.

In soldering up a thin wire ring, greater care is needed than we found necessary in joining the ends of the strip for the foot. Having boraxed the join, play the blowpipe flame firstly on the wire at a point exactly opposite. Bring the heat gradually round, first on one side and then on the other, until the borax has ceased to bubble. Then put the panel of solder on the seam and proceed exactly as with the foot.

Another method of holding the joins of rings in position for soldering is to hold each side an inch or so away from the ends with pliers, and when 'n position, duly charged with solder, bring the seam into the blowpipe flame. This is a usual trade method. Sometimes one may take two fairly heavy bricks and weight with them the ends of the wire in the right position; sometimes one is able to spring the ends of the wire into position; lay the ring on the brick, and by careful manipulation of the flame in order to avoid displacements due to expansion, successfully to solder the ring. Adopt that method which proves, after trial, best suited to the worker.

After the ring has been pickled and any surplus solder removed with a file, it is malleted truly circular on the mandrel and truly level on the iron flat die. When levelling it is often necessary to turn the wire over and mallet it on the opposite side. If at all stubborn, the wire will often come flat if a piece of cardboard is put on top of the iron plate. When truly shaped, the wire is tried in position. If too small to push on to the rim, it is malleted again on the mandrel until it can be forced on. If too big, a piece must be cut out and the ring soldered again. Rings of wire can be stretched very expeditiously by driving them down a tapering mandrel, using a hardwood punch to apply the force.

Before soldering the wire on the bowl the flat side of the wire and the outside rim must be made clean and bright, either by scraping, by filing, or by the use of emery cloth. This is to ensure that two bright clean metallic surfaces are brought to each other to be joined by solder.

Fig. 22 shows two methods of securing a wire on the rim of a bowl. A and B show the first step in the making of a "cramp." A piece of soft iron

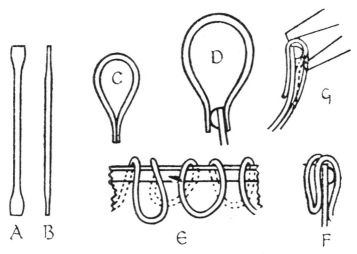

FIG. 22.—*Securing wire on rim of bowl.*
(A and B) *The making of a cramp.* (C) *The bent shape.* (D) *Showing its use.*
(E and F) *Indicate a second method.* (G) *Shows how loops are tightened up with the pliers.*

wire about $\frac{1}{8}$ inch diameter and, say, 3 inches long, is taken; the two ends are hammered out, and the wire bent into the shape shown at C. D shows how cramps are used to hold wires in position. Care should be taken that the flattened ends are parallel so that there is no tendency to push the wire out of position. E and F show another method. Here, binding wire, usually of a fairly stout gauge, is used. G shows how the loops are tightened up with the pliers.

Just as in the seaming of a wire we may sometimes dispense with wires, so we may in the soldering of a wire on a rim. The bowl, with the wire in position, may be placed mouth downwards on the fire brick, or wire gauze; a small weight placed on the bottom of the bowl will keep it in position.

Fig. 23 shows yet another method of using binding wire. This is effective in cases where the rim of the bowl slants inwards at a considerable angle, and gives the wire a tendency to slip upwards. The figure itself shows the most useful and usual way of securing a foot to a bowl for soldering. The hooking of the wire over the rim, instead of taking it right across the bowl, avoids any tendency the iron wire may have to distort the rim. The wires should follow truly radial lines as far as possible, thus crossing each other at a point on the axis of the vessel.

We have assumed that the wire will be soldered on the rim before the foot. Sometimes this is the better course, but sometimes we shall find it better to reverse the order. We must use our judgment to determine the right thing to do.

FIG. 23.—*Another method of using binding wire.*

The first step towards the actual soldering is to paint the parts to be joined very carefully with borax water, taking the greatest care that it shall go into every crevice into which we want our solder to flow. It will perhaps be well if we dry the first coat off, and then repaint. Cut a sufficiency of panels of a good solder of ordinary grade, much more easily fusible than that we have used for the seams. Cover these on both sides with the borax water.

Place the bowl mouth downwards (sometimes it is necessary to place the bowl mouth upwards and apply the solder from the top; to an experienced worker this is easy, but the novice will find the solder has an unpleasant tendency to run inside the bowl into places from whence it is difficult to remove) on the grooved fire brick, or on wire gauze. Heat it very carefully and evenly, taking care not to heat the half-round wire too quickly, or it will expand and become too loose. On the other hand, be careful not to heat the

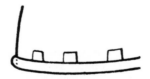

FIG. 24.—*Panels of solder placed around bowl.*

bowl so that it expands before the wire is hot. This, too, will enlarge the wire we are soldering on the rim and spoil its close fit.

As soon as the borax has given off all its water and has ceased to bubble and swell, we place the solder panels around at intervals, as shown in Fig. 24. This can be done either with corn tongs or tweezers, or the panels can be taken up from the borax slate, on the tip of the borax pencil, and transferred to their proper place. This should be done before the bowl has cooled, so that the borax will dry instantly and cause the panels to adhere. Some judgment is needed, for if we apply the panels when the work is too hot, the steam that is generated will dislodge them or the hairs of the borax pencil will stick.

The panels being safely in position, we may begin to apply the heat gently, watching carefully to see that the panels remain in position. Have ready a strong pair of corn tongs, so that any panels can be adjusted the moment the need arises. The annealing pan or hearth is turned slowly and steadily round, and the blowpipe is kept constantly on the move. As the melting-point of the solder is approached the blast is increased and the gas supply lessened. The blowpipe is moved more quickly so that bowl and wire each get their due proportion of heat. Then, as the solder fuses, a still sharper flame will make it flow swiftly along between the bowl and the wire. We now turn the hearth more slowly and look carefully to make sure that the solder has flushed soundly all around. It is well to mark the spot where the flushing begins by a piece of coke or brick. Then we shall be certain, when it comes around, that the whole circumference has been soldered.

As soon as the bowl is cool (the cooling can be hastened by quenching in cold water as soon as the heat has moderated), file round the top edge of the wire. If any gaps between bowl and wire are visible, more solder should be added until a perfectly clear edge is produced. It is sometimes a help to force the wire closer to the bowl by mallet blows. Take great care that the head used fits the mouth closely.

The soldering of the foot will present no difficulty. Fig. 23 shows how it may be securely held in position. For a first attempt the panels of solder may be put inside; a sharp flame from the outside will make the solder flush through to the outside. Strictly speaking, this is not good practice, the rule being always to apply the solder on that side from which any surplus may be most easily filed away.

The absolute beginner is urged strongly to make his first attempts at soldering with panels. If, however, the student has already had some experience, he should at once try the "strip" method.

The work to be soldered is prepared, bound with wire, and boraxed exactly as for panels.

The solder is cut into long strips; about $\frac{1}{8}$ inch wide is a usual size for solder rolled to a thickness of 8 metal gauge. If it curls up, it is straightened by running the strip between the pliers—take care of fingers when doing this—a sheared edge can inflict a nasty gash. The strip is filed, scraped, and emery-clothed to give a clean metallic surface. It is then painted evenly with borax and water.

As the work approaches red heat the strip of solder is held in the flame, and then at the moment the parts to be soldered are hot the end of the strip of solder is held on the seam or join. As it melts it is pushed gently until enough solder for the immediate purpose has flowed from the strip. In the case of a long join, such as that between a wire and the rim of a bowl, it will be necessary to apply the strip of solder at intervals of about $1\frac{1}{2}$ inches or 2 inches. This we judge by watching the glistening stream of solder as it flows. When this stream shows the least sign of failing we apply the strip again.

We shall find there are two extremes to guard against. If we do not heat the strip of solder sufficiently it will not flow freely, while if we get it too hot the end will run into a bead, or even drop off before we get it to the desired spot. Any little lump or bead that may form on the end of the strip should be removed at once by touching it lightly on the brick or whatever we are using to support our work, when it will break off.

It is fatally easy to put too much solder on when using the strip. One may, to some extent, guard against this by using strips of solder just long enough, or by taking hold of the strip with the tongs so as to leave only half or quarter of the strip available.

It will be well to get into one's mind the fact that a strip of silver solder, when applied to a join, at the right heat, melts away just as a rod of wax would do if we touched the top of a stove with it.

It will be seen that the joins must be hotter than any other part of the work so that the solder may flow there.

The brazing of a gilding metal wire, such as we should use on our bowl, gives excellent practice. The whole ring must be heated and the brass wire—50 per cent. copper, 50 per cent. zinc—must be heated and dipped in powdered borax. It will be found that when soldering base metals the flux must be applied much more freely than is the case with silver. The oxide that forms when precious metals are heated arises from the copper with which they are alloyed, and is therefore, by comparison, negligible.

When we have gained some proficiency in the use of the brass wire we should essay the use of brass-filed, or grain, solder. This is mixed with an equal amount of dry powdered borax, and is applied on a tiny spatula, or "toucher," made by hammering out the end of a piece of $\frac{1}{8}$-inch iron wire. Once the use of brass solder is acquired silver soldering will present but few difficulties.

An unmounted bowl will most probably be free from fire marks. A mounted one, from which surplus solder has to be filed and polished away, will as probably show them. Unless they are very troublesome, they may be removed by painting the whole surface with a thick cream of borax and water. Then anneal slowly and carefully, avoid overheating, and pickle clean. If this is done a few times the fused borax will dissolve the excess copper oxide.

CHAPTER 5

EXERCISE 3 : A SIMPLE BOX

OUR third exercise is one which has been thoroughly well tested. It gives most valuable experience in soldering.

Begin by cutting a strip of 10 gauge metal which will bend into a tube of $2\frac{1}{2}$ inches diameter and 3 inches high. File the sides and ends parallel and at right angles. Scrape the ends bright on both sides. Roughen as shown

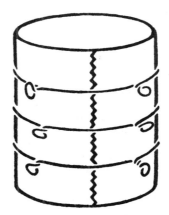

FIG. 25.—*Wiring the body of the box. The roughening of the seam is exaggerated in this figure.*

in Fig. 19, Exercise 2. Wire as in Fig. 25. If of silver, solder with the hardest solder. If of gilding metal or copper, braze the seam. The easiest and most certain method for the beginner is to lay a number of panels of solder, say eight or ten $\frac{1}{8}$ inch by $\frac{3}{16}$ inch, or near that size, along the seam inside the tube. Hold the tube horizontally in a pair of light iron tongs, with the seam at the bottom, and direct the flame upwards from underneath. This will ensure that the inner edges of the seam are secure. More solder may be added from the outside if necessary. Take especial care that the ends are securely soldered. The iron wire may give a little trouble by clinging to the solder. If the whole piece is made just red hot it will pull off with ease. The use of sandiver* will prevent this, but for most things it is not an urgent necessity. File off the surplus solder inside and out. Planish the tube carefully on the largest mandrel available. Begin in the centre of the tube and work outwards, evenly in both directions, gradually decreasing the force of the hammer blows as the ends are neared. If we begin by planishing the ends we shall probably make our tube waisted, *i.e.*, smaller in the centre.

---

* Powdered glass gall, a scum that forms when glass is first melted.

Rub both ends level on coarse emery cloth; see that they are accurate so that the sides of the tube are vertical.

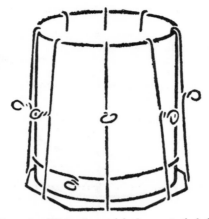

FIG. 26.—*Wiring the metal for base on to the body.*

Cut a piece of the same metal for the base. Planish it till it is slightly domed. Scrape or scour the edge clean and bright and wire the tube on to its convex side, as in Fig. 26; the wire around the lower part of the tube will prevent any tendency for the solder in the seam to give way. Borax inside

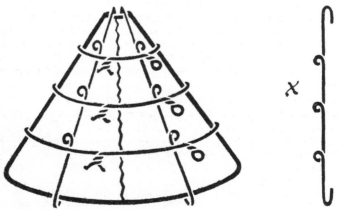

FIG. 27.—*Three shaped pieces of binding wire as* X *are clipped on the cone.*

and outside, not forgetting the seam, and solder carefully with solder of ordinary grade. The tube and its wired-on base should stand on something which will allow the heat to be applied equally to both.

Although the encircling wire will keep the joint intact, we should avoid letting the flame play on the actual seam for more than the fraction of a second. To this end we should make its position on the hearth quite clear. A chalk mark or a bit of breeze or brick will serve for this.

We may fit a domed lid to our box, but a conical lid will give the better practice. Blanks or templates for conical vessels are set out thus—draw an elevation to exact size, produce sides till they meet, from meeting point as

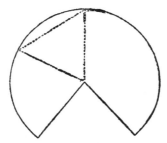

FIG. 27a.—*Template for a cone of size and shape drawn in dotted lines. The length of the arc—continuous line—equals the circumference of the base of the cone.*

centre draw arcs with radii equal to distances to smaller and larger diameters; along the bigger arc set off a distance equal to larger circumference, join each end to centre; this gives exact shape. Normally the conical tube will be hammered and so stretched. To allow for this the arc is reduced to three times the length of the horizontal lines of the elevation. Where a cone comes to a point, Fig. 27a, the arc of the blank must equal the circumference and the actual centre must be opened with a small round file. This prevents binding at the tip and allows the cone to form properly. To be on the safe side, for a first attempt we will cut this from thicker metal, say 12 mg. First, the two ends of the strip are bent, then the whole is rolled up until a cone is formed. Make three pieces of binding wire as X. Clip these on, and wire as shown. This is the only and universal method of binding tapered tubes (Fig. 27).

Solder soundly and planish.

A flat-faced hammer makes elongated facets on straight-sided things. A far more pleasant texture is given by the use of a collet hammer, such as shown in Fig. 11c, which has its face slightly curved in one direction only. A useful wrinkle where a polished hammer is not suitable, as in the first hammerings of a seamed tube or cone, is the emery clothing (use FF), of both work and hammer face, the direction of the emery marks on the latter being exactly at right angles with those on the former. Every mark of the hammer will show clearly.

The cone may be perfectly straight, or, if desired, the rim may be thrown out a little.

With the scribing block mark a clear line ½ inch below the top of the tube to mark the point at which it will be cut to form the lid (Fig. 28). Take a back saw and cut along this line for about 1 inch. This is for a vent to allow the hot air and steam from the borax to escape when soldering on the lid. If we choose the conical lid with an opening at the top, there is no need for this; with a domed lid it is essential. There is always an element of possible trouble, and even danger, in soldering up any hollow space without providing a vent.

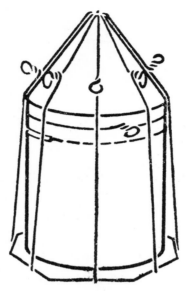

Fig. 28.—*A 1-inch cut is made ½ inch below top of tube.*

Allow the box, as it may now be called, to cool—on no account put it in the pickle at this stage. When cool, finish sawing along the scribed line. We have now a box and a lid. Rub the sawn edges true and level. Pickle both clean.

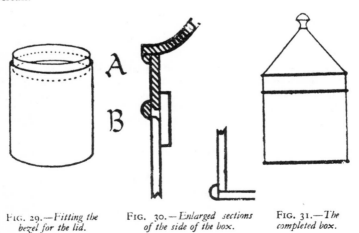

Fig. 29.—*Fitting the bezel for the lid.*   Fig. 30.—*Enlarged sections of the side of the box.*   Fig. 31.—*The completed box.*

For the bezel, on which the lid will shut, take a piece of 10 m.g. metal strip $\frac{1}{2}$ inch wide. Bend it carefully to fit inside the body of the box, solder it soundly with hardest solder, round it with hammer or mallet on the mandrel, scour the outside of the bezel and the inside of the body of the box for about $\frac{1}{8}$ inch down all around. Tap the bezel lightly on the mandrel to stretch it and ensure a good fit (Fig. 29). File a bevel on the inner edge of the body at an angle of 45 degrees until the edge is about half-width. Fit the bezel in position—it should go about $\frac{3}{16}$ inch into the box—wire to keep seam from opening, and solder with ordinary solder.* The solder will fill the angle left between the bevel and the bezel and leave a sharp angle. Without the bevel the angle would be filled up and thus prevent the lid from shutting down.

The box is now made, but will look rather bare and uninteresting. Fig. 30 gives an enlarged section of one side of a box with wires added to give interest, and Fig. 31 shows the completed box in elevation. The upper and lower wires may be put on the tube before the bottom and lid are soldered on. A, Fig. 30, shows a quarter-round wire. This would probably be got by first soldering a half-round wire and filing and rubbing half of it away before putting the lid on. The centre wire (B), is the only one that presents any difficulty. Note that the outer edge of the rim of the lid is bevelled off, and that scarcely a half of the flat side of the wire bears on the rim. Great care in fitting, in cramping, and in soldering is called for.* Do not forget, when rounding a flat-sided wire on a taper mandrel, that the diameter of one side of the wire will be perceptibly greater than the other. This may be remedied by reversing the wire on the mandrel and tapping it gently with a mallet. A knob, filed or turned from a rod of metal, soldered on the top, completes the box.

After careful and thorough pickling, all surplus solder should be filed off very carefully. Avoid filing the actual metal as far as possible so that the planished surface is not touched in the slightest degree. Use a smooth file and be careful not to let the edges cut gashes into the body or wires. Smooth the file marks away with an emery stick made by wrapping a sheet of FF cloth around an oblong piece of wood. A sharp point drawn along the back of the cloth close to the edge of the stick will ensure a sharp fold. Then, having made sure that no deep scratches are left, rub all places that have been touched by file and emery cloth with Water of Ayr stone until a perfectly smooth surface is produced.

In order to ensure a close fitting of lid on body, it is well at this stage to paint the rim and bezel, where they fit on each other, with loam and water. Tie the lid to the body with fairly thin binding wire and anneal the whole. It will then be ready for its final processes.

If we have handled our work with proper care, and have remembered that a hammered surface of metal is something beautiful and precious, there will be nothing more needed to polish the box beyond brushing it lightly on the spindle with pumice and oil.

If our box is of metal we can finish it as we did the bowl, or we can colour it with a solution of liver of sulphur. If of silver, we should anneal it after

* See Figs. 42 and 43, page 61. "Stitches" will ensure accuracy.

polishing, pickle it clean, scour it with fine powdered pumice, paint it thickly with borax and water, anneal it slowly and carefully, taking care that every part is covered with borax, and pickle it again until white and clean. Darken it with the sulphur solution and then brush it bright again with tripoli composition and paraffin. Wash in very hot water and give the final finish with a swansdown mop, using a minute quantity of rouge. The inside may be left from the pickle. The finished box should be a pleasant piece to see and to handle. The half-round wire that actually covers the opening between body and lid gives a note of distinction. Even in the working of such a rigid exercise as this, one gets a chance to express one's own ideas and to find out a little of what design means. The proportions of height to diameter, of lid to body, of the wires in relation to the whole, and, finally, of the knob on the lid, are all matters on which we have to exercise our æsthetic judgment.

We shall learn something of the secret of the charm that simple, straight-forward work made honestly and lovingly always possesses.

If we are fortunate enough to work out this exercise side by side with others we shall see how the personality of each craftsman will assert itself. We shall understand as we never understood before the meaning and value of what the artist speaks of as handling and feeling, qualities which have been left out of modern trade silverwork.

CHAPTER 6

THE DUCTILITY OF METALS

METALS are ductile. They may be drawn into long, thin wires. Draw-plates are made by filing a long tapering punch, called a drift, and driving it to varying distances according to the size of the wire needed, through holes previously drilled in a steel plate, about $\frac{3}{16}$ inch thick. We thus get a series

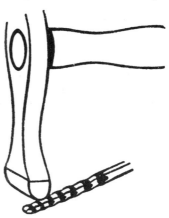

FIG. 32.—*Section of draw plate.*

FIG. 33.—*How the end of a thick wire is drawn out thin with a hammer.*

of holes of the shape of the section of our wires, diminishing in sizes and tapering gradually from back to front, so that no cutting action takes place as the wire is pulled through. The rear half of the hole is opened previously to a much wider angle (Fig. 32).

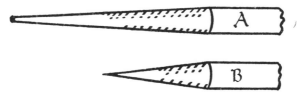

FIG. 34.—*Right and wrong points for wires to be drawn.*

For the worker in silver the most convenient and cheapest form in which to buy wire is slitting—that is, a strip, roughly square in section, that has been made by passing a piece of plate $\frac{1}{8}$ inch to $\frac{1}{4}$ inch thick through slitting rollers. This is charged for at the same rate as sheet.

When handling heavy wires, the best way to point them preparatory to drawing is to draw them out with a hammer, as shown in Fig. 33. This shows a square wire. For a round one the corners are hammered off.

As soon as we find it inconvenient to use the hammer we shall point our wire with a file, holding it in the hand-vice and resting the end to be tapered in a groove filed in the edge of the bench or in a peg. With the left hand we turn the wire slowly around while the file does its work.

In pointing wires for drawing, a long, gentle taper with a not too fine point is far better than a short stumpy one that comes to a needle point (Fig. 34, A and B).

The actual drawing is a quite simple matter. The one thing to avoid is exerting full strength until a considerable length of wire is available to grip with the tongs. This means that at nearly every pull we shall need to draw our wire a very little way and then grip it again close up to the plate; we may even have to wait for a third or fourth grip before pulling our hardest. Drawing metal hardens it just as hammering does, and our wire will soon need annealing. Unless it is thick, $\frac{1}{8}$ inch or so, it will need to be coiled up carefully (Fig. 35) before applying the flame to it. The flame should be a soft one—much gas and little air—and should be kept in constant motion. If we leave any loose ends, or if any of the coils are too large or too small, we shall see that these will catch the heat long before the close coils are heated. With fine wire it is extremely difficult to avoid melting these loose pieces.

If we are handling wire of less than about $\frac{1}{32}$ inch it will, until we have had a good deal of experience, be well to guard against the danger of melting our wire by binding the coils tightly together with iron binding wire. In a strong light it is difficult to tell whether silver is red-hot, which it should be if properly annealed. If there is any doubt it is well to hold a piece of sheet

FIG. 35.—*Wire coiled ready for annealing.*

metal to prevent any direct light falling on the hearth. Even quite thin wire will show red in a dull light for some seconds after the flame is withdrawn.

It is often necessary to make wires perfectly straight. This is done by stretching. If we fasten the end of a wire of, say, $\frac{1}{16}$ inch diameter, in the vice, and, gripping the other end in the draw tongs, pull it, we shall feel it stretch and become perfectly straight: that is, if the wire has been sufficiently and evenly annealed.

A little thought will show us that there are many sections for which it would be extremely difficult to file a drift. Indeed, for any but simple shapes the draw plate is far too costly.

The swage block (Fig. 36) is a simple and efficient tool which helps us out of the difficulty. This is a strong steel frame with the long sides grooved for about five-sixths of their length. In these grooves slide steel dies which have lugs at each end. These dies are forced together by the pressure of the powerful screw.

To make the dies, take a piece of cast steel rod of a convenient size, $\frac{3}{8}$ inch square or round is a standard, and file each end so that projections or lugs are left which will slide in the grooves. If we use square steel, one face is filed until the section is like Fig. 37. If we use round steel, the face is flattened to the same curve. Another die is now made identical with the first.

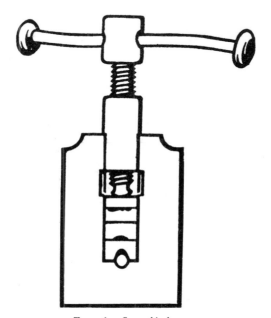

FIG. 36.—*Swage block.*

When the two rounded faces are screwed tightly together they should be in absolute contact from end to end. One of these dies is now taken, and in it is filed a gap exactly of the size and contour of the wire we desire. This gap is left untouched for a space of about $\frac{1}{32}$ inch on either side of the crest of the die, but beyond that it is smoothed and softened away on both sides in something the same way that the rear of a hole in a draw plate is made larger.

The dies are polished with emery cloth or with grain emery and oil used on a bit of wood; finally using flour emery. The smooth die is similarly treated. This done, both are hardened and tempered to a full yellow brown.

We now take a piece of wire of such a size and shape as will, when drawn, fill the gap completely (some judgment and experience are needed here), and, holding it in the contoured gap, we screw the plain die down with some force. A projection of about one inch of the wire is left to grip with the bench draw tongs. The wire, well lubricated with tallow, or a mixture of tallow and oil, is now pulled through the swage block. We shall find it necessary, even for a comparatively small wire, to use the full force of the draw bench. When only about one inch or so of the original wire

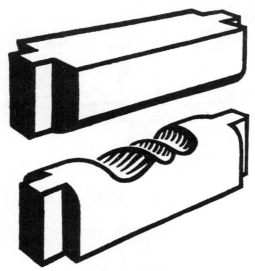

FIG. 37.—*Dies for swage block.*

remains undrawn we stop pulling. The screw of the swage block is tightened again and the wire is drawn in the reverse direction. This is repeated until the wire reaches the shape we need, or has become too hard to allow of further drawing. If we remove the wire for annealing we must be careful to mark the wire so that we may be sure of replacing our wire rightly in the die. We shall find that as our wire approaches the desired section, thin webs of metal spread out on either side (Fig. 38, *a, a, a*). These are cut away with curved shears as they form. Thus we continue pulling the wire backwards and forwards until the wire has filled every detail of the die. The thickness of the wire can be regulated if the back, or unmoulded side of the wire is flat. We can stop at any point we wish or we can go on until the two dies are in actual contact and our wire is the exact shape and size of the opening in the die. In the case of wires with a considerable projection on one edge and a very slight one on the other, we may have to draw a triangular wire before we use our moulded die. Thought and experiment will soon show us the best section of the wire from which to draw our moulding.

Fig. 38 shows how interest may be added to a swage-drawn wire. The thin thread is driven with a tiny, round-ended punch alternately, first from one side and then from the other. When the hollows in the wire tarnish the thread shows as a delicate waved silver line against a dark background. A study of the mouldings on mediæval work will show how all sorts of delightful effects may be produced by patterning wires with simple punches and stamps. Here a stamp means a tool cut in intaglio which, when struck with a hammer, will leave a pattern in relief.

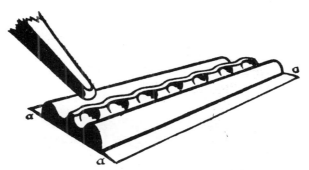

FIG. 38.—*How a waved thread moulding is made in a swage-drawn wire. Note the rough edged webs, a, a, a, that form in the drawing through. These are sheared and filed away.*

When we have become experienced in the application of wires to our work, or as the silversmith would say, the mounting of wires on our work, we shall find that more charming results can be got by using two thinner wires instead of one thick wire; by putting thin, round wires on one, or

FIG. 39.—*Right- and left-hand twists put side by side.*

both, sides of a half-round. The choice of wires of exactly the right sizes, and the putting of them in exactly the right places will present all sorts of interesting problems, and will test our capacity for design quite severely.

It is, of course, impossible to handle wires without finding that they can be twisted, and that the corded effect thus obtained gives us a delightful addition to the purely linear effects of plain wires.

Fig. 39 shows the effect of two pairs of twisted wires, one pair being twisted with a clock-wise, right-handed turn, and the other in the reverse direction. Here, again, is another delightful effect that has been used by metal workers in all places and at all times.

Fig. 40 shows yet another way of using a corded wire. A somewhat loose twist is flattened out by rolling, or, if no rolls are available, by hammering.

Wires are most conveniently twisted by a hook held in a lathe drill chuck. The ends of the wire are twisted together for about $\frac{3}{8}$ inch or so, and held in the hand-vice or slide pliers. The loop is then put over the hook, the wire is pulled until both sides lie evenly together, then the lathe is

FIG. 40.—*Another way of using corded wire.*

started and the twisting continued until the desired effect is reached. If with a moderate tension any sign of kinking is noticed, the twisting must be stopped at once and the wire annealed. At first there will probably be some trouble with the wires breaking. Almost always this comes from failure to anneal the wire evenly and thoroughly If no lathe is available, wires can be very conveniently twisted with a side wheel drill stock of the common American pattern; a wire hook is put in the chuck and the ends of the wire are held in the vice If we have no drill stock it is quite a simple matter to make a hook with a short cranked handle and a bearing for it that can be held in the vice For very fine wires this is the best device. Turning the hook with the right hand and holding the wire with the other makes it easy to regulate the tension with extreme sensitiveness.

If very thick wires have to be twisted we shall find it best, probably, to use a big hand vice to give the turning motion.

We may decide when our wires are twisted that they look too coarse in texture. Then we shall probably find that if we pull these through a draw plate the effect will be much more subdued. Remember that if this is done it will be necessary to twist the wire more tightly than if we use it undrawn.

Two extremes are especially to be guarded against in soldering corded wires. (*a*) It is very easy to use too much solder, thus clogging all the interstices and destroying the sparkle that corded wire work should have. (*b*) On the other hand, sufficient solder must be used to ensure absolute adhesion.

Despite all our care, it may easily happen that a corded wire will, in the soldering, spring away from its position on whatever we may be soldering it. We shall, of course, take every possible care to fasten it securely with wires or cramps on to its base; but even so, we may find we have failed to solder every part. Fortunately, it is generally possible to press the loose part back into position with the corn tongs, or with a piece of steel wire, about $\frac{1}{16}$ inch, pointed or flattened at the end according to the nature of the job.

If occasion arises to solder a thin cord against a thick plain wire, we shall probably find it best to solder the thick wire on first, using the solder rather generously. Then, after the angle in which the corded wire is to lie has been filed or scraped smooth and bright, the cord is wired in position, boraxed, and the piece re-heated until the solder just fuses and "sweats" into the interstices of the cord. If enough solder has been used for the thick wire it will rarely be necessary to add more. To solder a thick plain wire and a thin cord at the same time without clogging up the latter is an extremely difficult business.

Many applications of this principle will suggest themselves when working with corded wires, especially when two or more wires are used together.

In joining up the ends of a piece of corded wire to make rings, care must be taken to file the ends so that, when brought together, the twist shall be unbroken. This applies particularly to thicker wires.

The ends of thin wires can, of course, only be levelled when held in a groove filed in the peg. We shall, of course, use the hardest solder available when making corded wire rings. Care must be taken to avoid melting. Sometimes we may be unable to avoid a little lumpiness. A file will remedy this.

Sometimes we may have to put a corded wire in a position where we cannot first make it into a ring—for instance, on the stem of a cup after the whole has been soldered together. Such a job will tax all one's ingenuity, but some means of wiring it in position will generally suggest themselves. Do not solder all around at first, but leave a space of half an inch or so unsoldered. The loose end is then adjusted to the right length, wired, and the soldering completed. The ends of the wire should be filed as shown at C, Fig. 20. The bevels being thin are here an advantage. If we leave our cord a very little on the long side we shall find that the ends will crush together and make a neat join.

Corded wires have one drawback. Dirt tends to collect around them. They should not, therefore, be used freely on articles of silver for the table and such like. No one, for instance, would care for a dessert spoon with corded wires on the stem. On the other hand, there are many places where there cannot be the slightest objection to their use.

Obviously, cords must not come in contact with food. The following exercises 4 and 5 are given mainly because of the excellent practice they afford in neat, clean soldering. Pieces on which cords are used should be kept clean by frequent washing with hot water and soap. An occasional rub with a leather with a trace of rouge will keep them in good order. Avoid hard rubbing; worn-down corded wires are unpleasant.

CHAPTER 7

EXERCISE 4 : A PAIR OF SERVIETTE RINGS

As a study in the mounting of wires we cannot do better than make a pair of simple serviette rings. Take two strips of silver, 10 m.g. each 5⅜ inches long and about 1⅛ inches wide. See that the sides are parallel and the ends at right angles. Make them into rings exactly as described in Exercise 2; but use two pieces of binding wire. The hardest solder will, of course, be used.

The rings may be perfectly flat bands, or they may be slightly belchered, or bellied out. To do this, take a piece of thick, soft wood (deal) about 2 inches by 2 inches of any length, and put it in the vice with the cross, or end, grain section horizontal. With a ball-pane hammer strike a depression in the wood. Then, holding the ring over the hollow depression, strike it from the inside, gradually turning it round and striking it from both sides so as to ensure an even curve. Now push the belchered ring on a mandrel to bring it back nearer to its original circular shape. Take the ring off, reverse it, and push again on the mandrel. This done, anneal the ring.

Now take a stake that will fit as nearly as possible the inside of the ring. If none be available it will be a simple matter to make one by bending the extreme end of a piece of iron or steel bar, about ¾ inch in diameter, at right angles. This may easily be filed to the desired curve. Now planish the rings, beginning, of course, along the centre line and planishing outwards evenly in both directions. Anneal again and push on the mandrel to ensure roundness. If the edges of the ring have become uneven through the planishing, they should be rubbed level on emery cloth.

Make a flat board, well clamped to prevent warping, a little larger than a sheet of emery cloth. On this a sheet of blue back No. 2 or 3 emery cloth is glued. This forms a convenient appliance for levelling edges.

When the edges are level, that part of the ring to be covered by wires is emery-clothed bright to ensure sound soldering.

The wires have now to be chosen. Plain half-round wire, about ⅛ inch or a little less, across the flat face will make admirable outer edges. Inside these we may do what we will. We may put nothing more, or we may fill the whole space between the two half-rounds with any wires we please.

The exact sizes of these can best be determined by experiment. Having decided upon the general effect, we draw the wires until we get somewhere near what we think to be right. Then we hold them in position and consider any possible betterment.

Common sense will forbid the choice of absurd sizes, but no hard and fast rules can be laid down. Generally, it is better for wires to be thin rather than thick. A fine wire on either side of a thicker one will usually give a better effect than one single wire of equal substance to the three. As a rule, it is not well to put wires of equal size together. The effect of corded wires is often enhanced by the introduction of plain ones amongst them.

Having chosen our wires (for a first attempt one ring may have three plain wires of diminishing sizes inside the half-round. The other may have a piece of corded wire, right-hand twist, next to the half-round, then a piece of left-hand twist, and, lastly, a plain round wire slightly larger than the cord), we cut them to length, join their ends together with hardest solder, and round them on the mandrel. Then beginning with the inner wires we stretch them until they slip on the ring exactly to the right point. Lastly, we push on the heavier outer wires, having previously scraped them bright and clean inside. If our ring is straight-sided, or but slightly bellied, the wires should remain in their right position. It may be well to paint the ring over with very thin borax water and anneal it. This will give a surface to which the wires will cling.

At the first attempt it will perhaps be as well to solder one set of wires at a time. Put the ring with the wires in position, on a piece of flattened wire gauze, painted thoroughly, but not too liberally, with borax and water, and anneal very slowly and carefully. If the wires show the least tendency to spring off, weight the ring to prevent them moving. A short piece of $\frac{1}{2}$ inch square iron bar will serve.

When cool, the wires may be secured with binding wire, using one of the methods described in Exercise 3. Then solder with panels of good ordinary grade solder. Absolutely sound soldering is essential for the outer wire. Here a generous allowance is needed, but care must be taken not to let it flush away from this into the wires.

If we accomplish the first soldering of wires successfully it will be well to try soldering the second set with strip instead of panels. We shall now have some idea of the size and length of the strip of solder that will do the job.

When soldering seamed wire rings on to a seamed article it is always well to put all the seams together and to mark their position clearly. Then we can avoid playing the full force of the blowpipe flame directly on the joins. We shall thus have no trouble with the solder fusing out of the seams and leaving, in consequence, ugly gaps.

CHAPTER 8

EXERCISE 5 : A BEAKER DECORATED WITH APPLIED WIRES

THIS exercise combines in itself all the processes we have tried so far. The body of the beaker may be raised from a circular disc of sheet metal. The early stages of raising will be identical with those of the bowl given in Exercise 1. For the later courses of raising, which will take the metal from a shallow wide-mouthed vessel to a deep narrow one, the side stake A, Fig. 7, is used entirely. The planishing, too, will be done on the same stake. For this use a collet hammer (Fig. 11*c*). Such a piece gives excellent practice in raising accurately.

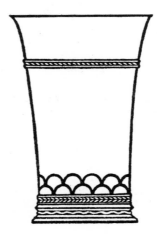

FIG. 41.—A diagrammatic elevation of a beaker. The semicircles, etc., are drawn as if they were on a flat surface.

It may happen, however, that time will not allow us to raise the beaker. It can be made quite well from a seamed taper tube. The principles laid down for making the conical lid to the box in Exercise 3 will guide us in this, and will serve for the setting out of the size of the "blank" for all conical vessels. In the case of our beaker, the centre for striking the arcs giving the right curvature for the upper and lower rims of the tube will be some distance, 12 inches or so, away. With vessels of still more gradual taper this centre, found by producing the sides of our drawing in elevation until they meet, will be at such a distance as to make it impossible to strike the arcs with ordinary compasses or dividers. In such a case the usual practice is to cut three elevations of the vessel in paper and, laying them side by side, to draw the curves free-hand. This, while not geometrically accurate, works quite well.

Having made the taper tube exactly in the manner of the conical box lid, we have to make sure that the axis of the tube is vertical. If we have a lathe,

the simplest and best way is to turn a piece of wood to fit the tube tightly; and then to turn the edges of the tube on this chuck. If we have no lathe we must use scribing block and dividers, as we did when trueing up the raised bowl, remembering that a bottomless vessel is more difficult.

Our tube being round and true, it is annealed. We then shape it with a mallet on a side stake. It is always well to make tubes to be shaped so that they will need to be raised inwards rather than bellied or stretched outwards. A soldered seam will stand being raised easily, but often gives way if stretched.

The bottom of the beaker is put on, again as described in the making of the box. Then, after filing flush with the sides of the beaker and polishing the whole with pumice and oil or composition, we are ready to mount the wires.

Firstly, make the four lowest wires—the two cords right- and left-hand twist, and the plain wires on either side. The lowest wire is, of course, actually on the edge of the bottom of the beaker. The wire which forms the base may be made of a swage-drawn wire, as shown in Fig. 38, with the centre thread punched into a wavy line. Or, of course, a wire of much simpler section may be drawn, or a plain oblong wire used which may be moulded by filing.

The semicircles may be half rings of round wire. Soldering these on—they will need to be bent to the curved surface—will give admirable practice. Now for the three upper wires. It is essential that these be perfectly parallel

FIG. 42.—*Raising a "stitch" with a flat scorper. The dotted circle shows how a wire will rest against it.*

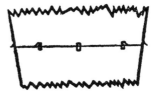

FIG. 43.—*"Stitches" on a conical tube ready to receive a wire.*

with the base. How shall this be ensured? Fig. 42 shows how, with a narrow flat scorper, a cut can be made in metal in such a way as to throw up a tiny spike or "stitch" of metal. Fig. 43 shows a section of a taper tube with a horizontal line marked upon it with a number of these "stitches" raised ready for the reception of a wire.

In the case of our beaker, after we have marked the line and raised the "stitches," we shall first put the plain wire on. Stretch it on the mandrel until it almost goes right on to the "stitches," but does not quite touch. Then anneal it, and we shall find that we can place it exactly into position with the gentlest push. Solder this and it will be an easy matter to put the two other wires on. The slight projections left by the "stitching" can easily be filed away. The cuts made into the substance of the sides of the beaker are, of course, completely covered by the wires. The use of this simple means will often help in the most difficult fixings and solderings.

The rim or lip of the beaker may be treated as we please. It may have a half-round wire outside, or inside if it is never to be used for drinking from; or it may have a "knife-edge" wire inside; or if made of thick metal, 12 m.g. or over, it may be just rounded off and left.

If we choose to put on the semicircles of wire, we shall find any roughness left by the solder may be cut away with a scorper. The surface thus left may easily be polished with Water of Ayr stone.

This, again, is an exercise which will leave us a vast amount of scope for the exercise of our skill in craftsmanship and design. It may be varied to any extent and in any direction we may choose—for instance, after some practice with the hammer we might make our beaker octagonal instead of round.

In our first attempts we do not take time into account. Obviously the first thing to learn is to work with accuracy, neatness (perhaps distinction is a better word), and charm. But, as soon as we feel our feet we shall not be content to draw our work out at too great length. We should aim at completing this exercise in about twenty hours, if seamed, to twenty-five hours if raised. A good size would be 5 inches high.

The polishing and finishing present no special difficulties; but we must be extremely careful not to over-polish our wires, especially if they are corded. Corded wire work should have a delightful crisp sparkle.

Great accuracy is desirable in wire work, but, on the other hand, we must avoid dull, mechanical precision. Wire work should have something of the charm of a line drawn with a sensitive free hand. It may all too easily have no more vitality than a harsh ruled line.

To make rings of wire, take a rod of steel, or any other hard metal of the diameter of the inside of the rings required. Then, having drawn a sufficient length of wire of the right size, grip the rod and the end of the wire tightly in a hand vice, rest the end of the rod in a notch in any available piece of wood; and holding the wire taut, turn the hand vice steadily round until a spiral coil containing the needed number of rings is formed. Care should be taken so to guide the wire, as it is wound on the rod or "spit," that the coils lie closely against each other. Then, with a fret-saw, or a sharp pair of shears, cut up the spiral into rings. For our immediate purpose these are cut into half rings either with the shears, or if the wire be sufficiently thin with a sharp penknife, laying the rings on a plate of metal or hard wood.

CHAPTER 9

EXERCISE 6 : A CHILD'S MUG

Made by the usual trade method from a seamed tube; in London a "collet"; in Birmingham a "neck."

WHEN we begin the making of any particular piece we first consider what its main purpose is, and how to make it completely fit for that purpose. There are many things of commonly accepted form that obviously are not fitted for their purpose. In making these we should very rightly ignore precedent and custom, and experiment boldly, striving to realize in concrete shape the ideal image which forms in our minds when we use our creative faculties.

On the other hand, there are many things which even now retain something of the inevitability and rightness that we find in fine works of the past. Our present subject is one of these.

A good mug must be essentially a mug. To coin an ugly but expressive word, it must be a "muggy" mug. It must not in any way look as if it would make a better vase or other article. Our mug is a handled vessel from which a child can drink with perfect ease, and it must be at once recognizable without question as a child's mug, and as nothing else.

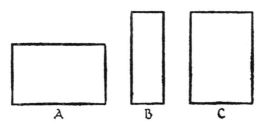

FIG. 44.—*General shapes for a mug.* (A) *and* (B) *are obviously unsuitable.* (C) *is suitable.*

The first points to consider are general shape and capacity. The formula for calculating the capacity of any circular vessel is:

(diameter^2 × 0·7854) × height = contents in cubic inches.

In the case of vessels other than cylinders the average diameter is taken.

1 pint = 34·6 cubic inches nearly.

It is obvious that a wide shallow vessel as Fig. 44 (A) is nothing like a mug. A tall narrow one like B would be inconvenient. But a vessel of the general proportions of C is essentially a mug. A cylindrical vessel of this shape, 2½ inches diameter and 3¼ inches high, holds rather more than ¼ pint when filled to the brim, a reasonable quantity for a child.

Cut a card template 3¼ inches high and 2½ inches wide, so that by marking round it with a lead pencil we can draw quickly a series of oblongs of the general size and shape of our mug. Fig. 45 shows how an almost endless number of forms may be developed by slight alterations of the straight lines into curves. Try the effect of altering the level at which straight sides begin to curve, at which convex curves change to concave, and so on.

In things of fine form the different curves and flatnesses are perfectly proportioned and related to each other. Short quick curves are contrasted with long slow ones; and the curves themselves are alive. A look at the curves of the simplest natural object when set side by side with a common-place manufactured thing will show us the difference quite clearly.

We shall make this piece in silver.

For the beginner B, Fig. 45 will probably be the best shape. The blank is cut (10 m.g. is a good thickness), prepared, and wired for soldering exactly as that for the box in Exercise 3.

The soldering of a seam that has to withstand the strain of raising and shaping must be done with the greatest care. First of all the ends of the strip are filed very accurately, and the roughening is done very evenly. When the cylinder is wired up there must not be the least vestige of a gap showing at the ends. See that the wires are in even tension. A very certain way of ensuring a sound seam is to put a number of fair sized panels of solder,

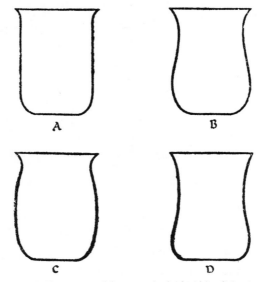

A

B

C

D

FIG. 45.—*Endless variety of forms can be developed by slight alterations of Fig. 44 (c), converting straight lines into curves.*

about $\frac{1}{8}$ inch by $\frac{3}{16}$ inch, inside the cylinder, at intervals of about $\frac{1}{2}$ inch along the seam—take care to have a panel at each end. Take a pair of light long-handled iron tongs, hold the tube horizontally with the seam at the bottom, and blow on the outside with a fairly large vertical flame until the solder fuses. Then if the seam is boraxed again and soldered from the outside we shall have ensured a perfectly sound join. Use the hardest solder available.

It needs some little experience to manage these very hard solders. The heat must be stopped the moment the solder runs, for not only is there a danger of scorching, *i.e.*, half melting the silver and making the copper "sweat" out in patches, but excessive heat makes the solder itself brittle.

The surplus solder is filed off, both inside and out, the seam is hammered smooth, the tube is annealed, hammered again, not closely, to make it round,

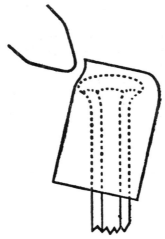

FIG. 46.—*The left side shows the end of the tube being "raised" in. The right side shows the process completed.*

and then annealed again. Note that in the annealing of a seamed piece the heat must be applied with the greatest care, and must be stopped well before the melting point of the solder is reached.

Make certain that the ends of the tube are level and at right angles to the sides. The quickest way of ensuring this is by turning it on a wooden chuck in the lathe.

We are now ready for the shaping. Mark with a pencil line the point at which the incurve towards the bottom begins. Then on a bottom stake as shown in Fig. 46, raise the bottom inwards with a mallet. Next the waist of the mug should be drawn in, using a mallet or a side stake, and working in both directions, from the point of greatest diameter upwards, and from the mouth of the mug downwards.

When the mug is shaped it is planished quickly—a process known to the Birmingham silversmith as "spot hammering," because the bright facets left by the hammer show as spots on the dull surface of the mug. For the convex curves a flat faced hammer is used, and for the concave curves a neck hammer.

We are now ready to put the bottom in. This should be cut from metal two sizes thicker in the metal gauge than that we used for the body—12 m.g. in this case. Begin by bevelling the opening at the bottom of the mug, with a rough file, at an angle of about 35 degrees with the horizontal. Now put the mug on a piece of 12 m.g. silver and mark from the inside, using a fine pointed scriber, the exact size and form of the opening at the bottom. Outside this, mark another line parallel to it and of such a size that when the disc is put over the opening it will project about $\frac{1}{32}$ inch beyond the outer side of the bevel. This marking will probably be drawn with a free hand. It is doubtful if the raising will have been of such accuracy as to bring the opening to a true circle.

Now dome this disc slightly and file (again using a rough one) a bevel, on the convex side, from the line marking the opening at the bottom of the mug to the edge. This outer edge should be as thin as it can be made without reducing the size of the disc (Fig. 47). This disc forming the bottom of the mug is now wired in position (Fig. 48), and soldered with the same

FIG. 47.—*How the opening at the bottom of the mug, and the disc that closes it, are filed.*

solder that was used for the seam of the tube. If great care is taken to keep the flame from actually playing on the seam for more than a moment the bottom can be soldered in without any undue disturbance of the solder. If, however, we are unsuccessful and some of the solder runs away, we must add a little more until all is sound again.

After the mug is thoroughly pickled and is free from the least trace of

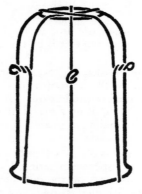

FIG. 48.—*The bottom disc wired in position for soldering.*

borax the surplus solder must be filed away very carefully. Here a caution is needed—it may happen that solder will run away from the seam and settle as a lump, at some distance from the seam: the chances are that such lumps will not adhere to the tube firmly enough to stand hammering. Any such excrescences must be removed completely. If we fail to do this we may have trouble while planishing. These lumps tend to work up as thin flakes, and as they have been hammered right into the underlying metal an unpleasant and troublesome scar will result. At all times any projection which might develop into a flake under the hammer should be filed clean away.

Should there be any lumps of solder inside the mug that cannot be filed away with an ordinary file, we may be able to get rid of them by bending a file (this is easily done when red hot—when the right curve is obtained the file is again made red hot and quenched in water) that will reach the spot. Sometimes a scraper may prove more effective. Fig. 49 shows two usual

FIG. 49.—*Side and end views of scrapers made from old files.*

forms. They are conveniently made from old files, and should be hardened, tempered to yellow, and sharpened on an oil stone.

The thin edge of the bottom disc should be filed away, stopping short just before the last trace of the solder disappears. Here, again, our object is to avoid leaving anything that can' hammer into a flake.

At this stage it will be well to mark clearly the exact centre on the bottom of the mug. This can be found by a wide opened pair of compasses used as shown in Fig. 50a. It is generally best to make a tiny four- or six-sided figure, within which the exact centre can be marked with ease. If bent dividers are not available the arcs to form the tiny square or hexagon can be struck

FIG. 50.—*The two arms are for larger and smaller vessels. The curves are near those of the inside of the mug but slightly quicker, i.e., of shorter radii.*

from any line drawn on the body of the mug parallel to its mouth, or at right angles to its axis. Then, after all deep scratches and lumps have been removed with smooth file and emery cloth, the mug is ready for its final planishing. A cast iron cranked tool (Fig. 50) will probably be the best choice. For the bottom, a stake (Fig. 4), or one similar to that shown in dotted lines in Fig. 46 will be good.

The mug will be planished exactly as was the bowl. Draw circles with the pencil compasses as far as convenient, and when this proves troublesome mark them with a pencil using it as the needle of a scribing block is used.

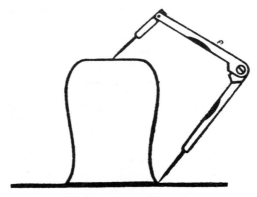

FIG. 50a.—*Finding the centre of the bottom of the mug.*

The first course of planishing is done on the join between the disc and the raise in bottom of the mug. Some force will be needed. This will soon begin to change the outward concave curve of the disc to a convex one. Any remaining concavity can be tapped out from the inside with a long bellying hammer, or the stake we are using can be used as a punch for the same purpose.

From this soldered join, work inwards towards the centre, taking great care that the bottom of the mug is kept from becoming too rounded. To do this use blows just hard enough to ensure that the hammer smooths the metal and no harder. The bottom of our mug being planished no difficulties will arise in working outwards, until the convex curve begins to change to concave. Any ordinary flat hammer, provided the edges of its face are rounded off, will serve for more than half-way up the mug. A sharp look-out must be kept on the hammer facets. The moment the front or upper edge of the hammer shows any sign of "pecking," *i.e.*, leaving an imprint of the corner, the flat faced hammer must be changed for a neck hammer. There is no special difficulty in using this, but some care will be needed to make the hammered surface of the mug look all of a piece. Do not be content until the form and surface are as perfect as they can be made. Do not forget that our sense of touch will often reveal defects that are not apparent to sight. It may happen that, despite all our care, some defect of surface will show inside the mug, so stubborn that no planishing will take it away. Such a defect will very often yield to the following treatment—put the mug on the stake on which it was planished, with the defect in contact with the iron or steel; over it, on the outside of the mug, hold a piece of sheet lead, about ⅛ inch thick, and hammer vigorously. Soon we shall find that the blemish has been transferred from the inside to the outside where it can easily be filled up by solder. The planishing done, the next thing is to mount the rim with a half-round wire. The rim should be slightly smaller than the broadest part of the mug and we are thus prevented from slipping the ring of wire into position from underneath. It is sometimes possible to solder a ring up and to spring it into position over a rim, even when that rim has a diameter slightly greater than the inside diameter of our wire ring. A better, or at least, a more certain way is to "lead" the wire on. Bend an inch or so of a length of wire long enough to go around the rim of the mug, and see that it fits nicely under the overhanging rim. Fasten this with cramps, having previously brightened both the rim of the mug and the flat face of the wire. Borax carefully, and dry off. Then with a few, very tiny panels of solder, fasten the end of the wire in position. Here we must "hasten slowly." We must, at all costs, avoid using solder so liberally as to run along the wire before it is pressed tightly to the rim. Carelessness, or failure here, will mean lumpy outline where there should be a flowing curve. At the first soldering we should not attempt to fix more than about an inch of wire. Afterwards this distance can be increased as found convenient. When we are approaching our starting point, the filing of the end of our wire will need great care. We must cease soldering well before we come to the end of the wire. If we fail to take this precaution we shall find it impossible to file the end of the wire properly without bending it out sharply. To do this will make a kink in the wire extremely difficult to remove or remedy; $1\frac{1}{2}$ inches is not too much to leave loose for this final fitting. We must be careful to arrange for the seam of the wire to coincide with the seam of the mug. This makes it absolutely imperative that the cautions about the avoidance of a direct steady flame on the actual seam be most carefully noted. The end of the wire should be bevelled as C, Fig. 20, so that it can be forced with pliers tightly against the other "soldered" end. We must aim at such a close and even fit that when the top of the rim is filed level, no pin holes in the solder should be visible.

Which way up are we to stand our mug while soldering wire on the rim? This is a question which everyone will have to settle for themselves. If our wire fits very closely and evenly we may have it uppermost and apply the solder from the top. But if we fail to get this, and it is not easy, we may reverse this procedure if possible. We cannot, of course, let the cramps that hold the wire in position carry the whole mug while it has its wire rim soldered on. Our aim will be to keep the solder where it is wanted. It is fatally easy to let it run in lumps and blobs where it is not only useless, but difficult and troublesome to remove.

The top wire being on, we begin on the foot. This may be made in a number of ways. It may be made from a raising. It may be a ring of metal It may be made by soldering plain or corded wires, or a combination of both, on a strip of metal. It may be made of simple wire, when interest can be added by filing or punching. That shown on the drawing (Fig. 51) is a plain oblong wire in which a groove has been turned or filed, or it may equally well be drawn in a swage block. Whatever method we choose we must be careful with the seams. Sound soldering with the hardest solder is essential.

We shall probably find that a foot that rests on the join between the bottom disc and the incurve of the tube will be in right proportion. This is a clear case of method of execution determining form, or design, as some would call it. Certainly it will be right from the practical point of view: the solder join will be completely covered and there will be no difficulty in finishing.

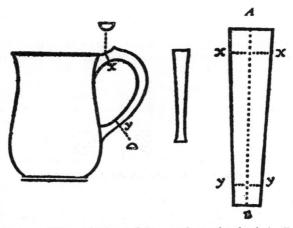

FIG. 51.—*The completed mug. Setting out the template for the handle.*

It will pay to file the upper edge of the ring foot so that it fits quite evenly.

A circle that will be just visible inside the foot should be scribed with dividers, striking it from the exact centre of the bottom of the mug. This should enable us to bind the foot in exactly the right position for soldering.

In the case of such a simple piece as our mug the trouble is not likely to arise, but it often happens that it is extremely difficult to wire a foot on exactly, so that its centre and the centre of the vessel it carries coincide. This difficulty can often be overcome by the use of "stitches" (see Exercise 5). These give a series of spikes which keep the foot from slipping out of position. They may be either outside or inside the foot as is most convenient. The graver cuts will, of course, be made on the part that will be hidden by the foot. There will be no trouble in soldering the foot. Do not forget the rule to apply the solder at the point or points where any surplus or roughness can be most easily removed. Obviously in our case this is the outside.

The rim and foot finished, we can think about the handle. A handle of the type shown in Fig. 51 will be found satisfactory. It will afford an easy and pleasant hold, will be in keeping with the plain vessel, and will give excellent technical practice.

Within limits, the general size and shape can be determined on paper. Firstly, then, we make drawings of the whole mug and its handle that satisfy us. We need side and end views.

To cut the blank for the handle—first take a piece of soft iron wire and bend it to the outer curve of the handle, straighten it out, and, on a piece of paper, draw a straight line AB, Fig. 51, of the same length. Think out what the sections of the handle are to be at top and bottom, and make careful drawings. These will, of course, be D shaped. The completed handle will have a D section. Before the back, or cover, is put on the section is a U. On AB mark two points X, Y, at a distance from each other equal to that between the two section points—it will probably be better to have these at about ¼ inch from each end.

Bend pieces of wire of the exact lengths of the U's; straighten them out and measure them.

At the section points, draw lines at right angles to the line AB, and equal to these last determined short lines; the centres of these short lines will,

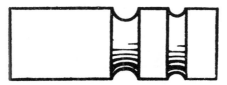

FIG. 52.—*The grooved cylinder of hard wood.*

of course, be on AB. Join the extremities of these short lines, produce them until they are long enough to touch lines drawn at right angles to, and at the extremities of AB, and we have the shape of the blank. Extend this wedge-shaped figure by ¼ inch or so, at each end, and cut the blank of this shape from 11 m.g. silver. This is to form the inside of the handle (Fig. 51). Take a piece of box, or other hard wood, and turn from it a cylinder that will just fit inside the curve at the top of the handle. In this cylinder turn two grooves as shown in Fig. 52, the smaller of these must be rather quicker in curve than the section of our handle is to be.

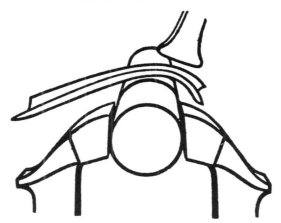

FIG. 53.—*Bending the handle.*

Fix this wooden cylinder in the vice as tightly as possible without cracking and crushing. Fig. 53 shows how the tapered strip of silver is bent with a hammer, not only into the curve of the handle, but into the U section also. A considerable amount of force is needed and the left hand will get jarred severely in holding it against the hammer blows. Any expedient that can be thought of to ease this jarring should be tried. A heavy pair of pliers would be useful. Shaped lead clams* in the hand vice may be tried. It might even be worth while to solder a thick piece of copper on the end of the strip, having, of course, first shaped it to a curve identical with the U.

We shall find that as we deepen the transverse curve the curve of the handle will tend to straighten; and as we bend the handle to its proper shape the transverse curve will open out wider. However, by frequent annealings and by humouring and coaxing the silver we shall find we can make it approach the right shape. The edges may be levelled by malleting, or gentle hammering, on the thin edge of the "throw back tool" (Fig. 9), or a collet hammer held in the vice. Here, again, we may use our judgment and press any odd piece of iron or steel into service.

We shall notice how any hammering on the outer edges tends to make the handle curve inwards, while hammering along the crest of the transverse curve will tend to make it straighter. We shall soon ask ourselves—how shall we planish the handle smooth without altering the curve? If we attempt, at this stage, to achieve anything like a smooth surface we shall be disappointed.

Fig. 54 will explain what to do. In this case a strip of stout sheet metal, silver or copper, whichever is to hand, will serve (brass or gilding metal should never be used, as these zinc alloys have a strong tendency to amalgamate with silver). Often a piece of thick wire will be better than sheet.

FIG. 54.—*The strip soldered on the handle preparatory to planishing.*

Before the planishing is begun the roughly shaped handle should be pickled until it is quite clean and white. This done, a clear pencil line should be drawn along the crest of the transverse curve. For the actual planishing we may use any hammer that will serve. A small neck or collet hammer will be very useful. We may find, however, that a small full-faced hammer of about ⅜ inch or ½ inch diameter will be even better. The curve of the hammer face should, of course, be a little quicker than that of the handle. There must be no risk of making ugly pecks with the corner of the hammer face.

* Clams, pieces of sheet lead or metal, bent at right angles, to cover jaws, thus preventing damage to work held in the vice.

For a stake anything that will serve will be used. A long thin beaked sparrow hawk is useful; but perhaps best of all would be a piece of thick steel plate about 3 inches by 3 inches by $\frac{3}{8}$ inch, with one of its edges rounded to fit the inside curve of the handle. Having chosen the stake, fix it firmly in the vice and see that its curves are suitable. Then begin to planish the inner curve of the handle. First planish as far as possible along one side of the pencil line, then along the opposite side. Continue thus, taking care that each side of the handle gets exactly the same share of planishing as the other. As the work goes on keep a sharp look-out for any defects in the curve. These are easily remedied by putting the handle on a large mandrel, or any other stake that fits the inner curve, and hammering along the bottom of the U curve from the inside. This will make the curve even. Note that this will be done with a narrow neck hammer, striking as in the first shaping on wood, on a part that will not be seen in the finished handle. The planishing proper is done on the curve of the handle where the fingers will rest.

Fig. 55.—*Testing the edges of the inner part of the handle. The right-hand drawing is, of course, wrong.*

When our handle is as shapely and as finely surfaced as our hammer can make it we anneal it, having first boraxed the solder join between handle and strip. After it has been at a low red heat for at least a minute we can increase the heat, melt the solder and pull the strip away from the handle. If working alone, with no one to hold either handle or strip firmly, it is well to bind the handle on to a piece of brick heavy enough to keep it still while we pull the strip away.

We shall have found it impossible to planish properly the extreme ends of the handle while their nearness to the strip has prevented the hammer doing its work; but when they are free from the strip we shall be able to do this easily, and to make any little adjustment, such as the slight quickening of the curve at the lower end where it is to join the body, that we may wish. The next thing is to shear (be careful to do this in little snips so as to avoid undue bending) and file the edges of the U-sectioned piece until the outer and inner curves are properly related. Here we must remember that the thickness of the outer plain part of the handle must be allowed for. At the conclusion of the filing the U-sectioned piece should look quite on the slender side. Another point to note with great care is that each edge of the U is exactly level with the other. If we hold a short length of straight steel wire across the tops of the U, we shall see at once if it is at right angles—as it should be—to a line that goes straight down the centre (Fig. 55).

The strip that will change the U section into a D can now be prepared. This should be of 10 m.g. The metal of the inner part will by now have become considerably thinner than it was at the beginning, so that 10 m.g. will be amply thick. The whole handle might well be wrought from thinner metal by an experienced worker. The strip should be well scoured, bent to fit the edges of the U, and planished. This may be done on the rounded end of a stake like Fig. 7, when it will take on a slight fullness. This is more pleasant than a simple flat strip bent into one curve.

Fig. 56 shows how the strip is wired on the handle. The concave curve at the extreme top is added as a separate piece. When all is well fitted and wired, borax carefully. To ensure the inside of the handle getting its proper share it should be filled with borax water, shaken, and emptied. Solder without stint with the hardest solder available. Pickle carefully, file up, taking care not to remove more of the hammered surface than can be helped, and if any gaps or pin holes show in the solder fill them up. Next fit the handle to the mug. This may, at the first attempt, prove a tedious matter. The one thing to remember is that we have to cut away those parts that touch the body until it fits. Do not hurry. Make quite sure of those points that are keeping the handle from fitting closely. The first approximate fitting may be quickly and conveniently done by snipping with a small pair of "crooked" shears. For the final close fitting, use a "smooth" cut file, half-

FIG. 56.—*Wiring the strip over the handle.*

round or 3-square, one which has lost its very tip, and is about $\frac{1}{8}$ inch wide at the end, is excellent. If the fitting is found difficult, it may prove helpful if a little rouge and oil is smeared on the body of the mug where the handle has to touch. Then the projections to be filed away will be clearly marked. As the fitting gets closer the red marks will increase more and more. Our handle has to be fitted accurately in two directions; it must fit closely against the mug, and at the same time its axis as viewed from above, in plan, must be in exact alignment with the diameter of the mug.

The fitting accomplished, the inner side of the handle and that part of the mug that comes immediately beneath it should be polished with pumice and oil, or any other smooth non-lustre raising abrasive. It will be impossible to do this as well after the handle has been soldered. We should provide a vent for the expanding imprisoned air. Two $\frac{3}{32}$ inch holes drilled $\frac{1}{2}$ inch away from each end of the handle will suffice, that at the big end should be through the inner curve, at the lower end it will be better and less conspicuous through the outer strip that covers the U.

See that the mug and handle are free from grease; again pour borax water through the handle, and wire it in position as shown in Fig. 56a. The soldering is quite a simple matter. The mug should be horizontal to avoid the tendency of the handle to slip down by its own weight. Borax again from the outside not forgetting all parts that have been soldered before. Use good easy running solder. Apply it where any excess can most easily be filed away, and see that the solder runs cleanly all around.

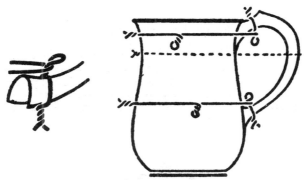

FIG. 56a.—*How the handle is wired on for soldering. For a beginner the two wires are advised. A practised craftsman would use one as shown by dotted line. The outer, flat side, of handle is omitted in sketch on left.*

Pickle the mug clean. After washing in running water, let it stand with the vents in the handle under water for some long time, or, better still, boil it vigorously for 10 minutes to remove all traces of acid that may lurk inside the handle. Then examine carefully for any defects of soldering.

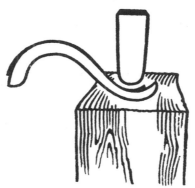

FIG. 57.—*Making a handle with a double curve.*

Remedy them if at all possible. Go over all soldering with a "superfine' cut file and a FF emery stick; polish inside and out. Anneal and pickle clean again. Darken with sulphur—liver of sulphur in hot water is the best form. As soon as the silver is a dark lustrous blue the sulphur should be thoroughly washed away in running water.

For the final polishing, after the darkening process, use tripoli composition (a little paraffin smeared on the silver will keep it from clogging), wash in hot water using a good soap powder, and, finally, after drying—take care to get all moisture from inside the handle—a slight application of a mop, a soft brush, used with a minute portion of rouge will give us a soft, pleasant, natural-coloured finish.

It may be that we shall wish to give our mug handle an outward turn at the bottom, like the handle of a seventeenth-century tankard. This is, of course, more trouble, but is not too difficult. The handle is made exactly as described, of course longer, and the lower end is shaped and bent with hammer and punch using the cross cut end of a piece of soft deal as a doming die (Fig. 57). The subsequent planishing is done on the punch that shaped the end curve. The fitting and soldering on of the usual heart or shield-shaped piece is a very easy matter. If, however, we want a scroll end we shall find it well to make a wooden pattern, get a cast from it in silver—any bullion dealer will do this—and solder it on. The solid scroll end should have a peg or tenon on the inner end to fit tightly inside the D-sectioned tube of the handle. This solid end would be soldered in before the handle is filed up.

This method of fashioning vessels from seamed tubes is a very regular trade practice. Although pieces made in this way have not quite the charm of one raised by hand from the flat sheet, it is a very valuable method, far superior to spinning. It is comparatively speedy, and in consequence inexpensive. Lastly, as a technical training it cannot be bettered. If we can make and mount a seamed mug without allowing any sign of the solder joins to show we may claim to have attained something like competence.

As an exercise in design, too, its value is great. The very severity of the limitations will force us to seek for rightness and reasonableness. There is nothing to tempt us towards strangeness, yet there is nothing that need cramp the exercise of our individual creative faculties.

Chapter 10

Exercise 7: A CREAM JUG AND SUGAR BASIN, AND A SIFTER

Let us first consider the purpose of the vessels we are going to make, and the nature of what they are to contain. A jug for a thick clinging liquid like cream will need a wide lip. For cream, unlike water, refuses to flow in a narrow stream. A silver jug with cream dribbling over the edges is not a pleasant sight. A cream jug must stand with reasonable firmness and its handle must afford an easy and firm grip, it must be right in balance, not only in actual weight, but in appearance also. Lastly, a cream jug must be easy to clean. It is no easy matter to remove every trace of cream from a vessel with a narrow neck, or from one that has not a reasonably smooth interior.

A sugar basin may be of almost any shape. One would not, of course, choose either a flat saucer-shaped vessel, or one that is tall and narrow. A rounded bottom is better for a sugar basin than a flat one that makes an angle with the sides, for it would be difficult, if not impossible, to empty one of the latter with a sifter; some sugar would certainly linger in the corner.

The sugar basin must be closely akin in general form to the cream jug. In fact, except for the rise of the lip, or spout, the two may be identical in type.

Two handles are customary on sugar basins, but there is no absolute need for them. Some shapes may be better without handles. Some may have one, and some three or even four.

In determining the shape of the sifter all we have to do is to think what will be best fitted for its purpose. For a shallow sugar basin the sifter will be nearer in form to a spoon; for a deep one it will be nearer to a ladle.

The shape of the bowl must be such that it will take up its full complement of sugar at one stroke. A circle, or oval, or pear shape attached to the stem at the narrow end, are all suitable. A sifter sharply pointed would be a tiresome implement when the sugar was getting low.

It is usual to pierce the bowl of a sifter; without the holes it would obviously be wrong to call it by that name. Although a spoon or ladle with an unpierced bowl might be efficient, piercing will give great charm. The sizes and shapes of the openings need thought, and at a first attempt, experiment, unless a perfectly satisfactory sifter is at hand to show us what is right. Roughly, openings of $\frac{1}{16}$ inch, $\frac{3}{16}$ inch apart, spaced over about half of the total area of the bowl will be near the mark. What is wanted is an arrangement of piercings that will let us convey the sugar from the basin without loss, and then allow it to shower through when shaken gently. The sifter must have a handle that can be held easily and firmly—there must be no danger of its slipping out of, or in, our fingers.

Fig. 58 offers three suggestions for shapes of cream jugs. None of them presents any serious difficulties in raising. The passage from the bulbous body of B to the neck will need care. Where, as in this case, the actual junction between the two parts is inclined to be sudden and sharp we shall find it best to leave it softer and more gentle in curve until the last possible moment. A clear pencil line marking the level of the junction, or change of curve, should be drawn.

We shall then take a square-faced planishing hammer, with its front edge, or corner, well rounded, and planish the bulbous body lightly and carefully *up* to the line. Then with the same hammer, if it serves, or with a

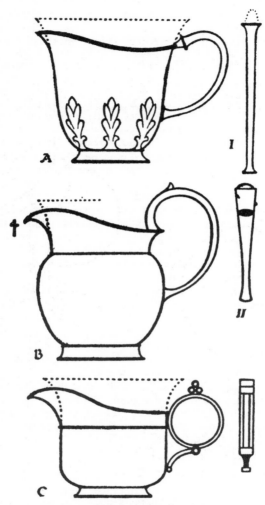

FIG. 58.—*Three suggestions for cream jugs.*

neck hammer not too full in curve (a Warrington hammer with its cross pane ground is admirable)* we planish the neck *down* to the line. There should then be little difficulty in smoothing over the junction of the two sets

---

* See page 19.
† The curve at the extreme end of the lip is exaggerated. It should be of such form that any surplus liquid runs back into the jug.

of hammer marks with a narrow neck hammer of suitable curve (here again a Warrington hammer can easily be made into a useful tool). The tools and methods suggested are good, but we must not assume that they are the only ones that can be devised.

We must see to it that the fitness of our jug is never lost sight of for an instant; and of equal importance is the need for realizing essential jug quality. It should look a jug first, foremost, and always.

In settling the type and general proportions of our jug rapid sketches will be of the greatest help. As we draw we must strive to realize the jug so clearly in our mind's eye that we actually apprehend it in three dimensions. Our minds should get all round it. The faculty to do this, one of the most essential for a creative craftsman, must be steadily cultivated.

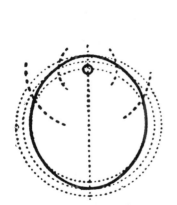

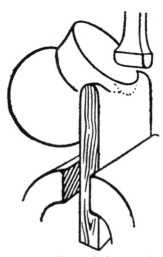

FIG. 59.—*How the contour of the lip and rim of the jug is marked.   Note the arcs struck from centre O.*

FIG. 60.—*Shaping the lip on wood.*

We can help our minds to take hold of essential jug form by carefully watching the flow of milk, or cream, from any jug, of whatever material it may be, that is at hand. One all important fact to keep in mind is that the surface of the liquid remains horizontal at whatever the angle the jug is tilted.

Having chosen the type of jug, we consider its capacity. Our jug will probably hold $\frac{1}{4}$ to $\frac{1}{2}$ pint; 9 to 18 cubic inches.

At our first venture it will be well to raise a completely symmetrical vessel, as indicated by the dotted lines in Fig. 58, leaving a little of the rim intact to form the lip, and cutting the rest away. The raising being completed and planished as usual (for a cream jug it is well to use a rather thicker gauge of metal than would serve for other vessels) we mark with a pencil wired to the needle of the scribing block, a series of horizontal lines, about $\frac{1}{4}$ inch apart.

We then draw a line from one edge of the rim to the other, through the centre of the bottom of the jug, thus dividing the jug exactly into two equal parts. This is done with a free hand. We hold the jug upside down. Then we can see the slightest deviation from the true line, just as a carpenter can when he takes a sight along the edge of a board he is planing. We now draw, freehand again, one half of the curve of the rim and lip of the jug. Then with dividers we draw on the other side of the medial line arcs equidistant from those where the curve cuts or leaves the horizontal circles. A curve drawn through these points will balance exactly that we drew first (Fig. 59).

Take a pair of "crooked" shears and cut away the surplus metal nearly up to the line we have drawn. Do this in little snips, holding the shears so that, as we cut, there shall be no tendency whatever for the shears to turn inwards—with straight shears this is most difficult to avoid.

The lip can now be shaped finally on wood (Fig. 60). Any odd bit will serve. The hollow should be rather quicker in curve than the rim of the jug. A rather unpleasant dent will probably develop just at the point where the lip begins to turn out. This is easily removed, either by a vigorous malleting from the outside, holding the lip on a side stake that fits the curve as nearly as possible; or we may have to knock it up from the inside with the ball

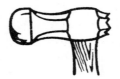

FIG. 61.—*Small full-faced hammer.*

pane of a chaser's hammer or some similar tool. The jug would be held on soft wood or a sandbag.

After the jug is annealed it is ready for planishing. Pickle and scour it quite clean and mark the medial line again, this time inside as well as out.

It is impossible to give any very definite instructions as to how best to planish the lip. In the choice of stakes and hammers we shall, of course, choose those that most closely fit the curves. Sometimes we shall find we can do nearly, if not quite, all the planishing from the outside; sometimes much will have to be done from the inside.

Probably a small side stake and a small hammer, very full faced (Fig. 61), about $\frac{1}{2}$ to $\frac{5}{8}$ inch diameter will be most useful. When working from the inside a neck hammer will be more useful.

A good deal of care is needed to keep the lip from becoming lop-sided. If we are careful to planish evenly on both sides of the medial line this trouble will not arise.

The first planishing of the lip being done, the whole jug should be very carefully considered. It may be that some alteration in the body of the jug is needed in order to bring about the right harmony between body and lip. We must not be satisfied until we have made a jug of distinctive and spirited form, until we have realized our ideal as far as we have power to do.

After planishing, the edge or rim of the jug will need filing into the finest perfection of curve within our reach. It may be necessary to use scribing block and dividers again to ensure symmetry. The jug is now ready for mounting. A half round wire will be best for a first effort. Cut a piece, well annealed, about ⅜ inch longer than is needed to go around the lip. Straighten it and scrape the flat side bright. See that the edge of the jug is also bright and clean ready to receive the wire. Find the middle of the wire and bend it for a space of about 1 inch on either side of the centre until it fits closely on to the centre of the lip. Paint with borax and water, fasten with cramps, and solder. Continue around exactly as the wire was mounted on the rim of the mug in Exercise 6.

The fact that we are not now dealing with a circular edge adds but little to our difficulties.

For the foot of our jug something like those shown will be quite satisfactory. They could be made by exactly the same methods as given for the feet of the bowl, beaker, and mug in former exercises. If we should feel that something different is needed let us experiment. Those drawn may all be made either by raising from circular discs, or from strips of thick metal bent up into rings. In either case a wire probably of oblong section rather less than $\frac{3}{32}$ inch by $\frac{3}{16}$ inch, would be soldered on the bottom. They may, of course, be decorated by applying wires or by notching with a file. A swage-drawn moulding also would make a satisfactory foot in some cases. None of the jugs shown are suitable for this, however.

We now come to the handle. If we are making a single jug only, with no thought of repeating it, we should forge and file this out of thick silver rod. But as we are making a sugar basin which will have handles identical, save in size, with that of the cream jug, we shall avail ourselves of the caster's services. To make the casting pattern of the handle on A, Fig. 58, find the exact length of the handle by bending a piece of iron wire to the curve and straightening it out. Take a piece of soft brass rod ⅜ inch diameter about twice the length of the handle and turn and file it down to the shape shown by the solid line. The long untouched piece of rod may be held so firmly that it will be quite a simple matter to bend the lower tapering part into shape over a beck iron by striking it with a mallet. When the right curve is reached, the untouched shank of the handle can be held in the vice, or hand vice, and filed into the shape shown by the dotted line. A 3-square file will do this. The handle can be severed from its shank either by filing till it breaks off, or with a back saw.

Casting patterns should always be left on the big side. Some shrinkage takes place, and ample allowance for the loss in thickness while filing up must be made.

So far it has been assumed that the section of handle for A is round. To file it into an octagon will test our skill severely, but will add very much to the charm of the handle.

Handle B presents no difficulty. This casting pattern may conveniently be made from a piece of brass rod flattened by rolling or hammering. Much of the filing to shape can be done before it is bent. The little projecting thumb bit is a separate piece soldered on. The section given is the obvious one, but all sorts of pleasant variations may be devised.

Handle C is wrought. The ring may be swage-drawn wire. The thumb piece is made of three pieces of tube. A piece of the same tube is put at the junction of the ring and the strut or support. The ring is, as a silversmith would say, "gapped" or grooved transversely, so that the short lengths of tube fit in snugly.

Great care must be taken to make casting patterns of such a section as will draw easily out of the mould (Fig. 62). Unless a pattern "leaves" well the castings will be very rough.

When the patterns for our handles are as perfect as we can make them

FIG. 62.—*Right and wrong sections of casting patterns for handles.*

FIG. 63.—*An elevation of a sugar basin to go with Fig. 58 (B). Often, as here shown, it suffices to draw one handle only.*

we send them to a caster's, or to a firm of bullion dealers who undertake casting.

So much time and practice are needed to make good sound castings that it is not advisable for the majority of students to attempt to do their own casting. Any good book on brass founder's work will tell us what we want to know.

It is advisable to have never less than two castings made from a small pattern in case of accident. It is also well to have two castings in brass as well as those in silver. These are especially useful in making patterns for similar handles of a smaller size. The pattern for the handles for a sugar basin to match the cream jug can easily be made by cutting a piece out of jug handle casting and soldering it up again.

When we get our castings we anneal them carefully and pickle thoroughly, taking every care to ensure complete removal of casting sand. Then with a rough file we dress away all seams and excrescences—there will be a little lump where the casting has been sawn off the "get," and there may be others. In the early stages of filing up castings it may be best to hold them in the vice between lead clams. For the final shaping and smoothing a hand vice, again using lead clams, or strips of leather or cloth as protection from the teeth of the vice jaws, is better. A 6-inch crossing file of the smoothest possible cut is a most useful tool for this kind of work.

After emery cloth has been used, worn FF or O for the last stage, the handle should be well brushed on the lathe. That part of the jug immediately beneath the handle, which cannot be reached directly by the polishing brush after the handle has been soldered on must also be polished at this stage.

The handle must now be fitted. Handles A and C are easy, the back of a half round file will serve quite well. B is more difficult, especially where the upper part of the handle comes on to the inner side of the lip. After it has been fitted, as nearly as possible, with the file, the centre of the upper extremity of the handle should be hollowed out with a scorper. Here the use of rouge or some strongly coloured matter (see Exercise 6) will help. We must aim at a fitting so close that the solder will flush easily and cleanly.

After fitting comes the problem of fixing the handle in position for soldering. Here again B is the difficult one. An expert mounter could, and probably would, "jump" the handle on. He would fuse some solder on to the part of the rim where the handle will rest. Then holding the handle with a light pair of iron tongs he would blow the flame on both jug and handle so as to heat them at the same time; then just as the solder reaches the melting point the handle would be held in position until the solder flushed. The flame would be withdrawn instantly after this had happened. The handle would, of course, be held firmly until the solder had solidified. The novice would find this holding the most difficult thing of all. It is so fatally easy to move the handle between the flushing and the solidification of the solder.

For the beginner the best course would probably be to fix a piece of fairly stout iron binding wire across the rim of the jug at the right distance from the edge so that the handle could rest against it. The soldering should be done with a strip. When we become expert we shall, perhaps, be able to solder both ends of the handle at one heating. At first it is not advisable to attempt this. Fixing one at a time, usually the top, we have a chance to adjust the other to its exact position very easily. On no account, as in all important solderings where the utmost strength is needed, must we omit the scraping bright and clean of the places to be joined.

With the sugar basin first consider the size. It will certainly need to be bigger than the cream jug. Make an accurate drawing of the jug to its exact size; then sketch a sugar basin of the size deemed right. Trace this sketch on tracing-paper. It is put over the actual size drawing of the jug, then we see at once if its size is in the right proportion with the jug. The exact size of suitable handles should also be determined on this sketch of the sugar basin. As suggested above, the casting pattern for these can be made easily by shortening a brass casting of the jug handle. Let us try to raise the basin exactly to the size of our sketch. Frequent and thoughtful use of callipers and compasses is essential here. Although for a very first attempt it may be well to finish the jug right out before starting the basin, it is not speedy. Much time can be saved by keeping two, three, or more raisings going at once.

The sugar basin we are making will probably be wider and rather lower than the jug. Basins to match either A, B, or C should have horizontal rims. Later we may find ourselves making a sugar basin with a shaped rim. To design such a basin satisfactorily is too difficult as yet.

Figs. 63 and 64 show sugar basins drawn to the same scale as the jugs. A simple sifter is also suggested.

To make the sifter, cut a circular piece of 10 m.g. silver for the bowl a little larger in diameter than the sum of the diameter plus the depth of the sifter we want to make. Dome it in a hollow in a wooden block, and planish it perfectly smooth; the inner side being more important, the face of the stake used must be highly polished.

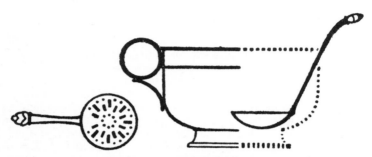

FIG. 64.—*A diagrammatic drawing of a sugar basin and sifter to go with Fig. 58 (c).*

The stem should be forged out of a piece of thick slitting, using a neck hammer as shown at Fig. 33, for roughing it out. As the shape is reached (the stem will, of course, be forged as a straight tapered rod) an ordinary flat faced hammer is used. The final shape is given with files. If we are thinking of making a number of sifters it would be worth while to make a casting pattern for the top of the handle. Castings from these would then be soldered on to the stems. Long thin castings are so liable to develop cracks that it is not wise to have these stems cast. Just before the filing is finished the stem should be bent by striking the concave side with the pointed end of a mallet (Fig. 10). A piece of wood with a groove rasped out into which the stem could be malleted would be useful.

The fitting of the stem on to the bowl will need care. The "rat tail" suggested, though not necessary, gives great strength. If a rat tail is not used the long slot and two drill holes omitted from the figure should be pierced. For soldering, the bowl is clipped on to the stem with a "cramp" bent to a suitable shape. The piercings suggested can be made solely with drill and file, *i.e.*, if the worker has had no experience in saw piercing. The long slots would be made by drilling a series of holes very close together and then finishing the openings with a thin flat needle file. The bud shaped finial at the end of the stem would be notched with a three square file.

The filing up of this stem, holding it in a hand vice and resting it on the peg will prove an excellent training. We shall learn something of the quality of form that a file will give.

So far no mention has been made of the leaf forms suggested as decoration on A, Fig. 58. It is intended that these be made by shearing out six pieces of silver, about 10 m.g., all alike and of such a shape that the serrations can easily be filed out of the edges. This done they may be rounded, grooved, and modelled by filing, thus giving us a further useful exercise. They should be bossed up slightly from the back, on wood, either with a small faced hammer, or with hammer and punch. They may then easily be bent until they fit closely on to the jug. When fitted, the backs should be scraped bright and soldered on, again giving valuable practice. If any doubt about neat soldering is felt, it may be well to run a thin film of solder on the backs of the leaves. Then after scraping the surface of the solder bright they would be wired on (an arrangement of wires like those shown for wiring up the conical lid of the box in Exercise 3, Fig. 27), carefully boraxed and fired with a gentle flame until the solder "sweats," leaving scarcely a trace showing outside the edges of the leaves. If a perfectly sound result is not reached, add more solder (if possible do this before pickling) in strip or panel. We could ensure a good fit by malleting the leaves on to the body, but then we should probably find the outline of the leaves showing inside; and this we ought to avoid.

The insides of the jug and basin will need perfect polishing. This is a job which may well and safely be left to the trade professional polisher. We want an absolute smoothness not easy to attain. However if we have used every care in polishing our stakes we should find it not too difficult. "Felt bobs" and stiff calico "end mops" will probably give us a better result than brushes. Here a power spindle is a boon. Polishing the interior of even a small bowl on a foot lathe is more than laborious.

"Fire marks" are frequently troublesome inside a vessel. Vigorous polishing in the professional trade manner with "leather bobs" and "Trent sand" will remove them; but this drastic treatment will remove an amount of silver, and make the vessel appreciably lighter and thinner. If a plating vat is available there is, in the writer's opinion, no objection to the common trade practice of "whitening," i.e., depositing a thin film of silver on the inside of the vessel before the final finishing. There is yet a further trade way of removing fire marks. The article is put in a plating vat as the anode. A certain amount of silver is removed evenly. The slightly frosted surface is then polished smooth. The process is known as "stripping." It destroys surface texture and blunts detail. Another entirely good and customary finish is to gild the inside of the vessel. A pale gold colour is a delightful contrast to polished silver.

CHAPTER II

EXERCISE 8: A POLYGONAL BOX WITH HINGED LID

So far, with the exception of the box with the pull-off lid (Exercise 3), we have made nothing with a moving part, and all we have made has been circular in plan.

This exercise presents two fresh problems. A flat-sided article is liable to distortion from expansion while soldering. The hinge joint demands a standard of accuracy in advance of any preceding exercise; and we have to reach this without the aid of any mechanical appliance.

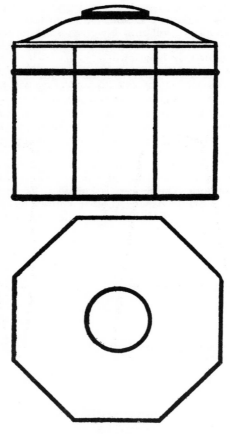

FIG. 65.
The detail shown as a circle in the plan may be omitted.

A hexagon or an octagon that can be drawn within a 3-inch or 4-inch circle is a suitable size for the plan of our box. Its height may be anything we please so long as its proportions are pleasant. There should be no indecision about its general form—its height should be distinctly higher or lower than its diameter. In a square or a polygonal thing we must never forget that the diagonals, from angle to angle, are greater than the diameters from centre to centre of opposite sides. This means that an object will look much larger when a diagonal is at right angles to the line of sight than when a diameter is in that position.

The difference is, of course, greater in a square or hexagon than it is in an octagon. Another point to note is that as a rule a 5- or 7-sided figure is not so satisfactory as a 6- or 8-sided one; somehow it seems unnatural for the front of a box to be an angle.

Fig. 65 is of reasonable proportions. If we adopt it, we can begin work from it directly. Measure one side and multiply it by 8. Then cut a strip of metal accurately to this length and a little—$\frac{3}{32}$ inch or so—wider than the height. Scour this strip bright and examine it carefully for blemishes; if any are visible (though rarely found on silver, they are unfortunately not uncommon on metal sheet), scrap the piece and cut another. Flatten the strip carefully with the mallet, and take all the buckle out with a hammer. To do this the metal is laid on the flat surface plate and pressed down. Though not impossible, it is extremely improbable that malleting will make the metal lie flat—it will spring up in places. Press the metal down, let it spring up again,

FIG. 66.

and, as this is repeated, note very carefully the exact position of these portions of the strip where no movement of the metal is visible. We shall find that if these rigid spots are hammered gently the strip will flatten. The process is repeated until the whole strip is flat. Buckling is due to parts of a metal sheet being at a higher tension than those surrounding them. The hammer equalizes this, and allows the sheet to lie evenly. This flattening and removal of buckle is usually spoken of as "setting."

FIG. 67.

Our strip of metal being set, we rule lines at right angles across it, dividing it into as many equal parts as our box has sides. We then take a short chisel with a wide edge (Fig. 66), and laying the strip on the surface plate strike the chisel accurately along the lines. Use a hammer of about 6 oz., and hit with some vigour. Fig. 67 shows the groove or nick we should make.

Another way of making the grooves is by scraping with a bent scraper (Fig. 68), or if the strip be narrow they may be filed. Whatever method we use, the grooves must be of such a depth that when the metal strip is bent to the right angle the outer corner shall be clean and sharp. The grooves should be so deep that distinct traces show on the opposite side of the metal.

If we use the chisel, we must be careful to anneal the strip before bending, and to scrape the two sides of the nick bright. The chisel will, of course,

FIG. 68.

harden the metal where it strikes. The bright surfaces are to ensure clean sound soldering.

The ends of the strip are filed at angles equal to half the corner angle of the box—for a hexagonal box this will be 60 degrees, for an octagon $67\frac{1}{2}$ degrees, and so on. This filing of the edges of metal so that they come together at the correct angle is called as in woodworking "mitreing."

The strip is now bent up. This is best done on a long narrow stake, usually the flat end of a "beck-iron." If no suitable stake be at hand, a piece of hard wood will serve.

The body of the box being bent up, it is wired and soldered as was the round box in Exercise 3, the only difference being that each corner is strengthened by running solder down the inside grooves. After pickling the inside of the body is filed smooth, the outer side of the corner seam is filed smooth, and the whole is vigorously emery-clothed.

Any blemishes that this may disclose are remedied, either with a hammer or flat mallet, or they may yield to a burnisher (Fig. 69), made from an old file, rubbed carefully and with much pressure inside while the facet of the box being dealt with rests on a smooth flat die or surface plate.

The question of hammer marks on flat surfaces arises here—are they right or wrong? It is clearly wrong to make a box smooth and then deliberately to mark, bruise, or dent the surface with a domed faced hammer. But if we have enough skill to hammer the sides with an ordinary flat hammer, we can make the actual surface of the metal of a better quality and more

FIG. 69.

lively and interesting; beyond this, the slight fulling out of the surface of each gives a subtle and elusive but distinct charm to the form of the box itself.

A useful wrinkle in hammering flat surfaces is to scour the surface with FF emery cloth so that the grain runs evenly in one direction. Then if we polish our hammer face on the same cloth, so that when we use the hammer the direction of the grain of its surface will be exactly at right angles to that on the metal, every blow will show clearly. A hammer that has been well used and polished until its face is distinctly rounded or "full" should always be used on flat surfaces.

The tube, or body, after flattening or hammering is ready to be trued, so that each of its faces will be exactly at right angles to the base. This is now soldered on as in Exercise 3.

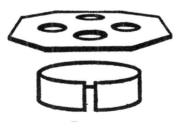

FIG. 70.

Now we are dealing with a flat-sided thing the difficulties caused by the expansion of the heated metal are vastly intensified. With the greatest care in the handling of the flame it is impossible to ensure absolute evenness of temperature, so that some amount of warping is inevitable. With practice this can be kept within such limits as may easily be remedied. For a first attempt, however, it will be well to cut a plate of sheet iron about $\frac{1}{16}$ inch thick that will fit exactly inside the body of the box. This is to be placed on a ring also of sheet iron, so as to lift it about $\frac{1}{2}$ inch above the bottom of the box. The ring should be about half the diameter of the plate (Fig. 70).

The presence of this plate inside the body, while it is being soldered on to the bottom, will ensure the retention of its true shape.

Now for the lid. There are, of course, any number of alternatives to that shown for the form of this. It might, for instance, be a pyramid—this would be set out as was the conical lid in Exercise 3, except that it would be divided by radial lines into eight equal triangular spaces. The radial lines would be nicked for folding and the two ends mitred.

At a first attempt, however, it will be well to choose the simplest form, as shown in Fig. 65. This is made from a simple domed circle, large enough to project about ¼ inch beyond the faces of the box. On this an octagon should be drawn in pencil, and the eight segments sheared away. Another octagon about ½ inch smaller than the box itself is drawn within this. With a mallet—shaped as for raising, but more carefully smoothed and rounded, each of the edges will in turn be flattened down. The inner octagon is a guide. The edge of the mallet must be watched carefully, so that the flattening proceeds for equal distances from the outer edge on each face (Fig. 71). If this is done carefully, there will be no need to planish the lid again.

The division of lid from body is marked and partly slotted for vent as Exercise 3. The soldering of lid to body is done exactly as there described, except that the iron plate is put inside to prevent warping.

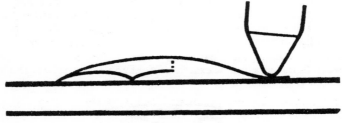

FIG. 71.

The chief difference between Exercise 3 and our present exercise is the fitting of a square wire about ⅛ inch inside both body and lid and the fitting of the bezel inside this wire (Fig. 72). The bevelling of the corner of the body wire to prevent the solder filling up the angle, as set out in Exercise 3, must be remembered. The lid wire also may need bevelling to ensure close shutting. Square wires and bezels will need to be carefully cramped for soldering. They will also need to be nicked to ensure sharp bending. Here it may be noted that when fitting a wire on a polygonal form we must aim at the utmost exactness. It is best, perhaps, to make inner wires slightly too large and outer wires slightly too small, and to make the final adjustments by filing.

As the box we are now making is to have a hinged lid, we shall put the outer half round wire on seven sides only, leaving the eighth for the hinge joint.

When we have taken our box thus far, loam and water should be painted on all fitting parts between body and lid. The lid should then be pressed home tightly and wired on firmly with many strands of binding wire, not too thick. After annealing the whole carefully a perfect fit should result. It is now ready for "jointing," *i.e.*, the making and fitting of the hinge.

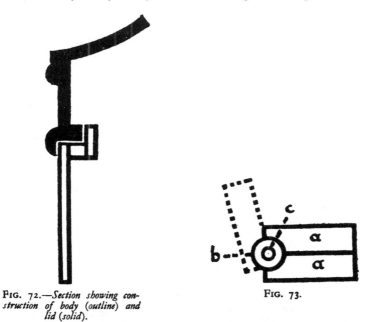

FIG. 72.—*Section showing construction of body (outline) and lid (solid).*

FIG. 73.

Hinge Joints.—To the uninitiated it may seem a matter of extreme difficulty to make a thing of such mechanical accuracy as a hinge with the simplest hand tools. It is indeed a fascinating and interesting bit of craftsmanship.

The simplest form of hinge for our box is what is known as a "book-joint." There are three parts of a hinge:

      (1) the bearers   (*a*)
      (2) the knuckles (*b*) (Fig. 73)
      (3) the pin   (*c*)

FIG. 74.　　　　　　　　FIG. 75.

To make the bearers for our hinge, take a piece of metal or silver $3\frac{1}{4}$ inches by $\frac{1}{4}$ inch by $\frac{1}{8}$ inch. File a bevel along one edge (Fig. 74). Bend it end to end, and mallet it close (Fig. 75). The folded metal is then put in the vice

(Fig. 76). The V-shaped groove is deepened and changed into a U with slightly incurved arms. This is done with a "gapping file," *i.e.*, a parallel flat file with rounded edges cut rather coarsely and smooth sides. The final shaping of the "gap," as the groove is called, is done with a parallel round file slightly smaller in diameter than the desired groove. For the joint we are making the gapping file should be $\frac{1}{8}$ inch thick, and the parallel round file $\frac{5}{32}$ inch diameter.

A little thought will show us the need for the U shape of the gap in a

FIG. 76.

hinge for a box whose lid has to turn through an angle of 85 degrees or 90 degrees only. If the gap were semicircular the lid would turn 180 degrees, and would therefore fall right back with the result that the weight of the lid, unless the box itself were extraordinarily weighty, would make the whole thing overbalance—note dotted lines on Fig. 73. What we have to do, then, is to ensure that when the hinge is opened and turned through the angle named, the outer edges, or horns, of the bearers will come in contact and thus prevent further movement Fig. 76.

To make the joint tube or "chenier" cut a strip of 12 gauge metal of any convenient length—say 4 inches to 8 inches and $\frac{17}{32}$ inch wide. File the edges smooth and exactly parallel. Shear one end to a blunt point. With a narrow

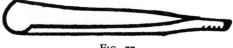

FIG. 77.

paned hammer strike the strip into a groove filed in a piece of hard wood. Then with a flat faced hammer close the edges of the point together into a roughly shaped tube (Fig. 77). This is now drawn on the bench through a

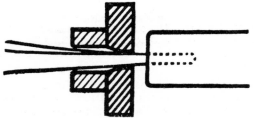

FIG. 78.—*How the seam of a "drawn" tube is kept from twisting.*

round plate until the edges of the strip meet and a tube is formed. In the earlier stages of the drawing it is well to get an assistant to pinch the tube as it closes in with flat-nosed pliers held at the back of the draw plate (Fig. 78). This keeps the seam straight. As soon as the strip has become a tube, take a piece of bright steel wire much longer than the tube (22 m.g. will be a good size), and file a point on it so that it may be forced right into the point of the tube. This wire is well oiled and driven into the tube. The whole is then drawn until the tube is as nearly as possible $\frac{11}{64}$ inch diameter. By this time the metal will be forced tightly on to the steel wire (Fig. 79). Had it not been oiled, it would be impossible to move it. If we now push the projecting pin through a hole that just fits it in the draw plate until it is stopped by the tube, we shall find it will draw out quite easily on the bench.

FIG. 79.

A watch must be kept on the wire as the tube lengthens very rapidly. If we find only $\frac{1}{2}$ inch or less projecting, we must withdraw the wire and cut the tube shorter before we finish the drawing.

The tube is now annealed, and the seam is notched with the edge of a three-square file (Fig. 80). This marks its position clearly and helps in sound soldering.

FIG. 80.—*Tube notched to show position of seam.*

We now file up the bearers accurately and saw off the folded end, leaving the two pieces of grooved bearer about $\frac{1}{32}$ inch longer than a face of the box.

We are now ready to cut the knuckles. There is always an odd number of these, in our case five. Using a fine back-saw, cut off five lengths. The ends of these are filed level and at right angles in a "joint leveller" (Fig. 81) made of hard steel. When the soft silver or metal is filed down to the level of the steel, no more can be removed.

The extreme sharpness of the angle thus obtained is taken off with a superfine cut file. On three of the knuckles a distinct bevel (Fig. 82) is filed off at the seam. The two remaining knuckles are similarly filed at one end only.

The soldering of the knuckles on to the bearer is done as follows. A length of joint tube bevelled at both ends is taken and wired at the centre of a bearer. Fig. 83 shows the position of bevel and seam of tube in the gap. This is a most necessary and important point to ensure great strength. If

FIG. 82.—*Each knuckle of the hinge is bevelled.*

FIG. 81.—*Joint leveller.*

FIG. 83.—*Note that this is one half of a three-knuckle joint.*

the seam should come outside the bearer it will, even if soldered, be liable to split open when being "pinned up." Though not the usual practice, it will be well to solder this in position right away, using a panel of the hardest, free-running solder available. The quantity of solder is a vital matter in making hinges; we must use just enough to solder the knuckles soundly, and not a particle more. The purpose of the bevelling will now be clear. The vertical faces of the knuckle will meet the groove exactly at right angles. There will be no need to use a graver to cut away the surplus solder. After removing binding wire and pickling clean we bring the other bearer into position; this done, we place the two knuckles bevelled at both ends in position. This second bearer with its two knuckles will be soldered to the lid of the box. The exact positions of these knuckles are carefully marked. The hinge, with its present three knuckles, is taken apart, the two knuckles are wired in position on the second or upper bearer, taking care that the seams and bevels are rightly placed in the groove. These are now soldered. All that now remains to be done is to find the position of the two remaining knuckles (these will come, of course, at the ends of the lower bearer), wire them into position and solder them (Fig. 84). After pickling, both parts of the hinge should be examined closely with a lens, and, if not soldered quite soundly, should be scraped bright along the solder joins and flushed again.

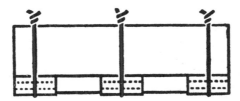

Fig. 84.—*The lower bearer with its three knuckles wired for soldering. The centre knuckle already soldered is wired so that it cannot move while the others are being soldered.*

When the soldering is finished, the hinge should be oiled, put together, and pinned up with a parallel bright, smooth, steel pin, not too tight a fit in the bore of the tube. The hinge should now open and shut—at this stage it will need an amount of force to make it do this; we shall probably need to prise the hinge open with a strong knife, and then to use pliers to make it open and shut. If the tightness is excessive, it can be reduced by adding a tiny portion of powdered pumice to the oil. The movement should be

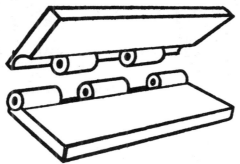

Fig. 85.—*A completed "book" joint ready for its pin.*

continued until we can make the hinge open and shut with our fingers. The pin is now withdrawn, and the two halves of the hinge are carefully annealed and pickled clean (Fig. 85).

The foregoing description of the making of a hinge must not be taken as an account of usual workshop practice. It is the method adopted in the writer's classes for a first attempt. Though not speedy, the result is thoroughly sound and workmanlike; with care the risk of failure is improbable. In actual manufacturing workshops a degree of skill and swiftness is developed that is almost incredible. All the knuckles are placed in position and "tacked" with tiny panels of solder with absolute certainty.

In the final soldering, a skilled man hardly ever fails to secure the knuckles soundly, and yet he never uses enough to fill the angles. It is all done so quickly that at a casual look it would seem that all sorts of risky tricks were being tried. Here, as in many another sphere, only those who have thoroughly mastered the canons of an art can afford to disregard them. It is an increasing practice to use solid machine-made joints for such purposes as hinging the box we are making. This is quite lawful, but it does not excuse lack of knowledge and skill needed to make a hinge joint by hand.

The next thing to do is to file the hinge on its back until, when placed on the box, it does not project unduly. For a first attempt a maximum projection of $\frac{1}{4}$ inch will be best. With experience this can be reduced until the bearer is narrowed almost to a thread. The risk of the solder used to attach the hinge to the box running into the groove and knuckles is too great to warrant the adoption of the lesser and neater projection at present.

When the hinge is ready it is taken apart and painted on every part and surface with a thin mixture of loam and water (except where the bearers are to be attached to the box). After drying it is put together again and pinned up with an iron pin (well annealed to ensure its having a thick coat of oxide) also painted with loam.

The box is also loamed to remove all possibility of lid and body becoming soldered. The lid should be wired firmly in position. A narrow strip of lid and body on either side of the parting is emery-clothed brightly. These bright strips and the corresponding parts on the bearer are painted carefully with a cream of borax rubbed with water on a slate.* The hinge is placed in position—the lower edge of the upper bearer (this carries two knuckles) comes exactly to the lower edge of the lid—the lower bearer (with its three knuckles) is similarly placed on the body, and the whole is wired carefully.

The borax is now dried off very slowly, and a number of tiny panels of easy-running solder are placed along the angles between bearers and box. All is now heated very slowly and evenly until the solder shows signs of melting, when a short sharp blast with a small flame, directed first on one side of the hinge and then on the other, should solder each part securely. The critical moment has now come. As soon as the box is cool the binding wire is cut away, and if all has gone well the box will open and shut. Sometimes the hinge may stick without any mishap in soldering. A little oil will release it.

If we are so unfortunate as to let solder run into the hinge, all we can do is to make the whole hot again, and at the moment the solder fuses lift the hinge off with iron tongs. An expert could take the hinge to pieces and put it together again; but for a beginner there is nothing for it but to make a fresh hinge and try again. However, if we have been careful to loam all moving parts and surfaces thoroughly and to avoid heating the hinge at the expense of the box (the flame should only play on the actual hinge for a moment), there is little danger of failure. Lid and body should be examined carefully, and if the solder joints between them and the upper parts of the hinge are not perfectly sound, more solder should be added. This is better done before pickling.

Any surplus solder will usually come away easily with a needle file.

* This should be thick and stiff, if thin it will mix with the loam.

The soldering done, we can oil our hinge once more, pin it up with a bright pin, and feel proud of our skill as we open and shut the box.

We shall now pin up our box with a steel pin, made exactly as the pin of nickel-silver which we shall use finally. This should be very slightly tapered, and should be forced into the joint until it is in close contact with the metal from end to end. If thought necessary, a "reamer" or "broach" may first be passed through. The pin now fits so tightly that the joint will hardly move. It is withdrawn, the hinge taken apart, and the pin forced through the two knuckles of the upper bearer a little farther. It will now be found on putting the hinge together again that the pin will remain stationary in the three lower knuckles, and that the two upper ones will move freely without making the pin turn round.

Another kind of hinge.—It may be that the projecting "book" joint will in no way be suitable for our purpose; and that a hinge that is nearly, or even quite, flush with the surface of the box be called for. Fig. 86 shows how this

FIG. 86.—*Section of joint, a hinge that projects but slightly. The lid is shown in solid black. In actual practice it would be well to ease the bezel with a file, thus avoiding the danger of binding when opening and shutting the lid. Some omit the bezel on the eighth, hinged side.*

can be achieved. The gap, or groove which carries the knuckles, is actually filed out of the square wires which strengthen the body and lid of the box. A glance at Fig. 86 will show us that with a gap but very slightly deeper the knuckles can be actually flush with, or even below, the surface of the box.

Such a joint is, of course, distinctly more difficult to make than the "book"; but there is no need for anyone who has accomplished that first described successfully to hesitate before attempting this second kind. The lid should be very firmly wired on to the body while the gap is filed; indeed, in some cases this end is reached by soldering with two tiny blobs of soft solder applied in such a way that they can be easily and completely removed. This must, of course, be done before the knuckles are soldered in.

The actual soldering will be best done as follows: every part where lid touches body must be most carefully loamed. Then body and lid are wired firmly together, and the gap or groove made perfectly clean and bright. The knuckles being cut and bevelled as before are placed carefully in position. Take a borax crystal, or cone, and rub on a slate with water into a thick cream. Then with a tiny borax pencil, dipped in the cream and shaken out, apply a very small amount of borax to the lower sides of the three box knuckles and to the upper opposite sides of the two lid knuckles.

The box is now heated until all bubbling of the borax ceases. The box is allowed to cool. Then, having cut some tiny panels of thin solder, drop them on the borax slate and apply, with pencil or corn tongs, whichever is preferred, a panel in the centre of each knuckle where the borax was put. Then the whole is heated until the solder fuses and holds the knuckles in their places. They are then said to be "tacked." The aim in this part of the process is to apply just enough solder to hold the knuckles, but not a fraction too much, so that there is no danger of the solder making the joint solid. The whole is allowed to cool.

When cool, the lid is very carefully opened. Avoid anything like forcing, and when it has moved a little, shut it again. Then opening and shutting alternately, it should be possible to take the lid off without breaking the knuckles away from their bearers. It must be remembered that at this stage the solder is so small in amount as to have no great strength. All that now remains to be done is to borax the knuckles again and apply such an amount of solder as will hold them with absolute firmness without destroying the clean sharpness of the angles that is so necessary to the right fitting and working of the hinge.

Finishing the box.—In polishing a piece of fine metal work that has flat sides, and consequently sharp angles, the spindle must be used with the greatest care and rather sparingly. Emery cloth and Water of Ayr stone must be relied on to remove all scratches and file marks. Then a few moments' work with a stiff brush, used with oil and pumice or composition on the lathe, will give the right surface for finishing. Avoid using a mop until the very last. These have a tendency to dull angles, and although our box should not have corners so sharp that they look as if filed out of thick metal, it should certainly not have its corners rounded and blunt. Boxes such as we have made are almost invariably lined with velvet inside. Any good case-maker will do this.

If a wood lining is necessary for our box, it may be made by first dropping in a piece for the bottom, wedging it in position by strips (the inner wire and bezel will prevent a piece of wood the actual size of the bottom from going in), and then fitting eight pieces of wood so that when pushed between the floor of the box and the underside of the wire and bezel they will hold in position. Glue will make them secure. As will be seen on reflection, this is a tedious and rather thankless task. If a wood-lined box is needed, the usual way is to leave the bottom off. Then the lining can be slid up into position.*

It must not be thought that the method given is the only satisfactory way of making a box, though it is probably the easiest one for beginners. A usual and excellent method for an oblong box is to cut a piece of sheet metal equal in length and breadth to the top and the sides, and front and back. The exact size and shape of the top is marked with a sharp steel point, or scriber, taking care that this is quite central. These lines are now produced until they come right to the edges of the metal. The four squares at each

---

* The wood bottom may be covered with a thin plate of metal or silver.

corner are cut carefully away with shears, and trued up with a file. With nicking chisel or scraper the outline of the top is notched for bending. The inner edges of back, front, and sides are bevelled at an angle of 45 degrees; and the angles at the corners of the top are notched with a three-square file very slightly, so that when the box is bent up all the angles come smartly and sharply to 90 degrees. Any box of geometrical form, and which has the edges of its angles straight lines, can be made in this way—by setting out what modern school geometry books call "the net" of the desired form.

Boxes, such as presentation caskets, and indeed any which have their sides moulded, are best fashioned by first making strips, soldering the moulding on them with hard solder, mitreing them, and soldering with an easier solder. The same method is used when making boxes of sheet metal wrought into moulded sections with the hammer.

A piece of stout sheet iron $\frac{1}{8}$ inch thick, $1\frac{1}{2}$ inches wide, according to the work in hand, and $4\frac{1}{2}$ inches long, bent so that the outer $1\frac{1}{2}$ inches at each end makes an angle of 135 degrees with the centre section, is useful. The strips when bound or cramped on the bent ends will come together at an angle of 90 degrees. The two pairs of long and short sides are first put together, leaving the two opposite corners to be joined at the final soldering. The lid of such a box is made and fitted after the body is complete. The bottom or floor is almost always a separate piece screwed or riveted in. The same methods apply to boxes other than rectangular in plan.

Chapter 12

Exercise 9 : A TEAPOT, RAISED AND HAMMERED FROM THE
BLANK

The working of this exercise gives great scope for using the knowledge
and skill that have been gained in the elementary exercises. Once a student
has made a teapot he feels that he is really on the way to become a silversmith. Its accomplishment marks a very definite stage of progress. Techni-
cally it is a recapitulation of the various processes that we have so far used.

A teapot must be efficient, it must pour well, be easily cleansed, easily
handled, well balanced, and stand firmly. Its handle must be strong, rigidly
and permanently fixed, with due provision made for its removal when the
pot needs repair. Its lid must be strongly hinged. Lastly, it must make good
tea. This will lead us to make our pot with a wide base so that the boiling
water can act on the tea in the shortest possible time.

The setting of the spout on the body and its relation to the handle are
points that call for great nicety of taste and judgment. Personally, the writer
holds that the line of the spout should be one which looks as if the liquid
can flow out with the least possible resistance. We should visualize our pot
in use, imagining the added joy that a delightful teapot can give to a meal.
The line of the flowing liquid itself should be thought of as a part of the
whole.

The handle needs, perhaps, even more thought. Efficiency, of course,
comes first, but a good handle has numbers of other points to think of.
Certainly its line should be related to the spout.

Fig. 87 gives a hint as to how a drawing will help to achieve this. A handle
must be right in size; this is no easy matter to settle upon; its sockets, if of a

Fig. 87.—*How the relation of spout to handle can be determined.
Insulated metal handle.*

non-conductor, or its insulators, if of metal, must be placed with extreme care, so that the handle will fit firmly and allow of easy removal when repairs are needed.

FIG. 88.

Fig. 88 shows a pot which fulfils these conditions and is certainly not too difficult to make.

The first thing is to decide upon the capacity of the pot, and to make rough outline drawings so that the right size can be determined. Then we make a final drawing from which we make our estimate of the size of the disc we shall need for raising the body of the pot. The thickness of the metal should be from 10 to 12 m.g. according to the capacity.

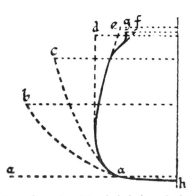

FIG. 89.—*Stages in raising the body from the flat disc.*

Fig. 89 shows, in continuous line, a half section of the body of the pot we are to make. The dotted lines show the stages of raising from the flat disc upwards. (*a*) is the blank cut from a sheet of 10 or 11 gauge metal or silver.

Its diameter is determined according to the rule given in Exercise 1—**average diameter** + height + $\dfrac{\text{average diameter}}{10}$ = diameter of blank—the figure 10 in the last is an average estimate. If the metal will stretch, as it often does in vessels with a concave contour, the fraction may be omitted. In the present case with a convex contour, little stretching will take place, and the addition of about $\frac{1}{12}$ diameter to the sum of the diameter and the height will probably be needed. If the student wishes, he may start with a larger blank and cut the edge down after it is raised. This will ensure that the raising can be made exactly to size, and will permit of the cracks, that are liable to form in the rim of a beginner's raising, being cut away, but it will involve more work. Individual touch and methods of handling make much difference in raising. Some craftsmen tend to stretch the metal more than others.

The various hints and cautions given in Exercise 1 should be read and carefully noted. With the addition of the following, the instructions given there should prove adequate.

The raising should be begun around a circle struck at the point where the dotted line (a) (a) meets the outline of the pot. Within this circle the base should be kept perfectly flat until the pot is ready for planishing; (b), (c), and (d) show the raising at different stages. By the time (d) is reached it will be well, if a mallet has been used, to put it aside and complete the raising to (e) and (f) with a hammer. Too much care in annealing (avoid over-heating as the plague) and in the use of compasses and scribing block for truing cannot be taken.

The fullness of the base shown at (h) comes easily by planishing on a rounded bottom stake. In planishing, as in raising, use the pencil compasses to ensure truth of form. This is most especially necessary at the points of greatest curvature, where the base merges into the body, and where the body turns inwards to the mouth. The mouth is planished while its shape is that shown at (f). The outward curve (g) is given with a narrow neck hammer, using a grooved piece of smooth hard wood as a stake (see Exercise 1, a similar problem). If we are fortunate enough to have a round mandrel that will fit tightly in the mouth, we can easily make it a true circle. Failing this mandrel, we can round the mouth by tapping the curved rim with the neck hammer whilst holding it on a stake whose curve is slightly flatter than that of the mouth. If we have nothing that seems large and flat enough for this, we can get the curve we need by holding the pot with its axis at an angle to the axis of the stake. A line drawn obliquely on a cylinder traces a flatter curve than one drawn at right angles to the axis. By remembering this we can often make one stake serve many purposes.

The pot we are considering at the moment can be raised and hammered on the stakes that are illustrated in Figs. 3 to 9, but it may be well to make one that more nearly fits inside our pot. This is easily done by making a model in plaster or wood and having it cast in malleable iron. Longitudinally, the curve of this will be almost identical with that of the pot except that the flatter part in the centre should be shorter, by $\frac{1}{2}$ inch or 1 inch, so that it may be used for other shapes, and that the concave curve of the mouth is omitted. Care must be taken that it will, when fitted in the crank or horse, pass through the mouth of the vessel.

Here it may be said that in the case of vessels with very small mouths it is usual to put the head inside first, and then to fit the crank on to it. No matter how tightly the shank of the head may fit, it may be loosened by striking the upper side of the crank smartly with a heavy hammer. Sometimes it will yield to a mallet blow. The blow should be aimed at a spot about 2 inches from the angle of the crank.

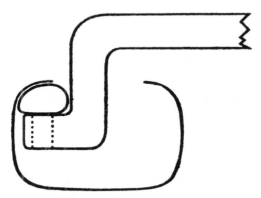

FIG. 90.—*Using the double crank.*

Fig. 90 shows the use of the double crank in shaping a vessel with incurved rim.

The raising and planishing of the body being as shapely and smooth as our hammer can make it, we make a ring foot of oblong wire, which may be grooved or moulded as we please, and solder it centrally on the bottom of the pot. This done, with the scribing block, we mark an accurate horizontal line around the mouth at the level of its lowest point. Then we cut as nearly to the line as we can with crooked shears, holding the mouth of the raising

FIG. 91.—*Section showing construction of lid, etc.*

towards our body. These crooked shears are necessary when dealing with vessels having incurved mouths. The levelling is finished by filing, followed by rubbing on the flat emery board.

The lid is now raised and hammered. This is quite a simple matter, even if we choose to flatten the top to make a good bearing for the collar of the knob. We first planish the centre of the lid into a rounded shape. A circle the size of the flat is struck with pencil compasses, and, using a hammer head held in the vice as a bottom stake, planish down with gentle blows from a full faced hammer.

We are now ready for mounting the lid and its seat. Fig. 91 will explain this. A square wire of about $\frac{1}{8}$ inch is soldered inside the mouth of the body.* Another ring of wire, slightly wider and thinner, say, $\frac{3}{32}$ inch by $\frac{5}{32}$ inch, is made and fitted loosely inside the wire soldered in the body. This second ring should have a distinct "shake" inside the first. Another wire of the same thickness, but wider, $\frac{1}{4}$ inch or so, is bent up flatwise and soldered to the second ring; this makes a ring of L section which will carry the lid.

The seams of these rings will, of course, be soldered with the hardest solder. The two forming the L can be joined with an easier solder. This will be used also to solder the lid to the L ring. After soldering, the rim of the lid and the edge of the L wire are filed or turned to a true circle.

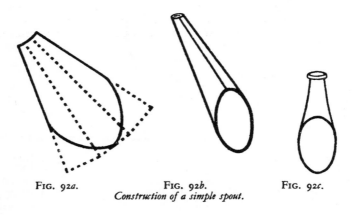

FIG. 92a.   FIG. 92b.   FIG. 92c.
Construction of a simple spout.

Next comes the spout. Fig. 88 shows the simplest form, a tapered tube hammered out at each end.

The exact size of this is conveniently determined by rolling up tapered tubes of stiff paper until we find a shape and size that is obviously right. We can then do one of two things. The paper tube may be cut, flattened out, and used as a template; or we may make a drawing of the actual size, and develop it as shown in Figs. 92a and 92b.

It is always well to make the spout of a pot one or two gauges thicker than the body.

The problem of soldering up the seam of this tube is identical with that of the conical lid of the box in Exercise 3. Use the hardest solder available. When pickled clean, the surplus solder is filed off and the spout emery-clothed.

The outward curve at the lower end can easily be got by planishing with a full faced hammer; a neck hammer with a gentle curve is admirable. The

* The lower, inner corner may be bevelled, or rounded, with advantage.

curve at the top is more difficult. For a stake for this it will probably be necessary to file up a piece of iron or steel to a suitable size and to bend it. We want something like a small "beck iron" or "sparrow hawk" with a bent beak.

We must take care to make our tube quite on the small side, especially at the wide end; if we do not, we shall find it is too large when the planishing is finished. It is, of course, possible to reduce the diameter by raising, but we should need a very sturdy stake to do this upon.

We have now to fit the spout to the body. This is done roughly with a small pair of bent shears and then finished off with a file. The problem is parallel to that of fitting the handle to the ring in Exercise 6.

The fitting done, we cut or file the top of the spout to the right height— very slightly above the level of the mouth.

For a beginner it may be advisable to solder the spout on before this is done; but we will complete the spout forthwith. The top of the spout can be strengthened in one of two ways. A half-round wire may be led around it, but this is a rather tedious business, and it is difficult to avoid bruising the wire whilst bending into the complex curve needed to make it fit closely.

The writer prefers the following: file the end a little shorter, and to rather bolder curves than the finished spout will show. Then take a piece of metal of about 20 m.g., cut an oblong about $\frac{1}{8}$ inch larger every way than the top of the spout. Then file, in a piece of hard wood, a groove into which this thick piece of metal can be driven with a narrow neck hammer (this may be used as a punch if struck with a mallet). The metal is then reversed and the process repeated so as to get the double curve.

This bending may be done quite well on a lead cake, but a solid punch is needed to stand up to the vigorous hammer blows necessary.

The bent metal is now pierced, by drill and saw or file, with a hole of the same shape but slightly smaller than the opening in the spout. This is soldered, with a reasonably liberal amount of solder, on the spout. It is then filed up, inside flush with the inner surface of the spout, and outside so as to form a pleasant rounded lip (Fig. 92c).

The handle next claims our attention. For a first attempt fibre is perhaps the best material. Though not quite as pleasant in colour as natural wood, it is practically unbreakable and stands up to constant use excellently. Make an accurate drawing the exact size of the whole pot. Take a tracing of the handle and the sockets. Get this cut out of a sheet of fibre of a suitable thickness: if the greatest diameter of the handle is to be $\frac{1}{2}$ inch, use $\frac{5}{8}$ inch fibre, and so on—any firm of hardwood workers will do it—or a piece of fibre may be bought, and the student may saw the shape out for himself.

Shaping the handle.—The first thing to do is to round the pegs or tenons at each end, and to make two short lengths of tube to fit on them tightly. These are the sockets. They are now sawn and filed, usually while actually in position on the handle itself, until they fit snugly on the body in the right place. Use a fairly heavy gauge, 12 or 14 m.g. Solder them on exactly in position. There is no great difficulty in holding the handle firmly and marking the position with a scriber or pencil. If it proves impossible to arrange the sockets so that they will rest firmly enough to allow of soldering, stitches (see Exercise 5) may prove necessary. Or it may be possible to arrange a support of stout binding wire. If the student doubts his skill to use strip solder without disturbing the sockets, panels dropped inside them may be used. Great care must be taken in applying the heat; the borax must not be allowed to bubble too violently or the socket will move out of position; the heat must be so applied that body and sockets get hot together. These short tubes can easily be made red hot while the body is still black. If this is allowed to happen, the solder will tend, if used as suggested, to flush inside the tube. This may disturb the fitting of the handle. Put the upper socket on first, and check the original marking of the bottom socket before soldering it on. A skilled man would probably "jump" the sockets on unhesitatingly.

For the present the roughly shaped handle is left as it is.

FIG. 93.—*The grid or strainer.*

Now for the spout. Fix the position very carefully. The tip of the spout should come very slightly, $\frac{1}{16}$ inch or so, above the level of the mouth of the pot. Mark around, with scriber or pencil, the large end where it fits on to the body. Within this shape, an oval in the present case, mark a series of $\frac{1}{8}$-inch circles arranged in a pleasant order. Put the pot on a suitable head, and mark the centre of each circle with a centre punch. Then drill them with a $\frac{7}{64}$ inch drill; a twist drill is perhaps the best (Fig. 93). Remove the burr left by the drill inside the pot with a half-round file bent to a suitable shape. Files can easily be shaped by making them red hot and, using a slotted piece of hard wood as a resistance, bending them while still red to the needed curve. This done, heat them again to bright redness, quench in water, and temper by dipping in turpentine or petrol, and flaring off. After the file, use emery cloth.

The spout is now tied on with binding wire, 22 or 20 B.W.G. Fig. 94 shows a usual way of doing it, but we must be prepared to devise our own methods. An excellent one is to make a counterpoise out of thick iron wire, which when sprung into the spout will have its greatest weight beyond the base of the spout. This will make it possible to hold the spout in position without using binding wire.

The spout being adjusted to the exact position, all wires are carefully and evenly tightened. Pour some thin borax water in the pot and pour it out through the spout so as to ensure the flux going where it is needed. Before applying the heat, take a last look to see that the spout is exactly right. Note most carefully that the axis of the spout exactly coincides with the line of the sockets, and also with the diameter of the pot. Then place the pot on the hearth in such a position that the wires are relieved of strain as far as possible. A short spout, for instance, will sometimes stand in position without wire.

The aim is to avoid a slip. Borax outside and solder with strip. Once the solder has run for one-third of the way round, there is no danger of moving. Sometimes it is necessary to remove the wires before the solder can be made to flush all around, especially in the narrow angle between spout and body. If the fitting has been carefully done, there should be little trouble in ensuring sound soldering. If the first attempt is not successful, try again before pickling. Then if there is any doubt, it is best to borax liberally, make the whole thing hot enough to melt the solder all around the spout, and lift it off with light iron tongs. It can then be fitted again more accurately.

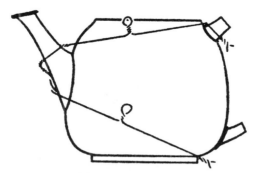

FIG. 94.—*The spout tied on with binding wire.*

Two points in the soldering of the spout to the body are: (*a*) the fitting must be even; it does not matter so much that every portion is in close contact with the body as that the points which are in contact are evenly spaced; if we fit a spout closely around the upper half, while the lower ɩ less closely fitted, the solder will rush to the upper half, and in doing so will widen the gap in the lower half; (*b*) when applying the heat, care must be taken not to overheat the wires in one place; the unequal expansion will pull the spout out of position. Go slowly, and bathe the whole in flame.

The soldering completed, pickle thoroughly, file off any surplus solder, and test the soundness of the soldering by filling the pot with boiling water. If there is the slightest crevice, the water will ooze through.

The shaping of the handle can now be continued. For this use a small half-round cabinet rasp, following with files of increasing smoothness. Take care to cross and recross the direction of the file strokes; fibre is a substance easily damaged by a rough file used unintelligently. After the files, use emery cloth; long narrow strips of "blue back" are excellent. Wrap the handle in soft thick rag, hold it firmly in the vice, and pull the emery cloth to and fro. The polishing can be done on the lathe with a brush, using oil and pumice. The final gloss is given with a mop, using a special substance similar to ordinary "Tripoli composition" sold by dealers in polishing materials. If this is not available, beeswax and turpentine will answer.

Shaping the handle will test our powers of design very severely. We must aim at making it not only pleasant to handle, but pleasant to the eye from every point of view. Take care to shape the handle so that there is no risk of burned fingers. The slight thickenings where handle goes into sockets, shown in Fig. 88, are for this purpose.

The sockets may now be drilled. Mark two points on each about $\frac{1}{16}$ inch from the open end, taking great care that they come exactly opposite and on a horizontal diameter. This marking is best done with the point of a graver or scraper. If no help is at hand to hold the pot, a jeweller's "pump'

FIG. 95.—*The two parts of the simple hinge. The two-knuckled part is soldered on the lid, that with three on the socket.*

drill stock that can be used with one hand is best. Choose a "spear" point drill rather less than $\frac{1}{16}$-inch diameter. The burr left by the drill inside the sockets can be filed, or cut away with a scorper.

Hinging the lid is the next thing (Fig. 95). Draw a length of tube from 12 or 14 m.g. sheet on to a $\frac{1}{16}$-inch pin. Cut two pieces of thick sheet a shade less than $\frac{1}{8}$ inch thick, about $\frac{1}{2}$ inch by $\frac{5}{8}$ inch. On these with the hardest solder put two $\frac{5}{8}$-inch lengths of tube. Gaps are now filed in each until the two can be put together to form a five-knuckle hinge. Take care to leave the outer knuckles on the three-knuckle piece a little wider than the gaps and the centre knuckle. This is to allow the whole hinge to be filed to size. This done, fit them together (they should fit very tightly), push a tapered pin through, oil the hinge, grip one bearer in the vice, and, with a pair of large pliers, work it to and fro until it moves smoothly. Fig. 88 shows how this simply made hinge can be fitted to the socket and the lid.

FIG. 96.—*The knob, collar, nut, and screw.*

When the upper bearer has to be fitted on to a rounded convex lid, it may be necessary to use a round nose chisel or scorper to make a close fit. The upper bearer can often be omitted in hinges made in this manner. The tube, or chenier, is soldered, before gapping, directly on the edge of the L wire of the lid, a flat to afford firm attachment being filed to take it. When making hinges in this manner, as a general practice, a flat should be filed on the seam of the tube before soldering it on the bearer. Sometimes it may prove to be more satisfactory to groove the bearer. The object is to ensure sound, strong soldering. Always use the hardest solder available. Then no risk of the knuckles falling off in subsequent soldering arises.

The hinge being fitted, the L wire and the rim of the pot are loamed. The lid is bound firmly in position. The hinge is also loamed and pinned with a black iron pin. It is then placed in position, boraxed where the bearers rest on the socket and the lid, and soldered with easy solder used in strip. This operation needs care, but is not extremely difficult.

We now make the knob, its collar, and the nut and screw (Fig. 96). If a lathe is available, the collar can be turned; if not, it can be hammered out of a bit of tube. This thin collar is soldered between two small domed discs pierced with holes the size of the screw. The concave surfaces of these domes allow the collar to sit firmly on the lid, and the knob to rest firmly on the collar. The screw is a piece of $\frac{3}{16}$-inch wire tapped with a $\frac{5}{32}$-inch Whitworth thread. The nut is a circle about $\frac{3}{8}$ inch diameter and $\frac{1}{8}$ inch thick, The loop is of stout half-round wire. A bead, or a section of thick wire, soldered on the head of the screw, and filed or turned to shape, forms the head of the screw.

The knob itself is of fibre. Care must be taken that the hole is drilled at right angles to the grain of the fibre. If drilled parallel with it, the knob would probably split in the turning. The screw must be just long enough to project about $\frac{1}{16}$ inch through the nut when all is screwed up tightly.

If we decide to decorate the pot, it is done now. The pattern shown in Fig. 88 is a suggestion of what it is possible to work by simple flat chasing. See chapter 16 for this.

Polishing and finishing the pot present no new problems.

After a teapot is polished, it is well to loam between the lid and the seat. The joint also should be loamed and pinned with a black iron pin. The lid is now wired tightly in position, and the whole is carefully and thoroughly annealed. This ensures that the lid shall sit rightly. The final adjustment by bending, shortly to be described, may often be avoided by this simple means.

Last of all comes the pinning up. Push the handle tightly in the sockets and mark the position of the holes on the pegs. Drill these with the same drill used on the sockets, $\frac{1}{64}$ inch farther from the outer end. This drilling is done from both sides. There is no great difficulty in making the holes meet in the centre. Then when a taper pin is pushed through it will pull the handle tightly into the sockets. Put a temporary pin in each end. Hard-drawn nickel silver wire is the best metal to use. The final pinning is done in this way. Take a piece of wire about $\frac{1}{32}$ inch thicker than the diameter of the holes. File this to a long and gentle taper. Emery cloth and polish it smooth. Hold it firmly in the hand vice, and push it with a twisting movement (use a spot of oil to prevent seizing up) until the pin fills the hole in the socket at its smaller end. Nip the wire off at the small end almost close up to the socket. At the large end make a tiny file notch $\frac{1}{8}$ inch away from the socket. Withdraw the pin, cut it off at the notch, and round each end up with file and emery cloth, finishing on a grease mop. This polished pin, with the smooth rounded ends, can now be driven with a small hammer through sockets and handle until there is an equal amount of projection on each side. It is well to put the pin in the lower socket from the opposite side to that in the upper one.

The same method is used for pinning up the hinge. In this case the pot is held with the spout towards, and the handle away from, the worker, and the pin pushed in with the right hand. On no account should the pins of handles and joints be riveted. If this is done, and repairs are needed, the sockets and joint will inevitably be damaged in extracting the pins. Moreover, the bright, glistening, rounded pin-ends add to the charm of the pot. Care must, of course, be taken not to leave the pins too long.

Great care must be taken to ensure that the pin remains fixed in the three lower knuckles. Before the pin is finally driven home we must remember to force the pin through the two knuckles on the upper bearer so that the bore in the two knuckles is very slightly larger than that in the three lower ones.

All that now remains to be done is to see that the lid shuts down properly, with no tendency to spring. With the simple type of hinge described there is little danger of this happening. If anything is wrong, a judicious twist, or a blow with a small mallet will remedy it.

Where other forms of hinge joint, book, flush,* or skittle† are used, it not infrequently happens that, when all is completed, the lid refuses to remain quite shut down. This defect is often remedied by putting a bit of wire in the hinge so as to stop it shutting right down. Gentle pressure on the lid, until it is felt to yield, will bend hinge, bearers, and lid sufficiently to let it drop into its right place. The possibility of having to do this makes it imperative that the soldering is absolutely sound. Sometimes a more yielding substance—leather, string, or rag—will prove better than wire. A final polish by hand completes the pot.

FIG. 97.—*A section of an insulated handle. As far as possible, the shape, as shaded, should be avoided.*

Metal handles of D section for teapots are made exactly as the handle of the mug in Exercise 6. The whole handle is soldered on the pot, a vent or vents being made with a saw-cut where the handle will afterwards be cut through for the insertion of the insulators. These are filed out of pieces of ivory or fibre (the former is the best), roughly turned to shape. Fig. 97 shows a sectional view of a handle and an ivory insulation. Although not absolutely necessary, it is certainly most desirable that the handle be cut at the points where the axes of the insulators will be most nearly parallel. If this is done, the insulators can be made to fit the handle and its sockets tightly for a considerable length. If one is compelled to have the insulators with their axes at an angle to each other, the insulators have to be filed away, as shown

---

* "Flush joint." A hinge made with chenier of large diameter and comparatively small bore, so that the projection above the surface can be filed off flush. Eighteenth-century teapots, straight sided, oval or octagonal, have "flush" joints. See Fig. 86.
† "Skittle." Joints which have in the normal position their bearers in a straight line on opposite sides of the knuckles. They are often bought ready made. The ordinary "trade" teapot has a skittle joint.

by shading. Plaster of Paris may be used to fill in the gaps; but when this crumbles away, as it will do sooner or later, all the strain falls on the pins, and the handle soon begins to wobble.

When a tubular handle is wanted it has to be made as a straight tube, usually circular in section, and bent. This is done as follows: The inside of the tube is painted very thinly and evenly with loam,* and carefully dried. The small end is now wrapped in paper, and the tube is buried in sand. The tube is filled with lead, and when cold can be bent to any curve desired. Doing this will inevitably alter the circular section. A flat surface will develop on the outer and inner faces as it is bent over the mandrel or beck-iron with a mallet. A round section is a bad one for a handle, so this happening is not unwelcome. The bending done, the handle is now planished. For the inner curves use a piece of hard wood for the anvil. For the outer curves use a mandrel or side stake that most nearly fits the inner curve. An oval section is the most easily worked; an irregular octagon, with its longer axis at right angles to the length of the handle, possibly the most pleasant.

In bending lead-filled handles the one danger to guard against is the formation of kinks, sudden sharp bends which may be difficult to planish away. If one can devise any slotted pieces of wood so that the use of the mallet can be avoided, or reduced to a minimum, much trouble can be avoided.

To melt the lead out of the handle, hang it on binding wire in the position from which the liquid metal will flow most easily. Then play a gas flame on the handle with no blast whatever, keeping it in constant motion; in a few minutes the lead will come out quite cleanly, leaving nothing but a few filmy fragments behind. Let the handle cool. Make a roughly shaped scraper that can be passed through the handle so that every bit of lead can be got out.

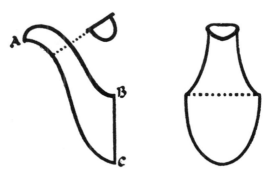

Fig. 98.—*Front and side views of flat-topped spout.*

If these instructions are carried out to the letter, no lead will cling to the inner surface of the handle, and it may safely be annealed. The two chief points to observe are that the coating of loam, while thin, must be even and quite free from gaps; and that no more heat be used than will suffice

* Use enough, but not too much, water; and see that the mixture is free from lumps.

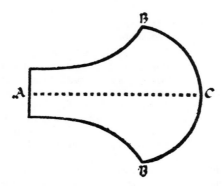

FIG. 99.—*The template for the* U *half of flat-topped spout.*

to melt the lead. When working in silver it is worth while to use the greatest care, so that the lead does no damage by alloying and amalgamating itself violently with the silver, thus eating into it, making unsightly holes, and ruining the work.

Spouts of D section—flat-topped—(Figs. 98 to 101) are made in almost the identical manner followed in fashioning a handle of similar section.

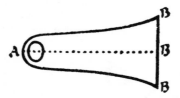

FIG. 100.—*Template for flat top of* D *sectioned spout. When fitted the line* BBB *will be curved to fit the body.*

Fig. 99 shows how the template for cutting the blank for the U, or lower half, is developed from the drawing. The distances are very conveniently taken by bending pieces of binding wire to the curve, nipping them to the right length and straightening them out, or bending them again, laying them on paper to mark positions and curves. In setting out Fig. 99 some little experimenting may be needed in fixing the points BB, and the curve BCB, on the flat template. Fig. 101 shows how the large convex end of the U is shaped by raising on a small round-ended stake. The end of the spout can be left D-shaped, or by curving the tip on both sides and piercing a hole in the end of the cover (see Fig. 100) the spout shown in Figs. 98 to 100 can be made. In spouts of this kind a pleasant finish is provided by leaving a narrow rim of the cover to overhang the U.

Curved spouts of circular section are made as shown in Figs. 102 to 104. The portion between AA and BB is a simple tapered tube, and is shaped,

FIG. 101.—*Using a small round-ended stake.*

soldered, and planished exactly as any other tube would be (Fig. 103). Next the curves BC BC are brought together with mallet or hammer, and soldered. The reason for the notch D to D now appears. This is closed and soldered. After filing off the surplus solder, the big end of the spout is planished on any suitable stake, or stakes, that can be found.

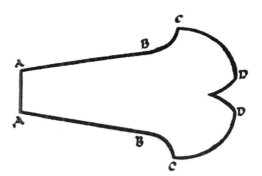

FIG. 102.—*The template for a circular sectional curved spout.*

This done, the whole is filled with lead. The spout is put in the sand at an angle, with the big end horizontal. The lead should come only to within about $\frac{1}{16}$ inch of the rim, so that the rim itself can be bent down with a hammer on to the lead. This will prevent the lead from working loose while the bending is done.

Such a spout as this can be bent by malleting, but the round taper tube will suffer in the process, and it will take a long time to coax it, with the hammer, back to its proper shape. Fig. 104 shows a method the writer has devised. The spout is made longer than is needed, and a hole of about $\frac{1}{16}$ inch is drilled at the extreme end. Then a piece of hard wood is shaped to the curve,

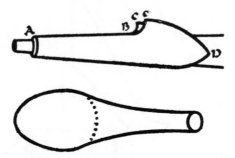

FIG. 103.—*The first stage in making the circular sectioned spout.*

and a groove is filed in this to fit the spout as nearly as possible. A hole is drilled through the wood. A wire is passed through spout and wood as shown. The whole is held in the vice (lead clams help greatly) and the spout bent by pushing or pulling the big end by hand. Here, as elsewhere, the student should be ready to devise details of procedure that will make

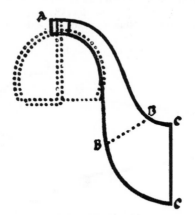

FIG. 104.—*How the lead filled spout may be bent. The wood and wire are shown dotted.*

operations like these easier and more successful. Everyone will find, as he grows more skilful, that he will acquire variations of method and procedure personal to himself.

If time allows, once the student has made a teapot successfully, and completely, to the limits of his powers, he should make another with the idea of testing his speed. If he, an individual worker, making only one pot at a time, can complete a pot such as Fig. 88 in forty to fifty hours, he may congratulate himself that he is well on the way to become a silversmith. This is, of course, a vastly longer time than can be given to the making of an ordinary commercial teapot at so much per ounce. But if our craftsman could make, say, half a dozen pots at once, the time would be halved. Still further reductions would come if such pots were made regularly and in larger quantities.

The making of things in a limited time should be part of the training of a silversmith, The writer would urge the industry on both sides, productive and distributive, to experiment in the making of some such piece as this teapot by hand, under the direction of an artist, so that all up and down the country simple, soundly wrought pieces could be shown for sale side by side with work made in the dull perfunctory way.

Repetition work, when the craftsman is free to enjoy the exercise of his skill and artistry, is entirely exhilarating. But if repetition work becomes a mere soulless task, we get manufactures. Fine work always retains something of the fire that burned in its maker's mind.

CHAPTER 13

EXERCISE 10 : A COFFEE POT, WITH CAST SPOUT AND HANDLE

FIG. 105 shows an elevation of a coffee pot following the tradition of early eighteenth century work closely. The only departure from precedent is that it shows a cast metal handle, not a wooden one.

In making a pot of this kind, a drawing to fix sizes and proportions should first be made. This done, we will make the plain body and lid. A rather stout gauge metal, 12 or 13 m.g., should be used, unless the worker has had a good deal of experience in making flat-sided vessels.

The simplest way of setting out the template for the body of the pot is to draw one of the eight faces with extreme accuracy, and from it trace the seven other faces with their sides and angles touching, the narrow ends all pointing the same way. This tracing is transferred to the metal and scribed in with firm lines. The blank should then be cut out as accurately as possible with shears, using a file for the final shaping. It is then flattened or "set," see Exercise 8. Each angle is now nicked for bending, and the ends are bevelled so that they will mitre properly when brought together. See that the nicks are sufficiently deep to ensure clean sharp bending, yet without breaking. Exercise 3 may be referred to for right methods of wiring. The actual join is soldered with the hardest available solder, and solder is also run along each nick so as to ensure strength.

The instructions given in Exercise 8 as to the flattening, hammering, and trueing up of the box will serve also for this coffee pot. It must be remembered, however, that this is much more difficult than the box owing to the greater length. An essential point here is to subject each face to exactly the same treatment. The greatest care must also be taken to avoid clumsy, heavy-handed use of the hammer. It is only too easy to stretch one facet unduly. If this should happen, the only remedy is to subject the other seven faces to the same amount of force.

If the worker is sufficiently skilled to make the pot of thinner metal, the burnisher (see Exercise 8) may be used almost to the exclusion of the hammer. The spring faced hammer (Fig. 11d) will be found useful in working this exercise.

Another method of making the body, serving equally well for either thin or thick metal, is to make it round. Then, having malleted or hammered it smooth (a finely planished surface is not an essential at this stage) and perfectly circular, the eight lines of the angles are marked and scribed just deep enough to be clear, but not so deep as to be difficult to remove.

A conical tube is most conveniently trued up in the lathe; a polygonal one may be done in this way if great care is taken to avoid the tool digging into the angles.

If we are fortunate enough to have an octagonal mandrel of the right size at hand, we shall find it a comparatively easy matter to mallet the round tube into an octagon. Care must be taken to ensure that the angles coincide exactly with the scribed lines.

If we have no mandrel, we shall be able to manage quite well with a piece of hard wood thin enough to pass right through the pot, with one face a little—about $\frac{1}{8}$ inch—narrower than the face of the pot. Using a mallet, or a small hammer with a distinctly rounded face, we shall find we can, with gentle blows, beat the round tube into an octagon. This done, it should be annealed and then planished on a straight stake. A bar of square mild steel a

FIG. 105.—*Coffee pot.*

shade narrower than the narrowest part of a face of the pot can be bought from any blacksmith quite cheaply. If we file and emery cloth one face smooth, we shall have an excellent tool to planish our pot upon.

It will probably seem, to the beginner, a rather difficult matter to get the angles exactly in the right place. Actually, it is not particularly so. If we have our work and hammer in that state where the mark of every blow is clearly visible, we shall find that we can move our work while the hammer falls, forcing the metal down on to the flat stake, and see the flat facet we are making creep up gradually to the line. A hammer, not too flat faced, and a bit of well worn emery cloth are essentials in the successful planishing of polygonal work.

FIG. 106.—*The fitting and mouldings of the lid.*

We now proceed with the lid. This is raised in the ordinary way, being at first circular in plan. It may be made octagonal by two methods. It may be malleted and hammered, first on wood and afterwards on steel. Both wood and steel should, of course, be shaped to fit the inside of the lid.

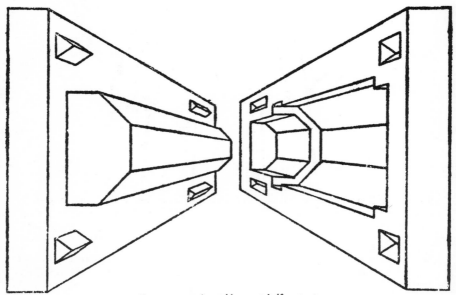

FIG. 107.—*A mould to cast half a spout.*

Actually, what is wanted is a shape exactly like one face of the lid, but slightly smaller. The other method is to fill the round lid with the pitch, tallow, and brick-dust or plaster used by chasers and to hammer down the centre of each facet until the angles, where the flat faces meet, coincide with the scribed lines that mark the eight divisions.

In the case of this lid it will be well to raise it $\frac{1}{8}$ inch or $\frac{1}{4}$ inch deeper than it is actually needed, especially if we use pitch in its shaping. The extra length will enable us to shape it without striking with great force on the extreme edge, a course which will be certain to make the pitch break and come out of the lid.

The exact size of the lid needs consideration. The section Fig. 106 shows the bezel, *i.e.*, the part of the lid that fits inside the body, as in one piece with the lid. To attain this we must make the circumference of our lid equal to the perimeter of the octagon. If we remember that it is easier to make a raising expand by planishing than it is to contract it by raising it, we shall certainly keep our raising on the small side.

If we deem the task of making lid and bezel in one to be too difficult the lid may follow the construction shown in Fig. 91.

Having made the body of the pot, we will consider the making of the casting patterns for handle and spout. Fig. 107 shows a mould for half a spout. (For the sake of clarity this has been made to show a very simple shape. In actual practice a straight spout like this would be cored; this

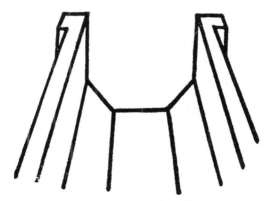

FIG. 108.—*The end of a half of spout.*

process will be explained later when dealing with the collar for the knob.) Fig. 107 must be taken as a diagram and not as a representation of an actual mould. It will be seen that when the upper and lower halves are brought together, a space, the exact shape of the half spout (Fig. 108), will be left between them.

For the handle and spout of our pot the problem is, of course, much more difficult, though the principles upon which we work are identical. The instructions given for the spout will serve equally well for the handle; though more care in regard to thickness may be needed.

The first thing is to take a tracing of the elevation of the spout, transfer it to a piece of metal 10 or 12 m.g., saw it out, file it up with extreme accuracy, and solder a piece of folded metal strip to make it easy to hold.

We now take hard modelling wax, break it up into small pieces with a little chisel, soften them by gentle heat, and build up on the metal template of the spout a model of the spout itself. Some little practice will be needed before the wax can be handled with ease. It will be found that the warmth of the hand alone will keep the wax plastic to a degree. For a first attempt the best method is to apply the wax liberally, making its mass bulkier than we need, and then trimming it to a size with a sharp penknife. It will be seen that the metal template in the centre of the wax enables us to obtain the most important contour with great ease.

The fingers are, of course, the best of all modelling tools, but something more is needed to make the facets sufficiently clean and accurate. Brass modelling tools, made from wire ($\frac{3}{16}$ inch diameter is a good size), flattened

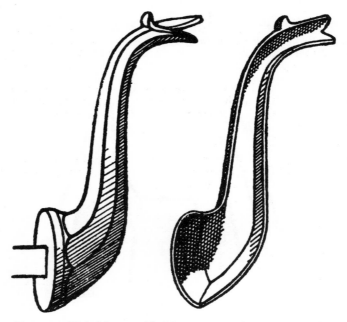

FIG. 109.—*The solid wax model of the spout.*
Note the folded strip of metal that is soldered
to the template.

FIG. 110.—*Casting pattern*
of a half spout.

out and filed up to a suitable shape (the human finger provides a good model) kept slightly warm, will enable us to carry our model as far as we please. Fig. 109 shows the wax model at this stage. Take the greatest care that the metal template passes exactly through the centre of the wax model.

Have some fine fresh Italian plaster ready. Make a box of card, wood, or sheet metal, so large that when the model is laid in it no part shall be nearer than $1\frac{1}{2}$ inches to any side of the box. Its depth should be equal to about two diameters of the thickest part of the model. Some arrangement which will enable the model to be held firmly, with the template exactly horizontal and on a level with the rim of the box, must be made. The wax model should be smeared thinly with oil.

In an earthenware basin put about twice as much water as would suffice to fill the box to the brim. Into this the plaster is sprinkled slowly and evenly until it just shows above the surface of the water. It is then stirred with a spoon until it is perfectly smooth and even. Its consistency is important; it should be liquid, but with distinct signs of thickening. As soon as we think the plaster is right we pour it into the box until its surface is just perceptibly above the centre of the wax model. It is then left until it is set. The surface of the plaster is now pared down exactly to the centre line with a flat chisel or a knife, and the wax model is lifted out. When the plaster is quite firm four pits are sunk (see Fig. 107), though there is no need to make them of the shape there shown. Actually, they are most conveniently bored out with the tip of a penknife. The surface is then oiled, and the wax model replaced. A wall of clay, wax, or card is put around the mould high enough to contain a mass of plaster equal to the lower mould. More plaster is mixed and poured in. When this is set the wall is removed and the two halves are prised apart.

We have now a mould in two halves in which we could cast a solid spout. This would be useless; we have to make it hollow, and beyond that quite smooth inside. Coring, a process to be noted later, is not available. We need two half-spouts which we can solder together.

Turn to Fig. 107 again, and note that, when the two parts are put together, there is a space of the exact size and shape between them. We have already the two moulds of the outside of the spout. How can we make the moulds for the inside? There are two methods available.

(a) We can oil each of the moulds of the outside, use the walls again and cast, in plaster, two halves of the spout, each of which is on a flat slab. When these are set we can pare away from each an amount of plaster equal to the thickness we wish to have our spout; a shade more than $\frac{1}{16}$ inch will be right. A convenient way of doing this is to make a drill which will go $\frac{1}{16}$ inch into the plaster and no deeper; with it we drill all over the last-made plaster casts, with the half-spouts in relief, a series of holes to serve as guides to show us how much we may pare away.

(b) The other method is to roll wax out into a sheet of the thickness of the spout, cut it in strips, and line the hollow mould with it. After plaster is poured on this, and it has set, the two halves of the mould are taken apart and the wax removed. Either method will give us moulds having hollow spaces into which we can pour tin, and so get two halves, right and left hand, of our spout in that metal.

Before pouring the tin into the plaster moulds they should be very thoroughly dried; "gates," or "gets," through which the metal is to be poured, are cut, and "vents," small notches, to allow of the escape of air are to be cut too. The moulds are smoked in a candle flame, wired together, and the tin poured in. The molten metal should always enter at the large end so as to avoid the pouring of a large quantity of metal through a narrow opening, involving a risk of chilling the metal and getting a "short run."

As soon as we have two clean sound castings in tin we scrape or file smooth (use old files), and emery cloth them. The tin patterns may now be sent to the founders to be cast in silver. The patterns for the handle should now be made in exactly the same way. Fig. 110 shows a half spout.

When the silver castings are to hand they should be annealed and pickled to remove all traces of sand. Any excrescences such as "gets" or "webs" along the joints should be sawn or filed off, and the halves rubbed flat on emery cloth to ensure a close fit or "mitre."

The in, or hollowed, sides of the castings are now filed, riffled,* scraped, and emery-clothed smooth. A final polish may be given with Water of Ayr stone or small leather bobs on a spindle.

Before the castings are wired together for soldering the edges should as always when using very hard solder, be roughened with a coarse file to ensure the flushing of the rather viscous solder into the joints.

In the soldering of the castings together, use a rather liberal allowance of the hardest solder available. The spout and handle are pickled clean, filed up and stoned, or brushed on the spindle. They are then fitted to the body, on a vessel with flat sides, a very simple job.

It is intended that all the details of this pot should be cast. Taking the patterns for these in order, going upwards, we begin with the base moulding. It would be possible by the use of "false cores," *i.e.*, moulds made in many pieces, to cast an octagonal ring with undercut mouldings as those shown in Fig. 111. This would perhaps be hardly worth while, and a satisfactory result may be reached in a much simpler way. Make a length of moulding, either by turning (if turned, the resulting ring will be cut through and straightened out), or by drawing in a swage block (Fig. 36) of the section we

FIG. 111.—*The base moulding of the coffee pot.*

FIG. 111a.—*Another way of applying the base moulding.*

need, but having rather more substance, so as to allow for subsequent filing up, with the members less deeply cut, and of such a shape that when the sand mould is made the pattern may be withdrawn without breaking the sand in any way. From this moulding the octagonal ring is made.

* Imagine a steel modelling tool cut like a file. That is a riffler. Effective ones are easily made from cast steel. When filed to shape and while still soft they are struck with the narrow edge of a flat file all over and from every angle using a bit of hard wood held in the vice as an anvil. Harden and temper as a bent file is treated.

Another way would be to make an octagon of stout oblong wire, and work the moulding in it with files and scraper. The scraper is easily made. It is like, except that its cutting edge is contoured to the shape of our moulding, that shown in Fig. 68. Such a tool will be found extremely useful in finishing the mouldings after they are soldered on the body.

The casting patterns for the moulding at the top of the body and for that on the lid immediately above it may be made exactly in the same way.

The bearers of the hinge should be cast from patterns filed up out of hard wood, box for choice. (See Fig. 105 for front view.)

Lastly, the knob (Fig. 112). This needs two castings. First, a small round one for the actual top, which should for convenience be cast with a short stem so that it may be gripped in the lathe chuck and turned. Second, the pattern for the shank should be turned as Fig. 112. The two projections are known as "core pegs." The shank will be moulded in the ordinary way; this will leave at each end of the mould cylindrical spaces. In these a rod made of sand and loam is laid, so that when the two halves of the mould are brought together finally and the metal poured in we get a casting with a hole the size of the "core pegs" right through.

We may note in passing that this identical method is used in casting stems, balusters, and so on of any shape. The difference being that instead of a straight cylindrical core a contoured one is used.

Briefly, the procedure is as follows: The pattern for the actual baluster is made with two core pegs as if a straight cylindrical core were to be used ; though in this case they may differ in size. Then another baluster is turned

FIG. 112.—*The knob. Note the* xxxx *here and in Fig.* 113.

everywhere of smaller diameter except the pegs. The difference in the two diameters is, of course, determined by the thickness of the casting. The contours are softer, blunted, less angular. From this second baluster a plaster mould is made in two halves just as in the first operation in making the patterns for the spout. If one or two castings only are needed, cores can be made in this plaster "core box" or "stock." If a number are needed, casts in iron or brass are to be taken from the plasters. It will be seen at once that when the core made in the stock is placed in the mould, a circular space is left into which the molten metal is poured.

The actual bulb of the knob is simply two domed circles of sheet silver, say 12 or 14 m.g., soldered together with a half-round wire around the join. The whole knob, being all of silver, is soldered to the lid. Do not forget the hole in the bulb for vent.

When all the parts are ready the whole pot is assembled. Fig. 111 shows how the casting is fitted on the base. The bottom of the pot is put on first. If desired, the bottom plate itself may be left as a wide flange and made to serve as a member of the moulding.

FIG. 113.—The pattern for the collar of knob. The part xxxx
only will be cast.

Fig. 111a shows another and perhaps better method. A thinner moulding is made, soldered on, and the bottom is finished off by soldering a heavy wire around it.

In soldering these mouldings a medium hard solder should be used, and in distinctly liberal amounts. The greatest care in even fitting and in every detail of soldering must be employed so that pin holes may be avoided.

In soldering the handle to the body, do not forget to saw a slit, a little way in, at one of the insulation points for a vent.

The hinge joint is a rather tricky matter for anyone but an experienced hand. For a beginner it is far better to use knuckles cut from a solid rod down which a hole has been drilled. This frees us from anxiety about the seam which is present when drawn tube is used.

Bullion dealers are now able to supply "solid drawn" tube, or "chenier." It is coming more and more into general use.

It may well be decided by some students who wish to make one pot only that it is not worth their while to make casting patterns for the mouldings, as these are usable for one sized pot only. Fig. 114 shows how mouldings are most conveniently applied to polygonal vessels. In the case of mouldings having a symmetrical contour, such as a half-round wire, notching the back deeply and bending is satisfactory. With mouldings such as we are here using, this method does not work very well. The one point is sound soldering with hard solder, so that when the surplus is filed away no join is visible. It will be seen that this is not on the angle as it is in moulding mitred in the usual way.

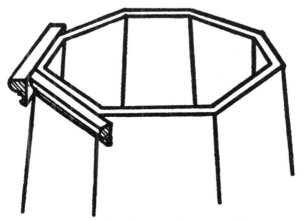

FIG. 114.—*How drawn mouldings are applied.*

It must not be forgotten that the grid, or strainer, in a coffee pot must be much finer than in a teapot. For a teapot $\frac{7}{64}$ inch is about the right diameter for the holes. For a coffee pot $\frac{3}{64}$ inch is nearer the mark. The whole of the available area should be covered fairly closely with holes arranged in a pleasing pattern.

In soldering the spout on to the body two methods of holding it are available. The spout may be wired on, or the iron wire counterpoise used.

We must not forget that both spout and body (at least the part that is nearest the spout) should be carefully polished before they are soldered together.

In soldering castings to a sheet metal body we must be most careful to give a greater share of the heat to the castings. Failure to do this may endanger the flatness of the pot's sides. The weight of the heavy spout or handle might push the sides and make them distinctly hollow.

The finishing of the pot breaks no fresh ground.

CHAPTER 14

EXERCISE 11 : A CONDIMENT SET

THIS exercise will introduce the process of stamping with the simplest of tools and appliances.

Anyone who has the slightest acquaintance with the silver industry knows that by far the greater part of modern work is produced mechanically, either by spinning or by stamping. This book, however, being a primer for the use of young workers and students, does not deal at any length with the specialized intricacies of modern workshop practice. Its aim is to encourage adaptability, resourcefulness, and understanding of principles.

The dies ordinarily used are cut in steel by professional die-sinkers. These craftsmen work solely in the harder metals, and normally have nothing to do with the actual making of complete pieces of silverware.

The process of stamping the sheet silver into the dies is also another specialized branch of the industry.

A stamp is usually a simple appliance, consisting of a heavy cast-iron base firmly fixed in the floor which, unless small work alone is done, must be actually on the ground. At four corners of this are four massive lugs, bored and screwed to take powerful screws; these keep the die in position. From the base or anvil rise two strong vertical and parallel guide bars 8 to 12 feet high, firmly fixed at the top. Between the bars slides a heavy iron weight, fitted with an appliance to hold the "force," a solid piece of metal, lead, tin, brass, sometimes even steel, that has been driven into the die. A pulley and rope are provided to hoist the weight. The impact of a 60-lb. weight falling 10 feet will drive metal placed on the die into close contact at every point. When thin metal is stamped a number of the blanks of metal to be shaped are placed on the die. Many blows are given until the lowest stamping is everywhere close up to the die. Then it is removed, another blank is put on top of the pile, and the stamping renewed.

Stamps must not be confused with presses. In these the pressure is slow moving, usually given by a powerful screw of very steep pitch. Presses are normally used for piercing holes in metal or for removing the surplus edge around a stamping.

Steel dies are expensive to make. This means that quantities of things have to be made in order to cover the heavy initial outlay. On the other hand, it often happens that small quantities of articles have to be made, when to make each one entirely by hand would be unduly tedious and costly. Here the methods given below prove of great use. They may be applied to pieces of any size not exceeding 5 inches or 6 inches square.

Fig. 115 shows a lead or tin die, and a wood or iron punch for stamping the body of the pepper pot (Fig. 116). Let us assume that we are to make a pair of these, one as drawn with its top drilled for pepper, and the other one with the knob on top omitted and replaced by a single larger hole (see Fig. 117) to fit it for use or as a salt pourer.

The first thing to do is to make a careful drawing, exactly full size, of the pot in elevation. From this we rasp and file up, out of a piece of boxwood, a punch slightly smaller than the drawing; this allows for the thickness of the metal. The greatest care must be taken to ensure accuracy. If a lathe is available, it will be well to turn a round punch—its diameter must be equal to a diagonal of the octagon—and, having marked eight equal divisions upon it, to file away the rounded parts between.

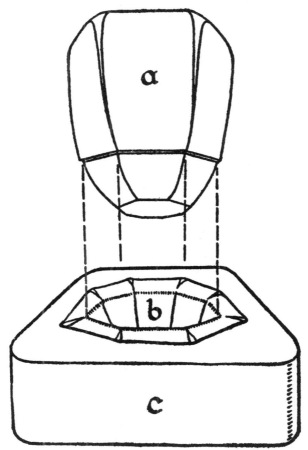

FIG. 115.—(a) *The Punch*. (b) *The thin metal lining of the die*. (c) *The lead*.

This will avoid much tedious work in measuring. If no lathe is at hand, the best thing to do is to begin by making a square punch properly contoured, and then filing the corners away to make the octagon. The punch must be as finely shaped as possible, and be glass-papered smooth.

A mould in which to pour the lead or tin that forms the die is now made. It is merely a tray with slightly sloping sides to allow the lead to come out easily. Make it from 10 or 12 m.g. gilding-metal or brass; see that it is amply deep—there should be at least ⅜ inch thickness of lead between the end of the punch and the bottom of the die. Fig. 115 shows a reasonable relation in size between punch and die. A smaller punch, mould, and die for the cover are made also.

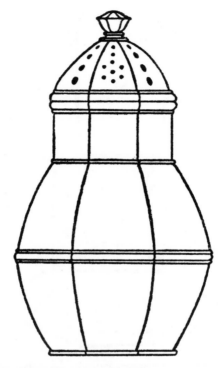

FIG. 116.— *Pepper pot made with the aid of punch and die, Fig. 115.*

An ample supply of lead and a sufficiently large pot or ladle to melt it in must be at hand. The punch is painted thinly but evenly with loam, or whitening, and water, and dried carefully. It is well to do the same to the mould too. The lead is melted—the dross, as it floats on the top, is removed with a bit of wood—and poured steadily and swiftly into the mould. While the lead is still liquid the punch is pushed into the centre of the mould until the little step at the top of the shaped part is just below the surface. It is held in position—see that its axis is quite upright—until the lead solidifies. As soon as the lead is reasonably cool the punch is removed and the die dipped in water or put under the tap, the loam is washed away, and the die dried. The loam is rubbed off the punch, and we are ready to begin stamping.

The die should rest on a thick iron plate or die, or, if available, on a big stake or anvil. The best hammer to strike it with is a mason's "lump" hammer of about $1\frac{1}{2}$ lb. to 2 lb. in weight.

Fig. 115 (*b*) shows a stamping of thin metal punched into the lead. This is of 6 or 8 m.g. brass, and forms the actual die into which we drive our silver. The stamping being deep, we shall need to do a good deal of shaping of the

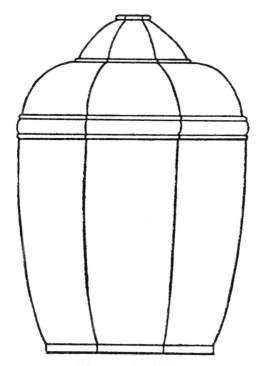

FIG. 117.—*Salt pourer, shaped body, stamped cover.*

sheet brass blank either by doming or raising. Were the die shallower, we could drive a flat sheet into it without any preliminary work. Having made our raising round, and of such a size that it reaches just above the step on the punch, we put it in the hollow in the lead and strike the punch with some force. It will be well to anneal the brass not only after it is raised, but at least once while it is being driven into the lead. Some puckering will take place at the corners when the surplus brass is malleted out flat on to the surface of the lead. (See Fig. 115 (*b*).)

As soon as the brass is well bedded into the lead—quite a number of heavy blows will be needed—the four silver blanks for the bodies, and the two for the lids, are cut, shaped, and stamped. If the work is done well, and the silver is not too thick—9 m.g. is about the thickest that should be used—the angles will need no further sharpening. With 10 m.g., or thicker silver, some planishing on a stake will be needed. A bit of mild steel bar, square, may easily be filed into an excellent stake. After the rims of the stampings are trimmed the shapes should again be driven into the die.

A wooden punch and a lead die will serve admirably for about six or eight stampings. If more are needed, it is a paying proposition to have a punch cast in malleable iron. This, used with a die of tin or type metal, would produce an unlimited number.

Assembling the pot.—Take the two stampings of the body, trim their rims with shears, file, and flat emery board until they fit, "mitre," as closely as possible. Cut the bottom out of one, leaving a narrow, under $\frac{1}{16}$ inch, horizontal piece of it all round. This is to make the fitting to the body of the vertical neck of the pot easier. The two stampings are then carefully wired together (the hook and loop method (see Exercise 3) will probably be the best to use), and carefully soldered with the hardest solder.

The neck* and a band about three-quarters of its width, that will fit closely inside it, are now made from 10 m.g. silver. These will best be made by cutting the strips with absolute accuracy, marking the eight even spaces and nicking them with a three-square file with equal care. The outer band, the neck itself, is made first; its two ends are carefully bevelled to ensure a close "mitre," then it is bent up into an octagonal tube, wired, and soldered with hardest solder. After pickling clean, the interior angles are filed smooth and true. Although not essential, it will help considerably if an accurate octagon be filed up out of $\frac{1}{8}$-inch iron plate to use as a template in the inside of the tube. (See Exercise 8 for a similar case.) When the outer tube, the neck, is finished, the inner one—which is soldered to the top, or lid, and forms the bezel—is made in the same way. Probably the best way to ensure an accurate fit is to make the bezel rather loose, and then to hammer each face on a bit of square steel held in the vice. The steel should be as nearly as possible exactly the size of the inner side of the bezel's faces. Another way would be to make the bezel of thicker silver, 12 m.g. or so, a shade too large. We could then do the fitting by filing the outside. An excellent thing to ensure that the fitting shall be good, whichever way we push the bezel in the neck, is to paint loam thinly inside the neck and outside the bezel, to force the bezel into the neck, and to anneal them. If this is done eight times, so that each face completes a revolution, the bezel should fit perfectly. As pulling them apart will be difficult, it may save trouble to make both neck and bezel $\frac{1}{4}$ inch or so too long, and to drill holes in four sides close to the edge. This would allow of stout wire being threaded through to afford a firm grip. We might even use the draw bench to get the necessary force.

If we are fortunate enough to have a very accurately made octagonal mandrel with a slight taper, we shall find it extremely useful and convenient in making the neck and bezel, but as an exercise in accurate fitting the student will do well to tackle the job using only a simple bar of steel.

The neck is now levelled at one end so that all its faces are exactly vertical. Then it is soldered on to the body with hardest solder. A flat to take the three wires, a half-round, and two fine round ones, that mask the join of the two

---

* The neck is to be of such a size that a very narrow portion of the bottom of the stamping, under $\frac{1}{32}$ inch, is visible all round. Upon this the fine wire at the base of the neck will rest.

halves of the body is filed; the wire rings are made and fitted. Unless an octagonal mandrel is available, it will be well to nick the wires before bending. The other wire mouldings on the pot, except that on the base, are to be drawn to the same sizes.

The base moulding is perhaps most conveniently made from thick plate about 14 or 16 m.g. After it is cut to size an octagonal hole is pierced out of its centre, leaving a width of about $\frac{5}{32}$ inch all round. This is soldered on with ordinary solder.

The other mouldings on the body are now soldered on. "Stitches" (see Exercise 5) will ensure that they are horizontal. Do not forget to use the hardest solder for the seams. The wire at the base of the neck comes next. Here it may be well to file a flat on the inner side of this wire either before or after bending.

The top of the neck is cut down to the right height, levelled, and the round and half-round wires mounted upon it. The filing away of any projection there may be inside the base of the neck—this would be the remaining portion of the bottom of the stamping—completes the body.

The soldering of the stamping of the lid or cover on to the bezel presents no difficulty. This done, the mouldings are put on. The knob has to be made either from a casting or by turning a round one and filing it octagonal. The holes are marked and drilled—$\frac{1}{32}$ inch is a normal size—but some latitude is allowable. The burrs are removed from the inside of the lid with a riffle. It will be easier to mark and drill them before the knob is put on. The knob is soldered in position; a little peg or projection on the bottom of the knob will ensure accurate fitting. The stamping will, of course, have a small flat octagon on its top.

Fig. 117 shows a salt pourer, or caster, which needs only the addition of a knob on the top and the drilling of holes in the upper part of the cover to make it into a pepper pot.

The two-storied or staged cover may be stamped in one piece, if the time and trouble can be spared to file up the punch. For one or two pots only, it would be easier and quicker to make two stampings, a large and a small one, and solder them together, having first pierced out the centre of the larger, lower member.

The body is, of course, too deep to stamp, though, were large quantities needed, it could be made in a drawing-press. This is a press in which blanks of comparatively thick metal are forced through holes in steel dies. Under the great pressure the metal is "drawn" up the sides of the "force" or punch. If we have a large draw plate and a punch, rather smaller than the hole we experiment with, we can try the experiment of forcing a tiny metal disc through the hole. This will show us how hollow shapes are drawn through.

For us the best thing will be to make a short mandrel, octagonal, in malleable iron; this will have curved sides instead of straight. A seamed tube open at both ends, or a raising with the bottom cut out, may be malleted on to this and then planished. Or a raised body might be shaped with a hammer, first on wood, and then planished on a bit of steel bar.

The assembling and mounting of these pots is done almost precisely as in Fig. 116. Differences are: the base moulding is merely an octagonal ring

FIG. 118.   FIG. 119.

of square or oblong wire; and for filling, a bezel and stopper in the bottom of each piece are made and fitted.

Fig. 118 shows the bezel: this is, of course, open to allow of the stopper (Fig. 119) being pushed in to close the aperture. These pieces should, if possible, be spun. The indented line going across inside the hollow of the stopper, or plug, shows a web of 12 m.g. to give a grip in removing and replacing it.

The student may well ask, "Is the brass between the silver and the lead necessary?" The answer is: "It has two functions; it furnishes a hard, smooth surface, and it removes any risk that may arise of lead adhering to the surface of the silver stamping."

Fig. 120 shows a mustard pot that will match either of the pepper pots that we have already considered. Its body is to be made exactly as described above. The rim is mounted with a half-round wire having a fine round wire immediately beneath it. The lower moulding, of the half-round and two round wires, is made and mounted as on the pepper pot.

The lid is to be stamped. The little octagonal boss on its top may be

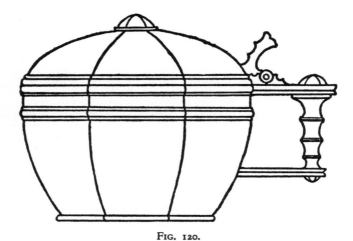

FIG. 120.

hollow; when it would be stamped, or solid, when it would probably be a casting. Fig. 121 shows the mounting of the lid's edge. This rests on an L-shaped wire with the longer side horizontal. The shorter side, shown rather thicker than the longer one—a point of little importance—forms a shutting bezel for the lid. It must be short, so that if a glass lining is used it may not come unduly low in the pot. The half-round wire that fits into the angle between the lid and the L wire has one of its edges filed away until it approaches a quarter oval in section. The small round wire, here above the larger member, is mounted as described earlier in this chapter. The octagon of L wire needs very careful making. There should be a small but distinct amount of "shake" when in position. Perhaps the best way of constructing this L wire "bearer," or "bezel," for the lid is to make an octagonal ring of square wire; the corners should be nicked and soldered with the hardest solder; this is soldered on a thick plate with an octagonal hole previously pierced in it. After the surplus metal inside and outside has been trimmed

FIG. 121.—*Section of a part of mustard pot. Body is shaded. Lid in outline.*

away, the bezel may be fixed in position with two tiny spots of soft solder (after unsoldering, all traces of the tin solder are most carefully scraped away). We can then file up the outer edge accurately and easily. If we intend to make more than one or two pots of this identical fashion, it will pay us to make a casting-pattern of the octagon bearer and have them cast. In this case we can make provision for the moulding to be cast on the bezel itself. Reverting to the body, we might have one moulding only for this, and make it from a casting too. We shall find the making of the facets and edges on the body and lid so accurately that their lines follow through will tax our skill very considerably. The fact that these difficulties do not arise in the making of such things from stampings is perhaps the greatest factor in lessening the cost of ordinary commercial productions.

Body and lid being made, we go on to the handle. As drawn in Fig. 120 it is intended that the plates, between which the spindle, turned or filed up from a casting (it should have a small peg or tenon at each end), is fixed, should be merely long isosceles triangles, with their bases the width of a face of the pot, cut off at their apices, and rounded so as to make a bearing of a reasonable size for the spindle. Cutting shapes out of cardboard will enable us to determine their exact shapes. Having found these, and having filed them up, either from thick sheet or from castings (the edges are grooved with a three-square file), we solder them on with hard solder—probably the middle grade—and then drill a hole in the upper one to take the tenon, or peg, at the top of the spindle. From this we determine the exact position of the hole in the lower plate, and drill this. These holes should be quite small, $\frac{1}{8}$ inch or $\frac{5}{32}$ inch, and the pegs need be only very short, less than $\frac{1}{16}$ inch, so that little bending will be needed to spring the spindle into position. If we make our octagonal bosses with pegs of the same size as those on the spindle, they will fit into the same holes. With careful fitting (do not forget cautions against absence of shake given in earlier exercises) there should be no difficulty in soldering spindle and bosses at one operation. Another caution: do not forget to polish every surface before assembling, so that the final finishing may be made easy.

The hinge of three, or better of five, knuckles may be made separately and applied, or the two bearers may be soldered on the pot, and then gapped to take the knuckles. These would be soldered in with the lid in position, a rather tricky business. Probably the best method here is to make it separately. Take a piece of thick metal, cut it roughly to the shape of the plan of the bearers of the hinge, then gap it deeply nearly through, cut the last bit with a thin saw, and solder the knuckles in. Exercise 8 gives instructions for this; the hinge will then be carefully filed up to the desired shape. The hinge is then pinned up to see that it works properly. The plan of the whole hinge calls for careful thought. The bearers are, of course, fitted snugly into position (it may be well to file a gap in the lid moulding to take the moving bearer).

To solder the hinge on, the whole pot is assembled, loam having been thinly but evenly applied wherever we do not wish solder to run—the lid is wired to the body—the moving parts of the hinge are loamed, an iron pin, well annealed to coat it with oxide and loamed also, is pushed in just tightly enough to bring the two parts in position. The hinge is placed in position and boraxed, taking the greatest care to prevent borax and loam mixing, and "tacked," i.e., soldered in position with a very small quantity of easy solder, probably applied in panels. Finally, the pin is withdrawn, the wires cut, the lid removed, and a further supply of solder to ensure sound joints is added.

The thumb bit comes next. This may be of any shape that we please, provided it is efficient in use—it must allow for the opening of the lid nearly to a right angle. The one shown (Fig. 120) is sufficiently spiky to work well. There should be no danger of the thumb slipping off. The other view of this detail would show it distinctly wider at the top. Properly, it should also curve out again at its junction with the moving part of the hinge joint.

Soldering the thumb piece in position: here the difficulties are more apparent than real. An expert would "jump" it on; but for a student there is a real risk of displacing the other parts of the hinge joint. It has to be put on with the same easy grade of solder. Lay the lid on a flat piece of firebrick, or iron-wire gauze, or better still, charcoal. If the thumb bit does not stand upright, the brick, or charcoal, should be tilted until it does. If thin rubbed borax is used, to obviate displacement when drying, it will be found quite easy to solder either with panels or strip. All parts, except the actual junction of thumb bit and bearer, should be carefully loamed.

Whenever we solder hinge joints we shall find that "to hasten slowly" is always the best policy. No worker, even the most experienced, can afford to risk the trouble of soldering hinges up solid. If this should happen, the only course is to unsolder everything, clean all surplus solder away, reassemble, and resolder.

We have now to think of the spoon for our mustard pot. Fig. 121 shows two views of one in keeping with the set. To make it: make a rough model in base metal to determine the right size and length. The length will depend upon the presence, or absence, of a glass lining. Normally this is used—any good glass firm will make a lining to shape.

The spoon stem is made from a piece of thick sheet, $\frac{1}{8}$ inch or so. For quantities, casting is advisable. The template for the bowl is conveniently made by folding a piece of paper and cutting a half shape. When this is flattened out it should be about $\frac{1}{8}$ inch longer and $\frac{3}{32}$ inch wider than the finished spoon. This is to allow for the "drawing in" when the bowl is domed. The template is cut with its point sharper than shown in Fig. 121.

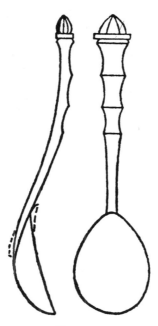

FIG. 121.

Ten m.g. is a usual thickness of metal. The bowl is domed in a hole in the end grain of a bit of wood. Its curves at this stage should exceed those of the finished piece. It is planished on the actual hammer, or doming punch, used to shape it. Begin by planishing straight along the centre line from wide to narrow end. Then go on, first a strip on one side of the centre, and then on the other side an identical strip. This will ensure that the bowl will be free from twist. The right amount of flattening of the transverse curve will inevitably take place. If the longitudinal curve is excessive, we may reduce it by a judicious blow on the convex side with hammer or mallet. Any dent that may result is removed by planishing.

The end of the stem is now shaped, front view only. A little concavity is filed to take the bowl. The two are held together by a cramp (see Exercise 2), with its ends suitably bent, and soldered with the hardest grade. The dotted lines in the left hand, side view (Fig. 121), shows the junction at this stage. We now file away the surplus until we have what is shown by the continuous line. Take great care to make the junction between bowl and stem as fine in form and in surface finish as possible. The edge of the bowl should be slightly rounded. The filed pattern as suggested for the stem is worked last of all. The harshness of the rigid lines of the drawing will be absent after the spoon is stoned up and polished. Take care that the angles where the stem joins the back, convex side of the bowl are rounded so that there is no lodgment for mustard. All must be so that simple washing will suffice for cleaning.

The last thing to be done in the making is to cut a slot in the front of the lid, opposite to the handle, for the spoon.

The pinning up of the hinge will need great care, especially if it has three knuckles only. The lid should just fall by its own weight, but shake must be reduced to a minimum.

A safe rule in the making of hinge joints is to have the knuckles as large as possible, either in diameter or length, or in both. Indeed, if it works well a large hinge is almost invariably to be preferred.

CHAPTER 15

EXERCISE 12 : A STANDING CUP AND COVER

A STUDENT who has worked out the preceding exercises may now feel, rightly and with confidence, that his training and experience warrant the attempt at something more ambitious. A standing cup and cover would appear to be a very suitable piece.

Following the precedent set in former exercises, we will begin by basing our cup on a traditional example of the first half of the seventeenth century. This type is an excellent one to begin with. Fig. 122 shows a reasonable version.

By now the student should be quite familiar with technical things, and able to give a much greater part of his energies and thought than he did in earlier exercises to æsthetic questions. Aesthetic here includes in its meaning not only the design, pattern, or fashion of the cup, but the finer qualitîes of its craftsmanship—subtleties of form, proportion, and outline, qualities of surface texture—contrast of light and shade, and suchlike.

The actual seventeenth-century cups—there are fine examples in the Victoria and Albert Museum—owe much of their beauty to the method used in raising the bowls, from thick cast blanks.

Some time in the middle of last century was published an English translation from the Latin of a medieval book of workshop practice, written by a certain monk in northern Germany, best known by his monastic name, Theophilus. The translator, Hendrie, having no practical knowledge, failed to make many points clear, but from his rendering a craftsman may make out much with a degree of certainty. One of these is the ancient method of raising from a thick cast disc. It would be an interesting experiment to have a disc cast of the diameter we need, and $\frac{1}{32}$ inch or so thicker. We should pickle it to ensure an absolutely clean surface. Then we should scrape it on both sides, and after that hammer it vigorously until we had a clean, clear disc. It is, however, doubtful if the result would differ in any way from what we should get by working on a disc cut from rolled sheet of the same thickness, i.e., approximately 24 m.g.

Let us assume that the bowl of our cup will be about $3\frac{3}{4}$ inches high and $3\frac{3}{8}$ inches in diameter at the top. Measuring this to determine the size of the blank by the Birmingham trade method (the height is added to the maximum diameter and a percentage added, here about 10 per cent.), we find that a disc of $7\frac{1}{4}$ inches is needed. The usual method would be to raise the bowl from 10 or 11 m.g. Circles of these gauges weigh approximately $7\frac{1}{2}$ oz. and 8 oz.

If we adopt the usual present-day practice, we raise our bowl exactly as described in former exercises, and strengthen the rim or edge by soldering a wire around it.

Seeing that the experience of working in the actual manner and method of the old masters cannot fail to teach us much, we will attempt the raising from the thick blank.

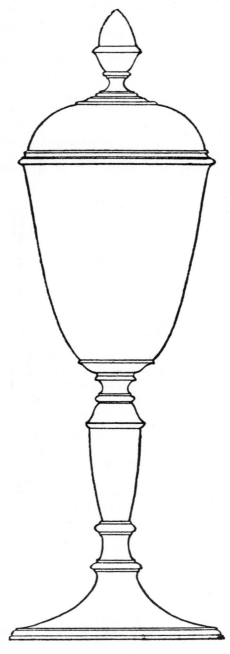

FIG. 122.

A simple calculation will show us that a circle of silver 24 m.g. in thickness, 4½ inches diameter, will weigh approximately the same as a 7¼-inch circle of 11 m.g. Cut the circle with great care to the 4½-inch diameter. Make

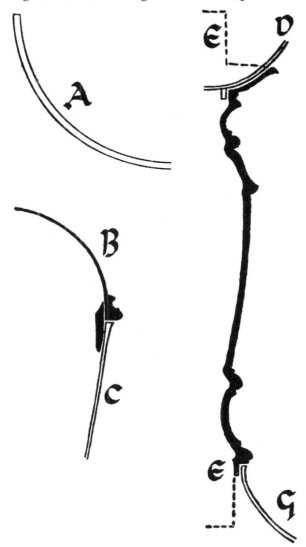

FIG. 123.—*Sections of the various parts of the cup.*

sure that it is exactly true, and remove the sharp arris edge left from the cutting with a file. Take a round-headed "bellying" or "doming" hammer, and "dish" or "dome" the thick circle in a deep hollow sunk in the top of the steady block (the end, cut across the grain, of a piece of thick soft deal hollowed out and held in the vice will make a good substitute) into a hemi-sphere of a little less than the diameter of the mouth of the cup. Take care that the centre mark is on the outer, convex side.

Fig. 123 (A) shows a half section. No thinning of the actual edge has taken place. After annealing, the beating from the inside may be repeated; care must be taken not to strike within $\frac{1}{2}$ inch or so of the edge. The aim should be the making of the uppermost $\frac{3}{8}$ inch or so of the rim nearly vertical, so that when the final planishing comes but little work is needed to shape this part.

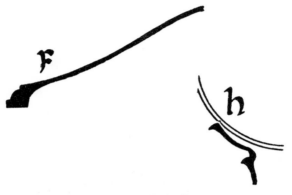

FIG. 123a.—F and H.

The next thing to be done is to stretch the whole of the metal in the bowl, except, of course, the rim. This remains throughout at its full thickness. The stretching may be done to some extent by a continuance of the beating with the round-headed hammer from the inside; but a more satisfactory method is to hammer the outside vigorously, the bowl being placed on a round "mushroom"-headed bottom stake. It will soon be found that the stretching can be continued with a raising hammer used just as in ordinary raising, and on a head fixed in a horse, but with probably harder blows. Care must be taken not to thin any part unduly. If it should be thought that the bottom of the bowl, obviously the danger-point, is becoming thin, the raising should be done in the reverse direction to the normal—from the rim downwards towards the centre.

From the account of raising given by Theophilus it would appear that in the Middle Ages it was customary to leave a thick piece in the centre of the bowl to attach the stem to.

In shaping the bowl to the drawing, if that is our aim, a template of sheet metal cut exactly to size will be extremely useful. It will be very helpful also to put the bowl on a lathe, and to hold a pencil against it as it spins to mark protuberances, if there are any. The parts that are too high may be "raised" in, or the parts that are too low may be bossed out, with a hammer on a bit of soft wood or a sand bag. Fig. 124 shows a useful tool. Sometimes a "snarling iron", Fig. 124a is even better.

The planishing differs in no way from that of former pieces, except that more thought regarding form, and more care to attain a fine surface, must be given, especially to the thickened rim, than is called for ordinarily. At this stage of his training the student should attempt a greater refinement and precision of form than he has yet reached. Hammers and stakes should be as smooth as fine emery will make them—indeed, the hammer should

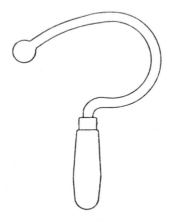

FIG. 124.—*The crook which can be made by any blacksmith from mild steel rod ½ inch to ⅝ inch diameter (a good one could be made from an old vice handle) is used to boss, or belly out raisings or seamed collets, or necks, from the inside. It is possible with such a tool to rectify, or adjust, the form of a quite deep vessel. Different bendings may be needed for different jobs. The end, away from the ball, is forged out thin and driven firmly into a big file handle. The size is normally about 6 inches to 8 inches from the knob to the inner curve.*

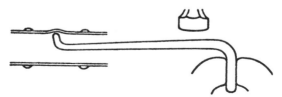

FIG. 124a.—*A "snarling iron," made of ½-inch steel, tapered down, about 12 inches long, as shown for bossing out narrow vessels, or tubes, in which it is impossible to use a hammer or punch. A hammer of 6 oz. or 8 oz. is used for striking.*

be almost "mirror"-faced. The worker must stand or sit at the level which gives him the greatest command over the hammer. He should arrange a background (light or dark, whichever serves best) against which he can see the contour of his bowl with absolute clearness. Then he must watch for irregularities, and smooth them away as he sees them. The work must pass the test of touch as well as of sight. The first-named is often more searching than the last.

It often happens that in order to get an exact shape it is necessary to turn the bowl around on the stake, so that the internal point of contact of stake with bowl remains constant in distance from rim or centre. A pencil mark on the stake will often be enough to ensure this; but a student may find it helpful to rig up a wood or metal stop against which he can press the rim of his bowl.

Fig. 123 (C) shows a section of the upper part of a side of the cup. Great care must be taken to ensure an even curve from the level at which the thickening begins up to the actual rim itself. If no very suitable hammer is at hand, we may take the head of an ordinary "Warrington" 4-oz. hammer, make it red hot, screw it firmly in the vice while still hot, and "upset" or spread out the face. This done, the face may be forged square, and then filed up exactly to the curve needed. The curve is, of course, only seen in a side view of the hammer just as in an ordinary "neck" or "collet" hammer. When shaped, the face of the hammer may be hardened and tempered. For such purposes as we are now dealing with there are, however, advantages in leaving hammers soft. Unless in constant use they stand up quite well to wear, and they may be easily and quickly altered to suit any particular curve.

The stem, Fig. 123 (E), is to be cast from a turned wood pattern as described in Exercise 10. The dotted lines show the pegs for the core. These are left on. It will, of course, be necessary to make a core "box," or "stock," to ensure getting a casting thin enough to be of a reasonable weight for silver. The actual technique of making the pattern and core, and of turning up the stem, is simple enough (see Exercise 10). The æsthetic problems involved, however, are quite difficult. We shall need to give our best thought to the relation between the different members. The quality of the curves, too, will tax all our powers. We must not be content until we have made every detail perfect.

Though the observation is hoary with age, it will do no harm to remind ourselves that the greatest masters of form, the ancient Greeks, invariably made the contours of their mouldings approach more or less closely to the curves of the "conic sections." These curves—ellipse, parabola, hyperbola— have something of the subtlety of natural forms, where we find long flattened curves contrasted with sharp quick ones, to the enhancement of the qualities of both. In turned work we shall find that the simple natural movements of the tool on the rest, if we let them, will give us fine quality of curvature.

It has been urged by extreme purists that a lathe, as it can give us nothing but mathematically accurate circular transverse sections, will fail to reach the highest forms. To the writer it seems far fetched to push our objections to mechanically produced form to such a length. If we have time, however, we may experiment, have two stems cast, and finish one by hand filing. One thing is quite clear—the result, whichever method, turning or filing, we adopt, will depend for its æsthetic qualities on the worker's sense of form and skill of hand. We may accept as an axiom—the more perfect technical method, turning, calls for a more precise and logical type of form than the easier softer method of filing does. The former will no doubt have "the defects of its qualities"; nothing can be left to accident. The latter may owe much to unforeseen accidents that always arise in work done solely by hand.

No new problems will arise in making the foot—if we choose to employ the ordinary methods. It may be raised from 11 or 12 m.g. sheet and mounted with a thick wire base moulding. On the other hand, if we use the actual methods of the old workers, we make a casting-pattern as Fig. 123a (F), out of thick metal plate with a thick wire soldered on to form the base moulding. The moulding may be turned to shape at this stage, or left until later.

When we have the casting we shall put it in the lathe and turn, "skim," the inner face lightly. Then the centre portion will be hammered up into shape, Fig. 123 (G). The outer surface will be smoothed as far as possible with the hammer. The remaining parts and the moulding will be turned to shape. So long as there is no possibility of its slipping out of centre, we need no more elaborate chuck than a flat piece of wood with a projection, about ⅛ inch high, fitting closely inside the base of the foot; the pressure of the back centre will do the rest. The top small end of the raising is cut off and the opening stretched with the hammer until it fits exactly over the projection at the bottom of the stem. Do not forget to put the foot back in the lathe and turn the edge of the opening at top true and parallel to the base. The stem may now be soldered on to the foot.

The fitting of the bowl on to the stem can be done as Fig. 123 (D), where a narrow ring, bezel, is first soldered on to the bottom. This need be only very narrow—half the width shown in the drawing would be ample. In making a cup without a lathe this is the only method to adopt. It would be almost impossible to wire a slender but fairly heavy stem on to a bowl securely enough to ensure its not slipping when actually soldering. It may be objected that an unduly large space between bowl and stem has to be filled with solder. A better method free from this drawback is indicated at Fig. 123a (H). Here a shallow recess, or "check," is turned in the bowl. Into this the upper inner edge of the topmost member of the stem, previously turned to a sharp edge, is fitted.

The cover comes next. Fig. 123 (B) shows a section with rim moulding and bezel. We may, if we wish, make this in the ordinary way, raise and hammer it, mount it with stout wires, outside for the moulding and inside for the bezel. Alternatively, we may make it from a casting in a manner identical with that suggested for the foot. The curve of the casting-pattern would, of course, be much flatter than that of the finished lid. The turning of the bezel out of the solid would need great care, but there is nothing really difficult in it. The domed cover being hammered out, it would be "chucked" in a recess turned in the wood, and the inside "skimmed" out cleanly. To turn the outside a chuck would be shaped to fit the inside of the lid as closely as possible.

The fitting of lids to cups is a matter that needs much care. Very little "shake" should be allowed, but the lid must lift off easily. It should not be necessary to hold the cup when removing the cover. Cup and cover must be truly circular, so that the fitting remains the same whichever way the cover is put on. The rim of the bowl and the lid moulding must be level too, so that the lid is free from the slightest tendency to rock. If any difficulty should arise, it will be well to paint rim and bezel with loam, wire the lid in position, and anneal it. If this is done four or five times, turning the lid around part way each time, a perfect fit, even if the case is a stubborn one, should be assured.

The knob is to be cast from a turned pattern. A core box should be made if a light knob is essential. As the core will not go right through, the one peg should be of ample length, 1¼ inches or so, to ensure the core being held firmly in the mould.

With the soldering on of the knob the cup is finished, save for polishing. If we make use of castings, the actual surface of the metal needs careful handling. It would never do, for instance, to have a smoothly turned stem and a roughly hammered bowl and foot. If the student can get access to a fine historic example, he should study every detail deeply so that he may capture the secret of the beauty of the old workers' craftsmanship and embody it in his own.

To conclude this exercise on the making of cups, we will assume that we are actually carrying out a commission to make a cup of a definite type.

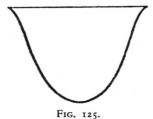

FIG. 125.

Suppose, then, a client comes along with a commission, insisting that the bowl of the cup shall be of the type of Fig. 125. We will further suppose that the client is one with a considerable knowledge of the arts, and whose taste is impeccable. He will be sensitive to qualities so elusive, subtle, and fine that nothing but our best will satisfy him.

Before we begin work we should, if we can possibly do so, look at all the things of fine shape, whether in nature or art, that we know of. The principles that determine fine form are to be seen in the shapes of flowers, leaves, buds, seed-pods, fruits, and in countless other natural things. If we can visit a good museum, we shall find that the forms of such things as

FIG. 126.

Greek vases, porcelain (especially Chinese), and blown glass will teach us the same lesson. To write down that lesson is not so easy. As in many things that really matter, we shall find, if we attempt a too rigid and definite statement, that the most vital things have escaped. We can see clearly enough that the value of long flat curves is enhanced by contrast with short quick ones, and that convexity may be balanced by concavity. Beyond this we see that a vital matter is the position of the changes of curvature. Thought about this will show us that the way in which the change is made is vital also. It may be done clumsily, it may be done in a commonplace obvious manner, or it may be done in such a way that our vessel will have something of the quality of an organic thing. It will look as if it had grown to its own delightful shape and could have grown in no other wise. The power to conceive and to embody fine, inevitable-looking forms is essential to the craftsman. If his work is to come to its full measure of fruitfulness there must be a sufficiently large body of educated taste to detect and to appreciate these finer qualities. The craftsman must be able to count on his work being received with something like enthusiasm.

The size and general shape being decided upon, the craftsman, who should at this stage of his training be able to get much help from drawing on paper, will draw his cup out. As he draws he will see in his mind's eye, not the mere pencil line on paper, but the actual metal shaped by the hammer. Fig. 126 shows how the writer decided upon the final shape of the body and cover, and determined a definite relation between it and the lid.

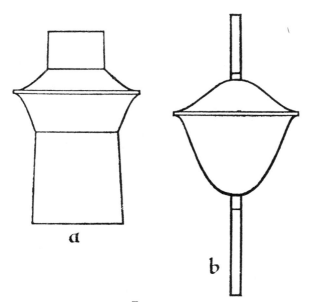

FIG. 127.

Our imaginary client has decided that he wants his cup to stand on a short stem, and as he has seen some lathe-turned work that has interested him deeply he wishes this stem to be turned also. How are we to find a good proportion for this? *Reductio ad absurdum* is useful in solving geometrical problems, and the designer can often make it serve his end also. Draw out a number of outlines of cup and cover, and consider them. Begin by drawing

K

a stem and knob (Fig. 127*a*) absurdly large—obviously this is impossible; equally impossible is (*b*), where stem and knob are as much too thin and weak as they are thick and clumsy in (*a*).

Having found what will not do, we begin experimenting until we find a size and shape that pleases us. Certain things are obvious here: one, the rightness of keeping the stem small enough to allow the curve of the lower part of the bowl to be well seen; another, the fact that normally a short stem is thick and a long one thin.

Fig. 128 shows how a reasonable proportion for the foot may be arrived at. The curves of the lip are produced until they meet the curves that may be drawn in a downward direction from the lower parts of the bowl. These

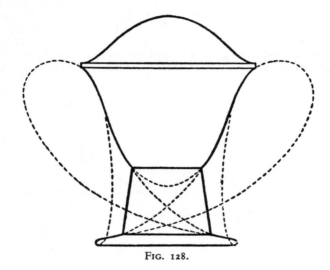

FIG. 128.

meeting-places fix with a degree of reasonableness the larger diameter of the stem and its length too. The smaller diameter is chosen as giving the fullest value to the convexity of the bottom of the bowl. The position and dimension of the actual base are decided by the same method of producing curves. The writer does not, of course, give this as an indication of a short way of learning design, but if we analyse any really fine thing we shall discover a definite relationship between all the parts.

To the writer it would seem that our fathers who worked out the system of art education that obtained at the end of the last and the beginning of this century were not so wide of the mark as we are apt to think. In those days every art student, no matter what trade or craft he followed, who took his studies seriously and got beyond the elementary stages gave a substantial portion of his time to the drawing of the human figure, either from life or from casts from the antique Though much time was wasted and many absurdities arose in the schools, the system did ensure that everyone learned something about proportion and of the relations between the different parts of the figure. Modelling the figure was widely practised also, and students learned the need for making their work look right from all view-points.

Everyone who draws or models a human figure uses something like the methods suggested in Fig. 128. Every designer too, no matter what craft or purpose he is designing for, is guided by the same principles. Sometimes he is conscious of it and uses it deliberately, but more often he follows it by intuition.

We must never forget that it is impossible to reduce this suggestion to a set of rigid rules. Principles are not formulæ, they are living things, and if true and sound will prove themselves to be applicable to the most diverse problems.

By this time the student should be sufficiently expert in raising to practise a well-tried "trade" method. This is the "creasing" of the blank with a "neck" hammer (see that its corners are well rounded) into a series of radial grooves, either on a sand-bag or on a grooved piece of wood. This is done before the first "course" is given and at the workman's discretion afterwards (Fig. 129). It will be seen that the method tends to thicken the metal. The force of the hammer blow—a mallet is not really adapted to the method, though it can be used—crushes the convex folds down into the concavities. Because of this it is well to take a blank of a slightly larger diameter than has been done hitherto.

We may also wish to thicken the edge of the bowl still more by beating the rim with a ball-pane or "neck" hammer used transversely at the end of

FIG. 129.

each course of raising. Fig. 130 shows how the metal behaves under this treatment. This process will, of course, entail the use of a blank still larger. The greatest care in annealing is needed. Over-heating causes what is known as "grain growth." The crystals grow to an undue size, and the metal loses its strength; instead of being plastic it tends to become "short" in nature. Tiny surface cracks will appear; these will deepen and widen with each "course" of raising, and finally the metal will split. Sometimes such a disastrous change in the nature of the metal will take place that solder will fail to fill up the cracks and to hold the metal. The only remedy is a drastic cutting away and the insertion of a fresh piece of silver. If time is not an object, it is always wise to scrap a "raising" when this happens and begin over again.

No problems beyond those dealt with in previous exercises arise in the planishing of the body and cover, though we should again aim at a quality of form and surface beyond anything we have reached hitherto.

The turned stem, the base, and the knob may be cast, or built up from heavy sheet of about 0.09 inch thick. If we choose the latter method, we shall need to use very great care in gauging the diameters of the deeper parts. Callipers will serve, but a quarter of an hour or so spent in making fixed gauges will relieve us from all doubts as to how far we may go. We have to find the interior diameters accurately, and then make gauges from stout sheet metal for the exterior diameters wider by double the thickness of the metal at its thinnest points. Thus if the interior of the tube be 2.25 inches, and we decide that its thinnest part must be at least 0.04 inch thick, the gauge will measure 2.25 inches + (0.04 inch × 2) = 2.33 inches from side to side.

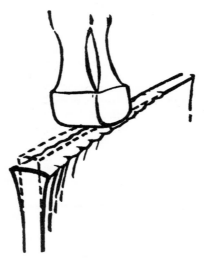

FIG. 130.—*"Caulking" or thickening the edge.*

Having made the tubes for the stem and knob as accurately to size as possible, they are to be "chucked" on hard wood. Take care that wood and metal are in contact everywhere so that the risk of "chatter" marks, due to vibration, may be eliminated as far as possible. The forms should be roughed out first with a diamond-pointed "graver." The final shaping and smoothing will be done with a round-nosed turning tool. The natural curves this gives us will be far better than those of any line we can draw on paper—that is, provided we use the tool with intelligence and sensitiveness. There is an idiom of turned form as truly as there is one of hammered. In turning the hollows suggested we shall find the inevitable movements resulting from the opposing forces of tool cutting the revolving metal, of turning tool held on the rest, and the resistance of hand, arm, and body will give a quality of form that we shall recognize as belonging essentially to the turning process.

The dominant feature of stem and knob being a rhythmic series of hollow curves, we must take the greatest care that all the other members of the mouldings shall enhance their value. If time allows, it would be excellent practice to turn two or three variations of the different parts of the cup in hard wood. The two materials, hard wood and silver, are of course very different, but there is enough similarity to warrant the experiment being tried. One important thing to remember is this—the lustre of the metal tends to emphasize the sharpness of the angles, or corners, of a moulding. A section of a moulding in silver that we imagine to have quite sharp angles will, if examined through a lens, prove to be rounded and smooth.

Cups in ordinary practice stand on wooden plinths. Too often these are of "ebonized" wood with a shiny, objectionable surface and of very "questionable" shapes. Natural woods such as mahogany, or better still, walnut, are far more lively and attractive. Again, every cup should have its own plinth designed to set it off to the best advantage. There is no need for

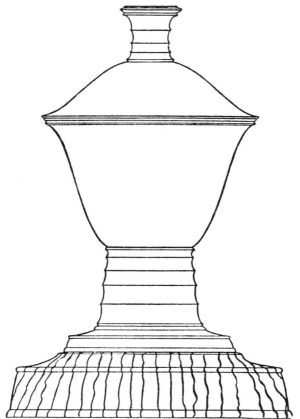

Fig. 131 *gives a suggestion of the completed cup on its appropriate plinth of wood.*

plinths to be circular; they are often better adapted to display the beauties of a round cup if they are polygonal in plan. Again, there are cups which look their best when standing on simple slabs of wood. The commonplace fashion of fixing shields with winners' names engraved thereon to plinths will often spoil the effect of the whole piece. The provision of a ring of silver completely encircling the wood is far preferable. If separate pieces are imperative, they should be considered as integral parts of the design.

In conclusion, the writer would once again remind his readers that the illustrations are not to be regarded as ready-made designs to be slavishly copied. They are merely suggestions, or, if a metaphor be preferred, sign-posts pointing to paths leading to pleasant places where pleasant results will ensue. In technique, too, every worker worthy of the name of craftsman will invent little devices of his own. The success of the student depends absolutely on the value of that which his own personality contributes to the work.

A NOTE ON "SPINNING"

If we have the use of a strongly made power-driven lathe, it will be well from all points of view to attempt a simple spinning. It is a process which has become so general in the silver trades that some knowledge is absolutely necessary, even to those craftsmen who do not wish to make a constant practice of spinning.

Briefly, spinning is the shaping of sheet metal by forcing it with highly polished steel burnishers on to a shape previously turned in hard wood. This implies that both wood and metal are spinning round rapidly. A moment's thought will make us realize that the metal must be held very tightly against the wood. So much pressure is needed, the back centre is screwed up so tightly, as to make it impossible to spin anything but very tiny things on a foot lathe.

A study of Fig. 132 will give a fairly complete idea of the spinning of a simple shape that may easily be made into a cream jug on the lines of A, Fig. 58.

The circular blank is cut from 9 m.g. metal; copper is perhaps best for a first attempt. The size is determined as for raising. For a first attempt—as the chuck in this case has a rounded end we may sink a little depression in the centre of our blank—do this on the sand-bag with a round-headed hammer.

The blank is then held in position on the chuck, the "back wood" (this should be of the hardest wood) is put against it, and the back centre screwed tightly up. Oil is applied to the steel centre, and also is smeared all over the blank, taking care that none gets between it and the back wood.

We now take the long-handed tool as A, and, holding it firmly on the rest and against the peg, we start the lathe. Then as the disc spins round we burnish the blank from the centre outwards, trying to coax the flat disc to fit closely on to the chuck. We shall find the blank behaving not dissimilarly to a disc when being raised. We shall not get very far with our first course, and the edge will tend to become crinkled. This crinkling can be kept in check by holding a piece of hard wood, the "back stick," with the left hand against the inner side of the disc. It is impossible to avoid all creases, and so long as they yield easily to the mallet they do not matter.

The purpose of the long handle will at once be clear when we make our first attempt. Often the end of the handle is held under the armpit, and the movement is given by swaying one's body. The tool slopes downwards; the usual point at which the tool touches the disc is about midway between the horizontal and vertical diameters—the rest itself has its surface at the level of the centres.

As in raising, the disc must be worked evenly all over, and we must avoid taking the centre of the disc too far, and leaving the rim alone. The tool should be made to travel along evenly from the centre outwards.

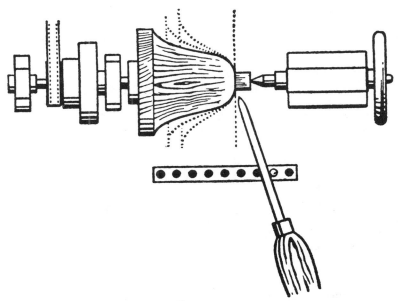

FIG. 132.

A diagram, drawn as seen from above, of spinning a shape as (A), *Fig.* 58. *The "back stick" is omitted for the sake of clearness. The dotted lines are indicative of stages of progress; they do not give the actual shapes the metal assumes. A plain back centre is shown; one with ball bearings is more efficient.*

When the disc refuses to yield further we take it out of the lathe, mallet it vigorously to remove all creases, and anneal it. Thus we proceed by stages; five or six courses will probably be needed before the metal is in contact with the whole surface of the chuck. The disc is, of course, malleted and annealed at each stage. If our tool is well polished, liberally oiled, and used intelligently, it will leave but few traces on our spinning. The least failure in any one of these will result in a most unpleasant surface.

As soon as the disc has been spun close to the chuck the rim will be turned true—a large "graver" pointed tool is used; then after annealing it is smoothed with the flat sides of the tool B on the convex curves, and with the flatter curves of A on the concave. Our first effort will probably not be a great success. If it fails, scrap it and wait for a good one before cutting the lip and mounting it with the wire.

The question as to what qualities we should expect a good spinning to have is a difficult one. The writer, without wishing to decry the work of the trade spinner, feels that the following should be kept in mind: (*a*) A form entirely right when raised and hammered is not necessarily a good model for spinning. (*b*) Similarly, a chuck turned to a shape that looks right and satisfying in wood may fail to give a good spun form in metal. (*c*) The best suggestions of the essentially right forms for spinnings are those we see the discs assume as they are shaped.

In short, we must endeavour to get hold of the right idiom of form if we are to use this method worthily. A personal notion of the writer's is that the forms of blown glass, such as that of fine sixteenth-century "Venetian glass," give a hint of the right quality of form to aim at. This notion may be

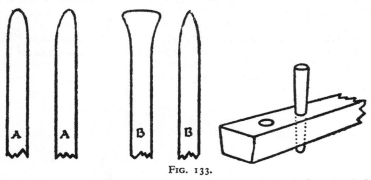

FIG. 133.

Two views of the ends of the tools necessary   *A detail of the end of a spinner's lathe*
for a first attempt at spinning. The total   *rest and peg.*
length of steel and handle often exceeds
2 feet 6 inches.

wrong, but is it not certain that the forms of good spinning should arise as directly from the process as do the forms of fine blown glass?

The whole question is extraordinarily difficult. It is clear that the usual view of spinning, as merely a quicker and cheaper way of making hollow vessels that were formerly raised and hammered, is quite wrong.

It is, of course, impossible that a purely mechanical process can ever give the living interest and charm that came from the skill of a man's hand using the simple, natural, traditional tools of the craft.

On the other hand, spinning is a perfectly legitimate process, capable in its own way of giving results of considerable charm and distinctive quality. This peculiar quality of spinning is what we must seek for. If the manufacturing silversmiths would bring trained and sensitive artists into their spinning shops, and the operative spinners themselves would try to understand and follow loyally the suggestions that such men could make, the dull, tiresome shapes that are so woefully prevalent might give place to something infinitely more interesting—possibly even exciting.

It will be said that the writer has urged students to attempt to spin a shape that he intended to be raised. In answer he would say that the sight of the contrast between the two shapes spun and raised will help greatly in the understanding of the problem, and therefore the experiment is well worth making. What is here suggested is, of course, merely a first exercise, more complicated work involving the use of "section chucks" for spinning work with drawn-in mouths smaller than the greatest diameter of the vessel—"rolled over" edges—mouldings raised from the inside, etc., should be left till a later stage.

CHAPTER 16

THE DECORATION OF SILVERWORK—ON CHASING

Although for some years fashions have tended towards plain surfaces and severe, often starkly rigid, forms, it does not follow that there is no place for decoration on silver wares. There is, indeed, much to be said in its favour even from the practical and utilitarian point of view. Well thought out and well placed patterning will often enable a vessel to stand hard and constant use. The inevitable scratches and slight bruises that are so difficult to avoid, and that would disfigure a perfectly plain piece, pass unnoticed on a patterned one. Furthermore, decoration may be used to add greatly to the strength of the piece it adorns.

It may be objected that the silversmith's business is to make things. Should he not hand them over to the engraver, the enameller, or the chaser if he wants his work decorated? To a great degree this objection is valid. Even if it were possible for a man to learn all these crafts it would hardly be practicable for him to follow them consistently. On the other hand over-specialization means unintelligent craftsmanship. The complete silversmith should be able to put his hand to the ornamental crafts; and the decorator should be able to fashion a piece in gold or silver throughout. In neither case will the absolute speed, precision, and certainty of the specialist be reached; but both, maker and decorator, will understand each other infinitely better, when each has essayed the other's particular branch of the craft. The added interest that this temporary change would bring to the work of both would repay, over and over again, any inconvenience or loss of time that might arise were the experiment to be made.

The decorative craft most generally useful to the constructive craftsman in metal is chasing, and that is the craft we will begin with. Chasing, here and hereafter, is to be taken as including chasing, embossing, repousse work, and the modelling of solid metal with hammer and punch. The chaser needs a substance that is at once hard and sticky, yet plastic enough to yield to the blows of a hammer and punch. Pitch tempered as described has all the necessary qualities.

Mixing the pitch. Take 7 lbs. of "Brown Swedish Pitch"—the quality may be determined by (*a*) colour; there should be a faint shade of brown in the lump, and, when broken, the dust is very distinctly of that colour; (*b*) fracture: this should be clearly "conchoidal," *i.e.*, the forms are shell-like; (*c*) tenacity: when a tiny fragment is held in the fingers until it becomes warm and soft it would pull out in thin strings several inches long; here again we should test by colour for good pitch pulled out until very thin and shows a clear translucent brown when held to the light; (*d*) Smell: pure vegetable pitch has an agreeable odour; but pitch adulterated with rosin and bitumen gives off acrid, choking fumes when melted. Break the pitch up into pieces of 2 inches or 3 inches, put them in the pot* and melt on a gas ring. With

---

* The usual one is known in the iron trade as a "Negro Pot" 10 inches or 12 inches are good sizes. A strong iron ladle is needed too.

the pitch put about 6 ozs. of best tallow. Have in readiness 10 lbs. of coarse, "Plaster of Paris" or powdered pumice, or "Bath Brick" dust. This powder must be dry and free from lumps.

When the pitch and tallow are completely melted, add three or four handfuls of the powder and stir evenly until it disappears; then add a similar quantity; go on doing this until the mixture becomes difficult to stir. If too much powder is added the mixture will become dull in surface and short in consistency. If this over-stiffening happens it can be remedied by adding more pitch and tallow.

When we think we have reached the right degree of stiffening, or hardening, we test the pitch by dipping a bit of wood, or scrap metal, into the pot, and cooling it in running water. When quite cold, well mixed pitch should be so hard that one can, by using considerable force, just make one's thumb nail indent it. We must not forget that in winter, more tallow, and in summer, more powder, will be needed.

Caution. On no account must pitch be overheated. Not only is there a danger of the pot boiling over and taking fire, but any undue heating will destroy the elasticity and stickiness so necessary if one's chasing is to be done happily.

Pitch bowls and blocks. The hollow hemisphere of cast iron filled with pitch is more pleasant to work upon than a block of thick wood; but if we have no bowl available the wood will serve quite well.

If we have a bowl,* we pour pitch into it until it is level with the rim (if we wish to save pitch we can economize by dropping lumps of brick into it; wood will serve, but it has to be held down to prevent its floating); this is allowed to cool, then a thin layer, not too liquid, is spread over the surface, allowed to cool, and this spreading is repeated until a thickness of from ½ inch to 1 inch is reached.

If we have only a piece of wood (get it as thick as possible, 2 inches at least) it must be covered by pouring, spreading, and allowing to cool until the needed thickness is reached. It is sometimes convenient to make walls of clay or cardboard into which pitch can be poured. However, every worker will devise his own methods of handling pitch. In use, the constant addition of pitch to the block will make it so thick as to be unwieldy. When this happens the surplus is chipped off with a broad "cold" chisel and a big hammer.

Pitch bowls can only be used when placed on rings or collars† while wooden blocks are put upon sand bags.

Sticking metal on pitch. If we have the pitch melted, the most convenient method is: cut the metal rather larger than the finished piece of chasing is to be, mallet it flat, lay it on the bench with about $\frac{3}{32}$ inch projecting over the edge, and bend it down by tapping it gently with a mallet to an angle of about 30 degrees; do this on the four sides.

---

* The writer has seen galvanised iron ladles, with the handles removed, used successfully as pitch bowls.

† A triangular frame of stout wood 1½ inches × 1½ inches is quite serviceable. Rings are made by coiling leather belting and fastening by stitching or riveting. Another way is to make a ring of iron strip about 1 inch to 1½ inches wide and cover it by winding thick, soft cord around it.

Smear a tiny spot of oil on the concave side of the metal. Place it greasy face upwards on an iron plate (the surface plate is generally used, but a piece of thick iron sheet ⅛ inch or so will serve well) until it cools. Meanwhile a pitch bowl, or block, of a convenient size should be flattened in readiness. This is done either by (a) pouring, or rather spreading, stiff, half melted pitch on the top of the block, or (b) heating the surface of the pitch on bowl or block by playing a gas flame on it until it softens so that it can be spread level with an iron bar—say 1 inch square. The final flattening is done either by putting the block pitch downwards on the surface plate, or by putting the surface plate on top of the block.

When we have a level pitch block, and a pitch-covered piece of metal, we stick the metal on by smearing a little pitch on the levelled surface of the block and bringing the two surfaces of pitch, on metal and block, together. Apply pressure or weight to ensure perfect adhesion and allow to cool.

If our pitch pot is not melted, and we cannot wait, we can stick our piece of metal on this way. Turn the edges down and oil as before. Warm a block with the gas flame, and as the pitch softens work it up towards the centre until a mound of pitch is formed. Then take the metal and, with it, scrape the pitch a little more to one side. Now press one edge of the metal on to the pitch and lower it gradually into a horizontal position, taking the greatest care that no pockets of air are imprisoned between metal and pitch. Metal is removed from the pitch either by driving a thin chisel between metal and pitch, not always a safe proceeding, or by warming the pitch with a flame. Do this first in one spot until the tang of an old file can be pushed under the edge of the metal. Then as the whole plate of metal is warmed, gentle leverage will lift it up. Sometimes light "soldering tongs" will prove excellent.

Very great care is needed to avoid burning the pitch. The smooth glistening surface should never be destroyed. The disappearance of this shows that the pitch has been burned and its nature destroyed. At the first sign of smoking and bubbling the flame should be moved away. A safeguard is to keep the flame in constant motion.

Until one becomes accustomed to handling hot pitch, one must take the utmost care in avoiding burnt fingers. The use of wood or rag will help, and with practice steel or iron tools of all kinds can be used in handling pitch successfully. As more experience is gained one learns the knack of shaping pitch with the fingers, and the heat at which it may be touched.

Hollow vessels are filled by pouring pitch into them. For this it must be sufficiently liquid to flow freely, otherwise air pockets may form.

A very simple and effective method of preventing pitch from spreading over the outside of our vessel is to wrap paper around it, cutting, or tearing, a hole big enough for the pitch to flow in easily.

If we should be unable to prevent pitch from going where we do not want it, we must wait until all is perfectly cold. Then with a hammer and chasing punch-tracer we can very carefully chip it off. When this is done some may still remain. If we hold our vessel in a gas flame so that a thin hot jet of flame strikes the pitch, we can, in a few moments, wipe it away with rag or waste moistened with paraffin or turpentine. Here great caution must be exercised to avoid setting fire to the rag.

When the vessel has to be filled through an opening so narrow that pitch will not flow down it another method is used. Pitch is poured in thin streams on the surface plate, and, as it cools, is worked with the fingers into long thin rods. The vessel is heated and the rods of pitch are pushed in through the narrow opening until the vessel is full. The whole must of course be kept sufficiently hot to allow the rods to go in freely; but if too much heat is applied, bubbles may form. There is also a danger that liquid pitch may spurt out when least expected.

One safe method would be to put the vessel to be filled in a saucepan of hot water or to imbed it in hot sand. In either case great care must be taken to keep water or sand from getting into the vessel.

Emptying pitch out of vessels. In large shops a specially constructed oven is used for this. In the ordinary workshop it is usual to devise an arrangement of binding wire and to suspend the vessel, mouth downwards, over the pitch pot. Then a gas flame is allowed to play around the vessel's mouth—no blast is used. The moment the smallest flame of burning pitch is seen the gas is withdrawn, and the pitch flame extinguished in the most convenient way.

In a few minutes the pitch will begin to flow freely. Then the flame may be played a little higher up. Finally with a plop the comparatively hard core will come out.

When vessels with large bodies and narrow mouths have to be emptied the utmost caution is needed. Pitch expands with great force when heated. If the mouth is allowed to become clogged with hard pitch, while above it is approaching the melting point, there is grave risk of a serious explosion.

As soon as the pitch is melted out, as cleanly as possible, the vessel should be put under the hood or in a fire grate while a flame is played on it until all flame and smoke cease.

The vessel can then be annealed. This should be done with a small hot flame kept in constant motion. If the pitch tends to cling to the sides of the vessel scrape it away with a bit of wood. The annealing must go on until the pitch is seen to be all burned to a white ash. The vessel should be allowed to cool. The ashes should be brushed out and if any black persists the vessel must be annealed again before pickling. If half burned pitch is put into acid pickle a substance very difficult to remove is formed.

Sometimes, especially when dealing with flat sheet work, there is no need to burn the pitch away. The metal can be heated until the pitch upon it glistens, when it is easily wiped away with rag. Paraffin will remove any pitch left after the first wiping. Here, of course, as noted before, the greatest caution is needed, if burns are to be avoided.

Chasing tools. These may be bought ready made from the tool dealers, but the serious student will certainly wish to make his own.

Blanks for chasing tools, sometimes called "brindles," can be bought, but as there may be some difficulty here, we will make them from cast steel rod for our first attempt. For this we shall need six tools, three made from $\frac{1}{4}$ inch or $\frac{7}{32}$ inch square rod, and three made from $\frac{5}{32}$ inch square rod.

Cutting the blanks. Mark off five lengths of about $4\frac{1}{2}$ inches. Cut the rod either by sawing through with the hack saw, or by nicking with the edge of a file until the steel will snap off when pulled or struck smartly.

Properly, a chasing tool should be thickest in the centre of its length, so that if we have any skill in forging, the ends of the rod may be drawn out with the hammer a little. Next the corners are filed off to make an octagon. The whole may then be drawfiled,* but should not be polished. A too smooth tool is difficult to hold. Where, as in tool (1), the end is broader than the stem one end only is hammered out on all four sides. This is the "striking" end. The lower or "working" end is hammered on two sides only so as to make the original square end into an oblong. A close study of Fig. 134a will enable

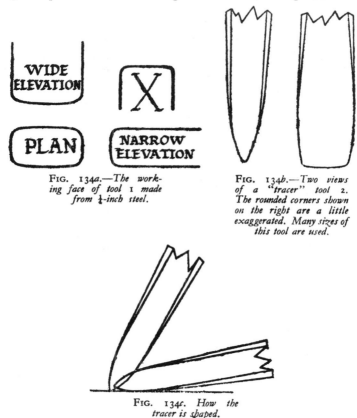

FIG. 134a.—*The work-ing face of tool 1 made from ¼-inch steel.*

FIG. 134b.—*Two views of a "tracer" tool 2. The rounded corners shown on the right are a little exaggerated. Many sizes of this tool are used.*

FIG. 134c. *How the tracer is shaped.*

us to complete the tool. Note that X is wrong, the centre part of the face is flat; such a tool would refuse to leave a clean clear trace behind, it would "peck." On the other hand, except for special purposes, tools should not be too rounded. The face of the tool should be shaped and polished with FF emery cloth with the greatest care. It is a frequent custom to use chasing tools "soft" for a while. Correction is easy and a tool that has "worn in" takes a subtle and delightful form. The "working" face of the tool and about ½ inch of the stem above is finally hardened by heating to a bright red

* Draw filing: the file is held at a right angle to the rod, the stroke is parallel with the length.

and quenching in water (beware of burning the steel). The face and end are again polished bright and tempered by blowing a small gas flame at a point about 1 inch up the stem. As the colour appears and travels down the stem it is watched intently. The moment the face turns a full yellowish brown, the tempering is arrested by quenching again. In the case of small tools one has to plunge the tool in the water with the utmost swiftness. Otherwise the temper will be too low. Beware of hardening too long a portion of the stem. If this is done, the end of the tool may break suddenly.

Tool (2). This is a "tracer," the most important tool in the chaser's kit. Fig. 134(b) shows exactly how it should be formed. The working edge is not a chisel, nor is it merely rounded, but is formed of two intersecting arcs with the tip rounded off. This is best shaped by holding the tool, as one holds a pen, and rubbing it to and fro on emery cloth, letting the tool rise and fall as it is moved. Fig. 134(c). A tracer must be perfectly symmetrical on its axis, both in width and thickness.

(1) and (2) are made from the $\frac{7}{32}$ inch or $\frac{1}{4}$ inch steel rod.

Tool (3). This is a tracer made from $\frac{5}{32}$ inch steel. It is exactly the same as (2) except that it is only about $\frac{9}{64}$ inch wide.

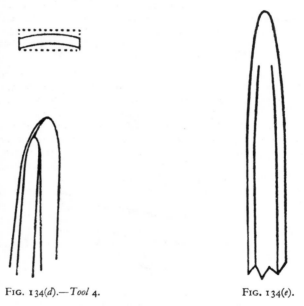

FIG. 134(d).—*Tool* 4.   FIG. 134(e).

Tool (4) is another tracer identical with (3), but curved instead of straight. Fig. 134(d) shows how the curve is worked out of the oblong into which the blank is first filed. The hollow is made either with a half round file, or, as some prefer, with the extreme tip of a three-square needle file. It is rather a difficult matter to get the intersection of the rounded bevils to follow the exact curve. One of the best ways is to wrap a piece of emery cloth around a wooden cylinder of the right diameter and to rub the tool along it, allowing the tool to rise and fall as did the straight tracer, excepting that the movement must be longitudinal (a transverse movement, at right angles to the tool's axis is best for straight tracers).

As soon as we have made our tracers we should strike them into a piece of sheet metal laid on the flat die. The mark or "trace"* is then examined carefully with a magnifying glass so that any defects, such as unevenness in width can be detected and remedied. A final polish on a bit of fine emery cloth should make them ready for hardening.

Fig. 134(e). Tool (5). A point or dot, made from $\frac{5}{32}$ inch steel tapered down so that its end is an exact hemisphere of $\frac{1}{32}$ inch. No. (6) is a tool similar to Fig. 1 but a rather pointed oval in plan, made from $\frac{1}{4}$ inch steel. We now have enough tools to begin with. Of course, we shall soon find more tools are necessary and we must be prepared to make more than one for each fresh job we do. Tracers of all widths and thicknesses and degrees of curvature; tools for embossing and for modelling raised parts on the front of all sorts of sizes and shapes and face curvature, some nearly flat and some approaching a semicircle in profile, will demand to be made. Sometimes one class of tool will approach so closely to another that it will be difficult to classify it; thus, a tracer leaving a broad line may be used as an embossing tool. Chasing tools should always be as shapely as we can make them. Using clumsily shaped tools inevitably results in clumsy work. Chasing tools are kept in cylindrical metal boxes. These are pieces of tube, about 3 inches high, from, say, $1\frac{1}{2}$ inches to 3 inches diameter, soldered on to a flat disc of metal.

Tracing. We must first learn to use the tracer. Study Fig. 135 carefully. This has been drawn from the writer's own left hand and shows exactly how the fingers hold the tool. The function of each digit is:—*Thumb:* this presses the tool tightly against the other fingers; *forefinger:* the upper part of the tool rests against the side of the upper joints, while the tip presses the centre closely against the end of the thumb; *middle finger:* the side of the end of this finger is pressed strongly against the lower end of the tool, the last point of contact being about $\frac{1}{2}$ inch from the working end; this finger does not rest on the metal; *third finger:* this is the most important and takes the most strain; it rests on the metal and acts as a guide and a pivot for the tool; the tip is pressed very firmly down on to the metal, on its outer face, towards the inner side of the root of the nail, and it takes great pressure from the side of the middle finger; the strain on this finger will make it ache at first until the muscles get used to the work; professional chasers usually develop a distinct flattening and widening of the tip; *little finger:* this is often held straight out so that three or four tools, other than the one in use, can be held in the left hand while working; but the knack of doing this is difficult to acquire, for the beginner its exact position is immaterial.

Many students persist in resting the tip of the middle finger on the metal; this is certainly a wrong practice, it prevents one from seeing clearly what the tool is doing.

Stick a piece of scrap sheet metal, any gauge under 12 m.g., about 3 inches square on a pitch block. On it draw two concentric circles about

* The line traced will, normally, be about $\frac{1}{50}$ to $\frac{1}{32}$ inch in width.

$2\frac{5}{8}$ inches and $2\frac{1}{8}$ inches diameters. Within the inner one draw any pattern of interlacing arcs that may occur to one's mind.

Now arrange the pitch block in a good light, coming from the right. Take the tracer (2) in the left hand as Fig. 135. Note that it should slant slightly away from the worker, so that the tool will, as it were, "walk on its heel." Place the rear end of the edge on the outer circle. Hold the tool with the utmost firmness and draw it along the curve. Do this until the action becomes familiar. Take a medium sized chasing or repousse hammer, about 2 to 3 oz. in weight, and practise striking the end of a chasing tool held, as for actual work, on a lead cake, until one can not only hit the tool unhesitatingly every time but can alter the angle of the tool and the direction of the hammer blow, so that the force is always along the axis of the tool. This may seem extremely difficult, but is not so in reality. One will soon find it possible to hit the tool unfailingly and rightly with one's eyes shut. Chasing will be

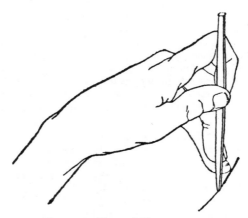

FIG. 135.—*How to hold a tracer.*

a very trying business until one can attain some measure of automatism in the use of the hammer.

Now for the actual tracing. Hold the tool on the line, as described above, strain the fingers and hand as if to draw the tool along the line, but press the tip of the third finger on to the metal so firmly that it acts as a brake. Now strike the end of the tool with steady, even blows, at a rate of about 140 a minute, and it will move slowly forward towards one. The tool will move a little way without any movement of the tip of the third finger; but we shall soon find that we have to move the whole hand. While this happens the pressure is, of course, momentarily relaxed. This, too, may seem a difficult thing to do, but actually is little more so than using the hammer. At our first attempt the tool will no doubt skid and slip just when we least expect it. Serious practice for an hour or so, however, will usually enable one to master it.

For a circle of the size given, and for arcs drawn with radii of 1 inch or over, the straight tracer $\frac{5}{16}$ inch wide will serve. It can even be made to follow a quicker curve if it is tilted more on to its heel, and the hammer blows increased in speed and decreased in strength. If this is done it will be found well to reverse the usual rule that the tool should move towards one. When tracing very small, quick curves the tool often has to be moved away from one.

After practice on curved lines, straight ones may be tried, then combinations of straight and curved, then compound curves, then parallel lines,

FIG. 136(*a*).

FIG. 136(*b*).

FIG. 136(*c*).

straight and curved, then curves which converge gently towards each other and finally meet at a point. Sometimes it is more advantageous to "jump" the tracer along straight lines rather than to run it. If this is done it is best to have the line to be "jumped" with the tracer at right angles to the lines of sight, like lines on writing paper.

Drawing on metal. For geometrical patterns, and these we shall most probably choose for our first attempts, the clearest lines are those drawn actually on the metal with dividers and scriber.

When it is necessary to make a preliminary drawing on paper we must make it on thin paper or trace it on tracing paper. These drawings can then be transferred to the metal by using carbon paper, or better still a piece of thin tough paper, one side of which has been coated with black lead. A soft black lead pencil will do this well.

Then if this is placed, black face downwards, between tracing and metal, and the lines are traced over firmly with a steel style, or a very hard lead pencil, the pattern will appear on the metal in clear black line. A little "lump gamboge" moistened with water, rubbed on the metal and smeared over thinly will give, when dry, a dull surface on which pencil lines show with perfect clearness. If the student is a draughtsman it is often best to draw the pattern straight on the metal with a lead pencil—the hardest obtainable. Here the use of gamboge is most necessary, especially for ease in making erasures and alterations.

Drawings and tracings on metal are far from permanent. Workers with moist skin will find that the lines rub off very quickly. Permanency may be achieved by going over the lines with a scriber. For the finest work this is, though somewhat slow, the best course. For ordinary work a drawing or tracing may be made sufficiently permanent for all practical purposes by painting it over lightly with shellac varnish thinned down with methylated spirit. If carbon paper is used, choose one whose colour is not soluble in spirit; otherwise the varnish will blur the lines.

As soon as we can trace a line that is reasonably firm and clear we shall want to do something more than practice pieces. It is not always easy to think of suitable exercises which may be put to definite use. A wooden box, covered with square panels nailed on, can be quite pleasant. These are of 8 m.g. brass. Simple finger plates also offer some scope. Figs. 136(a) and (b) give suggestions for patterns done with tracers alone.

FIG. 136(d).—*Simple type of foliage for embossing.*

FIG.   136(e).—*May   be traced or embossed.*

The next thing is to use tool (1) or (6) and emboss a pattern. Figs. 136 (c), (d), (e) and (f) offer suggestions.

It is quite a usual practice to emboss a pattern directly from the back and, if a more definite outline is needed, to stick the metal on the pitch, face uppermost, and to outline it with a blunt tracer. This, however, is not advisable for a beginner.

When we have traced in our pattern the metal is taken off the pitch, cleaned, perhaps annealed and pickled, if we do not like the rather "messy" paraffin and rag, and stuck on again back uppermost. Then with the broad smooth tool (1) we sink those parts that we wish to be raised on the right side. Usually it is better to begin on the edges of the shapes and work inwards. For the present we must be content to leave complicated modelling, and to attempt nothing more than simple rounded bosses.

It may be that our pattern is so simple that there is no need to stick the metal or pitch for embossing; it can be laid face downwards on a piece of cardboard or leather and bossed up with hammer and punch. This will, of course, destroy the metal's flatness. It may be restored either by the use of small boxwood punches, or we may choose to put our little panel on the flat die, or on the bench, and to go over the lines again with the tracer, hitting just hard enough to bring the metal, under the tool, in contact with the flat surface upon which it rests.

The flattening of chased work is a matter that needs care and thought. Take "flat chasing" work done with the tracer alone—we may wish to preserve the rippled surface that comes naturally; then we use a mallet with a leather or rubber face; or—we may find it necessary to hammer the whole surface flat. The case for and against each must be well considered. Sometimes utility will be the deciding factor, and sometimes appearance. On a small scale a smooth surface is more likely to be desirable than on a large one. Sometimes sheer necessity will decide. It may be impossible to make the floor of a tray sufficiently flat without vigorous hammering.

If we have no skill in drawing, or not enough confidence in our powers, we may make use of tracings of pressed leaves. Fig. 136(e) shows a maple leaf put to this purpose.

FIG. 136(f).—*Suggestions for border pattern, traced or embossed.*

Another field for the diffident draughtsman to work in is the making of chequers with "tracer" and "point" or "dotting tool." Figs. 137(a), (b), (c).

Some practice will be needed to use this "dotting tool" or "point." Even to make one impression in exactly the right place needs care.

When, as in Fig. 137(c), we have to cover a space closely with tiny point marks so as to produce a matted or textured surface, it is not quite an easy matter. The tool should be held in the usual way with its tip about $\frac{1}{16}$ inch above the surface of the metal. Then we shall find that when we strike it with the hammer it will be forced down on to the metal and immediately it will spring back again to its former position. The fingers actually function as a spring. Our aim should be to move it about over the space while the hammer falls quickly, lightly and regularly, thus producing an even texture. It is generally best to go around the outer edges first and then to work towards the centre.

Not infrequently, on old work, we find patterns, sometimes elaborate, done entirely with a fine point in this manner. Something of this kind should be attempted. Not only is it an excellent discipline for the hands, but it can give results of great beauty also. This work is often called "pricking" or "pouncing."

Every chaser will want to trace scrolls. If we find them too difficult to draw freehand we may make a scroll in wire and mark around it with a pencil

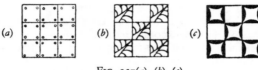

FIG. 137(*a*), (*b*), (*c*).

Chequers made with tracers and point. The black in (c) would be dotted closely all over.

A background of scrolls, such as Fig. 136(*e*), can easily be drawn if we first draw a series of circles or portions of circles to guide us. It is indeed quite an easy matter with a little practice to develop a circle into a scroll. The filling in of the irregular shapes of the background of this kind will help us to understand some of the fundamental principles of design.

It must be very clearly understood that these figures should not be copied. They are to be taken as suggestions only. The writer's aim has been to point out a way which should lead to right results. It cannot be too strongly urged that every silversmith should learn to draw to the best of his ability. Few can be so placed as to be out of reach of at least reasonably adequate art teaching. For those who wish to go beyond very elementary chasing, modelling is a necessity.*

So far we have worked on flat metal. In silversmith's work the surfaces to be chased are usually concave or convex; rarely are they flat. A good first exercise on such a surface is to dome and planish a shallow, saucerlike, circular dish or tray from 5 inches to 7 inches or so in diameter. Fig. 138 offers a number of suggestions for filling alternate radial spaces. This is, perhaps, the simplest layout that can be found.

It is not a very easy matter to get the whole of a shallow bowl stuck soundly on pitch; it is, however, quite a simple matter to get a small portion, such as one of these sectors, stuck on.

Having traced in the outline of the radial space—sector—we draw within it the pattern, we wish and trace it also. If it be at all intricate, or we doubt our ability to draw it again exactly in the next space, we may take a rubbing

* The importance of this paragraph cannot be over stressed.

of it on thin paper and from this transfer it into the remaining spaces. It must be clearly understood that Fig. 138 is given as suggestion only.

The background to patterns of this kind is very fittingly textured. A small tracer $\frac{1}{16}$ inch or so wide, struck evenly, and in as regular an order as the space to be filled will admit of, so as to cover the whole background with a series of dotted lines running at right angles to the axis of the sectors, is very effective.

If we choose a pattern of foliage we may emboss the leaves and stems slightly. The central ring, the cusped band within it, and the cusped boss in the very middle may also be embossed. To do this we should, of course, fill the bowl with pitch. The greatest relief should not exceed $\frac{1}{16}$ inch.

If, after all, we decide to forgo embossing, we have some choice in the treatment of the surface. We may subject it to a fair amount of hammering, when the effect of the chasing will tend a little towards engraving, or we may leave it with its slight surface play untouched save for a gentle malleting to make the bowl true.

FIG. 138.

We must remember when using dividers to set out patterns on vessels hollow either inside or out, that we are not working out geometrical problems on plane surfaces. Thus when we strike a circle on a convex surface we shall find that the radius we use will not divide the circle (as it will on a plane surface) into six parts. In drawing on surfaces other than plane, the centres are rarely on the plane of the circumference, but above it or below almost always. Division of circles, drawn on vessels, has always to be done by trial.

If we wish to make something of which chasing is an integral part, a Fruit Dish or Tazza (Fig. 139) makes an excellent exercise.

The chasing of a small round piece, such as the stem, or knop, of this piece provides some fresh problems. The first is : how is it to be held so that it will not move under the blows of the hammer and punch. If the whole tazza has been completed to the final solderings, a tall mound of pitch will have to be made on a block.* This may be built up from broken pieces, roughly 1 inch cubes, melting them together with a gas flame ; or the pitch pot may be heated until the contents are getting soft, thus allowing the pitch to be pulled out in pieces and moulded, using a heavy cold stake to shape it. If the knop is still a separate piece, the mound may be quite a low one. Often, things such as this tazza are screwed together.

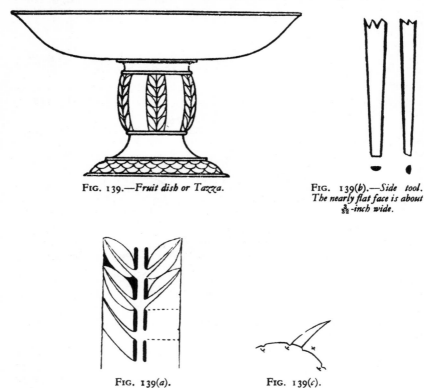

FIG. 139.—*Fruit dish or Tazza.*

FIG. 139(*b*).—*Side tool. The nearly flat face is about $\frac{3}{32}$-inch wide.*

FIG. 139(*a*).

FIG. 139(*c*).

In this mound we have to make an impression of the knop. We do this with a piece of cold iron or steel, a hammer head or what not. Then we heat the pitch again and while it is still soft we lay a piece of rag on the pitch and, with the actual knop, press the rag deeply into the pitch. As the block cools we keep the pitch firmly pressed up to the knop, taking care not to let the mould rise above the horizontal diameter. If this were allowed it would, of course, be impossible to pull the knop out of its mould until the pitch was heated or broken.

* The projecting dish and base must not touch the pitch.

There can be, of course, because of the rag, no adhesion between the pitch and the knop, and with a very little working it will come loose. To ensure firmness, an absolute necessity for the chaser who has just begun, we bore holes through the bench on both sides of the pitch block. Through them (they should be ⅜ inch or ½ inch diameter) a piece of thin strong cord is passed; this goes over the top of the knop down through the other hole and to a convenient length underneath the bench where the two ends are tied together. The chaser's foot or feet are placed in the loop as he sits at the bench, and the pressure from the cord on the knop will keep it quite firm. There is no trouble whatever in turning the knop around, all that has to be done is to lift the feet and the work is loose again. Where the work is larger, say 3 inches or more in diameter, the pitch block is often discarded and the work placed on a sand bag. The cord will hold it firmly. Sometimes the cord, as seen in plan from above, instead of being parallel with the edge of the bench, is at an angle with it. The thing to aim at is to arrange the cord so that it crosses the axis, of whatever is being chased, at right angles. There will, of course, be much friction between the knop and the mould, so that the only satisfactory way to mark the pattern on is by scribing; otherwise it would soon be rubbed away.

If we decide to adopt the suggestion in Fig. 139 and pattern the knop with vertical stripes, alternately plain, and chased with leaf-work, some thought about the best way of marking the pattern on the metal, and of chasing the foliage, is necessary.

To mark on a number of vertical lines on a rounded surface is not quite easy. Often a student is tempted to bend a straight strip of metal, and use it as a rule, with unhappy results. It is almost impossible to avoid distortion.

The best thing to do, after the number and width of the strips has been been chosen, is to divide one end of the knop, very carefully, with sharp pointed dividers into 6, 8, 10, or whatever number of parts is desired. Then take a small pair of pencil compasses, with the steel point very sharp, and from each point in succession strike arcs that intersect at points vertically above the starting points. These two sets of points are joined by pencil lines drawn free hand. Unless the knop is very much out of true, or we have been careless, these lines must be exactly vertical when seen in direct front elevation. Each line gives us one side of a strip.

Next we decide upon the width of the stripe (remember that these will be wider in the centre of the knop and narrower at the top and bottom), and set off, with the dividers, points marking the other sides of the strips. From these newly found points, vertical lines are drawn as before. These key lines should be scribed in to make sure they will not be lost. With every step we take, and each line we draw, the closest watch should be kept to detect the least departure from the vertical. Each line will, of course, show as a straight vertical line from one, and only one, point of view—from exactly in front.

If we have had no experience in chasing leaves growing symmetrically, it will be well to work a trial piece. Fig. 139(a) shows the best method of ensuring the right degree of regularity. A punch, in this case an oblong with rounded ends, is first struck in. This defines the central stem and the position and branching of the leaf ribs. Once this is done it is comparatively a simple matter to draw, and trace in, the ribs accurately. The tracing of the leaves themselves will now be found a fairly easy matter. The tracing done, the background should be sunk to the level of the first punch marks. If needed, this may be textured, or matted, with a single point or other tool. We shall probably need to make some tiny flat-ended tools to fit these background shapes.

A side tool, Fig. 139(*b*), will enable us to "set down" the leaves on each side of the ribs. The straighter edge of the tool is used as a tracer. Fig. 139(*c*) gives the section of the leaves. The slight ridge left by the side tool is smoothed away with a small tool, oval in plan, and very slightly rounded on the face. The leaves may be modelled or veined. Experiment on your trial piece.

If we feel that, although we wish to omit pattern, some relief of surface is needed. A tool, nearly as wide as the stripes, of the type of Fig. 134(*a*), can be used to produce a series of hollow flutes, of equal width. These will act as an excellent foil to the remaining plainer parts. Here again some practice will be needed before we can command skill enough to make flutes of an even depth and a pleasant surface.

FIG 140.—*Suggestion for pattern inside bowl.*

The first attempts at fluting should be done on pieces of metal bossed up to something near the contour of a section of the surface of the knop. The secrets of fluting are—extreme care in making the tool, it must be absolutely free from any tendency to peck (see Fig. 134(*a*), and remarks upon it)—perfect symmetry in curve so that it shall leave identical traces whichever way it is used—firm holding (there are two reasons for this, one that the trace, a groove the tool leaves, is not deep enough to act in any way as a guide, and secondly tools of any size, as this we are considering, have a strong tendency to bounce, or jerk, so that instead of an even groove we get a series of tool impressions)—and firm, steady, even striking with the hammer. This should be of ample weight. When we strike a large tool with a small hammer we fail to overcome the inertia of the heavy punch.

Hollow flutes, as a rule, should not be too deep. For this reason it will be well to begin them by running the tool down on the outer edges, rather than down the centre, as would be done were a deep flute desired. The method advised makes it easier to ensure a pleasant dividing ridge.

We should aim at a surface texture so smooth that nothing beyond a little emery clothing and stoning will be needed. This knop is a case where the marks of a skilfully used tool are wholly right and delightful.

Scale patterns, like those shown on the base in Fig. 139 and in Fig. 140, another suggestion for chasing the inside of the bowl, are done with punches, having tracer-like edges, but struck on with a single blow.

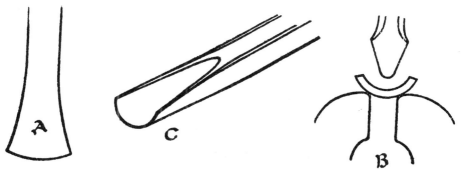

FIG. 141.

Fig. 141, A, B C, shows how they may be conveniently made. This method is useful for the larger sizes, ⅜ inch or so; the smaller ones may be filed out of the solid. To make a ⅜ inch semicircular punch out of a piece of ¼ inch steel, we first forge the end out as A. Then we heat the thin end again and hollow it as B. This shows the job being done across the jaws of a partly opened vice; though if we have a big piece of iron with a deep groove it will obviously give a smoother result. C shows the finished end of the tool. Care must be taken that the steel be left everywhere thick enough to stand up to the hammer blow without springing.

A round file will be used for the hollow curve. These are usually rather roughly made. Unless they are revolved constantly they will leave anything but a clear circular curve. An essential point to note is that a line joining the ends of the curve must be exactly at right angles to the axis of the curve. A pattern struck with a "staggered" punch is very unpleasant.

There is no need to worry about extreme exactitude in the measurement of these tools. First thoughts might lead us to assume that we should need to make two punches to strike, say, 24 semicircles around a circle of 3 inches and one of 3¼ inches diameter. We shall find that a single punch will answer perfectly. In the one case we shall place them very slightly farther apart, and in the other, very slightly closer together. The same principle makes it possible, within limits, but very wide ones, to take any punch and make it go evenly around any circle, or along any line and this without any measurement or "setting out." Let us assume that our circle has a circumference of 7 inches and that we wish to strike 20 semicircles of $\frac{3}{8}$ inch. We shall find that by allowing the imprints to overlap very slightly, but barely perceptibly, we shall do it quickly and with ease. Conversely, if we wished to put 16 semicircles only, the widening we should have to do would be scarcely visible. The distance between each one would have to be but $\frac{1}{40}$ inch wider; such a small amount would defy detection by the eye alone.

The finishing of the edge of the semicircle needs very great care. The curve has to be perfect; here emery cloth wrapped around a steel rod is excellent. The width of the impression when struck has to be even from end to end. Lastly the height of the tool; i.e., the measurement from the line, joining the two ends, or horns, to the highest part of the curve, has to be very carefully considered. It is possible to regulate the height of a row of semicircles in the same way as that adapted when fitting a given number in a certain space; but the range is far more restricted. Another point is that when the tool is held on a flat surface its axis should be vertical. It is impossible to ensure clean, clear impressions when the stem of the tool slants, even slightly.

Practice on scrap metal will be helpful. Clear lines marking the level of the horns should be drawn, and the work should be lighted so that the position of the horns can be clearly seen. At our first attempt it will be well to incline the tool forward, and to give it a very gentle blow, just hard enough to make the prints of the two horns, or tips, visible. If these are right, the tool can be put back into its position; we do this by feeling rather than sight; if wrong, we can make the necessary adjustment without fear that the faint trial marks will show.

It will be found that much depends on the quality of the hammer blow. To get a clear imprint from a punch at one blow needs something like a sharp rap; quite different from the blow that makes a tracer or embossing tool leave a clear trace. Another point to note is that the instant the blow is delivered the hammer is snatched away. Failure to do this may mean that a double blow is struck with the attendant risk of a double imprint of the tool.

The background of the interlaced letters in Fig. 140 is shown, in part, covered with tiny rings. This, an old and well tried texture, is done with a ring tool. Fig. 142 shows how these are made. A short sturdy steel punch with a rounded end is made carefully as regards shape of end, polish, and temper. With it a hollow is struck into the flat end of a piece of steel held firmly in the vice. The surplus is then filed carefully away in a long gentle taper, until an even circular ring thread of steel about $\frac{1}{64}$ inch wide is left. This is worked into a soft rounded edge with emery cloth until it leaves a circular print of the thickness of a thin tracer line, Ring tools need careful hardening and tempering.

To obtain an even texture with a ring tool it is best to follow the outer edges of the space and work inwards in, as nearly as possible, parallel lines. Overlapping should be avoided as far as possible.

The centre of Fig. 140 would need ring tools and semicircle punches of two sizes. The inside of the dish may be in flat chasing; when the whole will be lightly planished after the tracing and punching is done; or the pattern may be embossed.

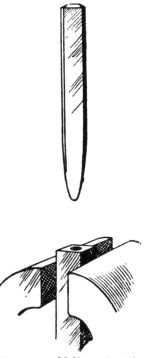

FIG. 142.—*Making a ring tool.*

There are three main divisions of the chaser's art. Flat chasing, worked on one side—the front—mainly with tracers. Backgrounds may be textured. Embossing, the raising of forms from the back. Repoussé, normally worked in three stages—outlining with tracers—reversing metal on pitch and embossing from the back—completion of modelling and giving texture; the metal is once more turned over, bringing the front uppermost. Very low relief may sometimes be got by sinking the background and modelling the parts left standing. The chasing up of castings is often regarded as a separate branch.

Progress beyond the elementary stage described depends entirely on a knowledge of drawing and modelling. To describe the technique of advanced work is impossible with the space available. Here are a few hints which will help anyone who wishes to try his skill. In raising bosses of any height avoid straining the metal; do this by inclining the tool and working outwards towards the edges of the forms. Anneal as soon as the metal hardens. If cracks should develop solder them at once.

Where a part in relief has much detail it is often necessary to boss up the whole mass. The traced lines, so clear on the front but soft and indistinct on the back of the metal, are easily obliterated and the position of the details is lost. To avoid this as soon as the metal is reversed and before the embossing is begun, the traced lines are marked with a fine point, lightly struck. The dots remain visible, even after vigorous work with the embossing tools.

The "snarling iron", Fig. 124(a) is the tool the chaser uses when he has to emboss a pattern on a hollow vessel. With practice it is possible to raise patterns of some complexity. Much experience is needed to get a relief that will allow all the remaining detail to be worked in it. For instance, a small flower is worked from a single circular boss; a larger one will have a smaller boss for each petal. Raised flutes, or gadroons, being of a considerable size and very simple form are not very difficult. The "snarling" of an elaborate pattern is usually a two-man job, one to strike, the other to guide the pattern on the vessel over the vibrating end of the tool.

There are few things the silversmith makes on which chasing is out of place. A dull, uninteresting form can often be enlivened by chasing a simple pattern. Endless suggestions can be found on the simpler pieces of English work from mediaeval times until towards the end of the XVIII century: after that chasing, except for the work of a few highly trained men, is almost invariably in a debased version of the rococo style.

CHAPTER 17

ON PIERCED WORK

If we think about the origins of metal work we shall see that the need for piercing holes in sheet metal would arise either for use or for decoration quickly and inevitably.

Doubtless, as a drill appears to have been one of the first tools that the wit of man devised, piercing began by drilling holes. Then would come the use of a chisel, quite an efficient tool, but limited. Openings of almost any shape can be made by using drills of varying sizes and then filing away the surplus metal left by the drill. This method is admirable for certain classes of work, especially when the metal to be pierced is thick. The locksmith of old times, as we may see in museums, produced results of extreme beauty in this way. Even here the range of what may be done easily and swiftly is limited.

With the discovery of steel the possibility of making tiny saws of steel wire arose, and the metal worker was not slow to take advantage of the wider range, greater freedom, and speed that the piercing saw gives.

THE TOOLS AND APPLIANCES

Illustrations of saw frames may be found in any good tool catalogue. Personally, the writer favours a light, rather springy, frame, with the lower arm adjustable, about 5 inches deep, for a first attempt. Present-day English frames are not adjustable and so none but whole length saws can be used in them. With the older, French, pattern shorter broken saws may be used, often effecting a considerable saving.

A good make of saws should be used, the cheaper ones are often extremely brittle. For a first attempt No. 3 is a convenient size. For thin metal, less than ·02 inch use a finer saw. No. 1, No. 0 or No. 00.

A piece of beeswax or the end of a wax candle should be provided as a lubricant.

Metal to be saw-pierced is held on a peg in which a V-shaped slot has been sawn. The slot is usually about 2 inches deep and $\frac{3}{4}$ inch across at the wide end. An ordinary beechwood "bench peg" reversed so that its upper face is horizontal is ideal for small work. For larger work a larger peg, say 12 inches × 3 inches × $\frac{3}{4}$ inch thick, tapering at the notched end to $\frac{1}{4}$ inch, may be screwed or nailed to the bench, or fastened in a vice. This will allow a piece of metal of any size to be moved freely without disturbing its horizontality.

As well as the frame, saws, and peg, we need a tool that will pierce a hole through the metal to allow the saw to be passed through. A drill is the most generally used, but some form of punch is often quicker. A short punch made of a 3 inch length of $\frac{3}{16}$ inch square steel, tapering from its centre to an absolute sharp point, struck with a hammer while the metal rests on a cake of lead, is quite efficient. The resulting burr can easily be removed with a file, or the punch may be driven in again the reverse way.

The use of this punch inevitably destroys the flatness of the metal. Usually this may be remedied with a mallet; where for any reason this procedure is inadvisable, the drill must be used. Professional saw-piercers use a screw press or, for small work, piercing pliers.

THE FIRST ATTEMPT

Take a few bits of scrap metal, any gauge from 9 to 12 m.g., and any size from $1\frac{1}{2}$ inches $\times$ $1\frac{1}{2}$ inches or upwards. Upon them draw first some circles $\frac{1}{2}$ inch to 1 inch diameter, and then a series of simple shapes with dividers and rule. Semicircles, triangles, oblongs, pippins, and such like. Within each shape pierce a hole, just large enough to take a saw easily, and $\frac{1}{16}$ inch away from the line.

Examine a saw carefully. Note especially its section. Fasten one end in the upper jaws of the frame with its teeth pointing downwards. It is obvious that this is right; were we to attempt sawing with the teeth upwards, the metal would tend to lift at every cutting stroke. There is no need to depend upon sight for finding out which way the saw is to go; touch will readily distinguish the direction of the teeth. Now pass the saw through the hole in the metal. Then rest the upper jaws against the edge of the bench and lean against the handle until the frame is felt to bend. Then the saw is secured in the lower jaws. The amount of tension we put upon the saw is, to a degree, a matter of individual choice. A reasonable tension for a No. 3 saw is one that bending of the saw is just visible when the frame is suspended by the middle of saw.

The metal is now pushed up to the top of the saw. See that the scribed lines of the piercings are uppermost. While the saw is horizontal and the hole in the metal is large enough to allow it to swing freely, no great care in handling is needed. However, when the saw is vertical we shall find that safety can be ensured only by holding the metal in the left hand, while the frame and saw are moved into position with the right. Metal and saw are now placed on the peg, the saw being about $\frac{1}{2}$ inch from the end of the notch and in a central position.

We shall have noticed that the section of the saw, at its widest, from the tip of a tooth to the back, is oblong. The cut made by the saw is but a very small fraction wider than the saw itself. It is, therefore, impossible to turn the saw in the cut. If we attempt to do so it will snap instantly. From this it would seem that straight lines are the only ones possible to cut. Yet we have all seen pierced work with every line curved. How is the saw made to follow them?

We will begin by piercing a circle. Small pieces of metal, up to $2\frac{1}{2}$ inches $\times$ $2\frac{1}{2}$ inches or so, are held on the peg by sensitive rather than forcible pressure of the tips of the fore and middle finger of the left hand, splayed out 2 inches, or near that distance apart. The hand itself is nearly horizontal; perhaps the wrist will be a little higher. The worker should stand or sit at such a level in relation to the metal as will enable him to look down on to it. If the eyes are too low, the consequent foreshortening will make the pattern look distorted.

Turn the metal around so that the drilled hole is towards the left. This will be convenient for starting to cut, and the scribed line will be between the eye and the saw. (This is a matter of some importance when, on rare occasions, we are compelled to work with the saw between the eye and the line we shall find our difficulties increased considerably.) The saw frame itself will normally point a little to the right of the right shoulder.

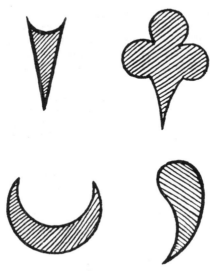

FIG. 143.

Now raise the saw as high as it will go. The handle of the saw is simply gripped lightly and sensitively in the closed right hand, the thumb does but little. Now pull the saw down with a stroke as nearly vertical as possible, and a very slight forward pressure. The saw will begin to cut through the metal as it rises and falls. The metal is now given a slight turning movement so that the cut approaches the scribed circle at a tangent. When it reaches the line itself the aim should be to move the metal so that the saw in its motion up and down shall cut around the circle on the line, but without cutting the line away. Normally the saw's motion is reciprocating only; it is the metal to be cut that is moved. Practice with circles should be continued until a fair standard of accuracy and speed is reached.

In saw-piercing circles the problem of turning sharp corners does not arise. For a second exercise, draw an equilateral triangle in a circle of, say, ⅜ inch diameter. Begin to pierce as before, letting the saw approach the straight line at the smallest possible angle. Saw steadily up to the corner of the angle. Move metal and saw until the saw is felt to be just touching the left-hand side of the notch in the peg. The saw should now be drawn back about $\frac{1}{32}$ inch or $\frac{1}{16}$ inch. It is safer to continue the up and down motion while doing this. Now using a rather quicker and shorter stroke, perfectly vertical so that no forward pressure at all is given, the metal is very slowly turned. It will be found that a hole large enough for the saw to turn is formed. As soon as the saw has fretted away a hole in which it moves freely, the second side of the triangle is cut. Continue until the triangle is completed. It may well happen, at a first attempt, that the corners are not quite sharp. They may be regulated and completed after the large mass is pierced out. Despite our utmost care we shall be certain to break many saws at first.

The insistence on the turning of the metal, while the saw moves only vertically up and down, being an absolute essential, will need modifying when very intricate forms are pierced. In sawing these the hands move; their motions are correlated, and a perfect sympathy established between them. Here practice is the one thing. Each worker will work out little peculiarities of his own.

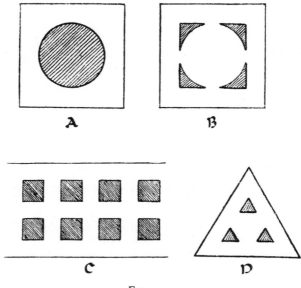

FIG. 144.

The aim of good saw-piercing should be such clean, precise workman-ship that no subsequent trueing up with a file is needed. For some time, however, this will be a counsel of perfection, and recourse to needle files will be inevitable.

After some proficiency in cutting thin metal is gained, thicker, say up to $\frac{1}{8}$ inch should be tried. This will be found much more difficult and the breakage of saws much more frequent. The one thing is to move the saw as nearly as possible in a vertical line. A moment's thought will show us that a slanting cut that would pass unnoticed in thin metal would be a glaring fault in thick. Another severe test of a saw-piercer's skill is the cutting of a series of openings of regular size and shape in a curved thing such as the rim of a bowl or a sugar sifter.

The saw will be found to move much more easily if, at intervals, a bit of wax is rubbed on the teeth. This allows us to blow the saw dust away, a proceeding impossible when oil is used.

Before we can produce pierced work that will give us real pleasure we must be able to use the saw with freedom. Timid niggling work will never look other than what it is. Although accuracy is an absolute essential, we must never forget that speed and directness are equally necessary.

As soon as we can manage the simplest forms, those of the type shown in Fig. 143 will give excellent practice. Choose forms in which inaccuracies will show clearly. Simple holes being mastered, we go on to the design and cutting of more complex work.

DESIGN FOR PIERCED-WORK

We will now take a brief look at the principles underlying the design of pierced-work.

Let us take the simplest unit, a circle. We may cut out a round hole A, Fig. 144, giving us, if our metal is bright and it lies on a dark background, a dark circle on a light ground. This will serve as an illustration of the simplest system of piercing. The unit of pattern is pierced.

The alternative to this is the piercing out of four spandrel forms B, Fig. 144. This gives us a light circle on a dark ground. Here the unit of pattern remains in the metal.

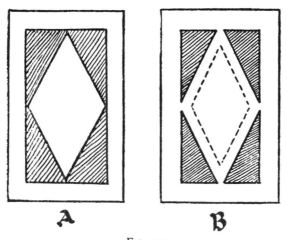

FIG. 145.

When we begin to devise pierced patterns we shall find that the two systems often become so involved that a pattern may seem to belong equally to both systems. C, Fig. 144, is an example of this; we may consider it either as a pattern of square holes, or as a pattern of crosses.

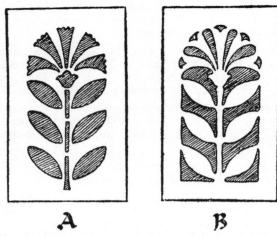

A   B

Fig. 146.

A point that must be noted, when piercing away the background, is that of strength. A, Fig. 145, if pierced as drawn would be so weak that the diamond would break away almost at a touch. B, in the same figure, shows how the diamond and its surrounding frame may be drawn so as to ensure sufficient strength. We must take care that this thickening of the points of contact is not carried too far. A pattern, Fig. 144 D, where the unit of form is confused may be said to be blind.

Fig. 147.

Let us now consider the principles embodied in Fig. 144 C at greater length. As we have seen, it may be thought of either as a pattern of square holes, or of crosses. If we add another row of holes we get a pattern of bars crossing each other. This may be thought of as a third principle on which pierced patterns may be made. If we draw several rows of squares, varying the size and spacing in each row, we shall find that with a certain proportion between openings and spaces the two elements will be so equally balanced in interest that we shall not be able to tell whether the pattern is intended to be one of holes or one of crossing bars. Though at times a pattern of this kind is right, usually either the solid metal or the openings should be stressed, so that one or the other tells clearly as the pattern.

Let us draw out two versions of a flower, adding any foliage we think fit, in the two main groups or systems. Fig. 146 A and B, show how this may be done. In a good pierced pattern, of whatever type, the background or the parts cut away should be pleasant in form, though as we have seen the actual pattern must always predominate.*

There are few motifs that cannot be adopted for pierced work. The student may do whatever he pleases so long as he obeys the rules and remembers that some things are impossible. Purpose, of course, has to be considered. To make a serviette ring with a pattern having spiky details that would catch in the linen would be absurd.

The size of the openings in relation to the solid parts left, or as an architect would say, the relation between the solids and the voids, needs thought. Purpose, and the thickness of the metal are the determining factors. For instance, Fig. 147, enlarged to 4 inches or 4½ inches, could very satisfactorily be used when placed on glass as a tea-pot stand pierced from 10 m.g. metal. If, however, we wished to make a tea-pot stand strong enough to dispense with a backing, we should find that the pattern would have to be made much bolder, and the pierced spaces correspondingly smaller. We should find that as a rule the thinner the metal the smaller the pierced holes would be.

Turn to Fig. 144, C. Here, if the squares are enlarged, the pattern may clearly be seen as one of bars crossing a space. Fig. 147 shows a pattern of this kind taken to a more complex stage. This is without doubt a pattern of bars, the openings play a secondary part. Fig. 145 B shows how this third system arises out of the first. If we pierced out the opening marked by the dotted lines we should clearly have a rectangular space crossed by four oblique bars. The obvious addition of two diagonal bars would mark it as belonging to group three still more clearly.

The student should practise the making of patterns for piercing as frequently as he can. If he will paint in the spaces with some dark colour he will be able to judge, with a high degree of accuracy, the effect of his pattern. This is a branch of the craft where paper design can be used to solve practical problems very successfully.

MARKING ON PATTERNS FOR PIERCING

The professional saw-piercer prefers to have his pattern drawn very accurately on thin tracing paper. This he pastes on his metal, a process of great difficulty when the pattern is a large one. It needs much care and skill as well to avoid stretching the paper and distorting the pattern.

* A good description of the two systems is positive silhouette B and negative A.

For the beginner the best method is to scribe the pattern with a sharp steel point. Then whatever happens the pattern is perfectly safe.

Another quite excellent method is to transfer the pattern on to a bright surface of the metal, very thinly coated with gamboge, as advised for chasing; a thin coat of hard shellac varnish when dry will protect it from rubbing and the dust made by sawing will not stick to it.

When a number of piercings all of one pattern have to be made, a convenient method is to cut the first with extreme care, and then to take rubbings or, better still, prints from it on thin papers. These are pasted on the metal. Professionals use printers ink, taking prints on damp paper. This method is rather a dirty one, but most efficient.

GOOD EXAMPLES OF PIERCED-WORK

Readers are doubtless familiar with some of the most delightful examples of saw-piercing. The cocks of verge watches, the frets of seventeenth century lantern clocks, and the older patterns of clock hands are all most valuable for study. The extremely skilful way in which drill holes are made to form part of the design should be especially noted in watch cocks.

Much may be learned from brass work made by casting from patterns made in pierced wood or metal. Amongst things answering to this description are horse-brasses, fender stools, and frets for the sides of striking clocks.

Pierced-work may be made the vehicle for the expression of the crafts-man's mind to a very full degree. It provides, perhaps, the very best exercises for the beginner in design. Its limitations are so very obvious. Again, principles of design, contrast, repetition, balance, rhythm, and such like are easily seen and understood.

A suitable exercise for a student who has worked through the first 12 in this book in which he may use pierced work is a Sugar Caster on the lines of those made in England in the late XVII and early XVIII centuries. Fig. 148 is a diagrammatic drawing of such a piece.

The leaf forms are akin to the "cut card" work of the late seventeenth century. The lines would be chased after the leaf forms were soldered on.

Let us assume that we are to apply this "cut card" work. The first thing to do is to wrap a perfectly parallel band of thick paper around the tube, thus finding the exact length of the piece of sheet needed. This is cut exactly to the greatest width of the leaf forms. It is divided into twice as many equal parts as there are leaves. Lines at right angles to the edges are ruled across each division. Let us choose six as the number of leaves. The strip will be divided into 12. A moment's thought will show us that the most convenient place for joining this strip together will be at a narrow point. We draw a leaf, its axis being the first line in from the end of the strip, and so on, on every alternate line to the end, where we shall, of course, get a narrow piece just as we did when we started. We shall find the best way of drawing a number of forms all exactly alike is to saw one out of a piece of thin metal and, laying it on the paper, draw around it with a fine pointed hard pencil.

Before we go farther, we will consider how best these leaf forms may be soldered on neatly and firmly. The problem would be a simple one for a trade worker, but for a beginner it is distinctly difficult. Here is a suggestion. On one side of the strip of silver a number of very shallow drill holes may be made; then easy running solder may be floated over the whole surface. When pickled clean, this solder surface may be malleted and hammered gently, and then filed until only a very thin film of solder will be left except in the holes. An alternative to drilling would be the filing of a series of deep

FIG. 148.—*The pierced top of this caster is fitted in the manner of the early examples—slots are filed in the uppermost moulding of the body into which will slide two or more lugs having their inner faces filed to fit the moulding—the lugs are soldered to the top. To secure the top, after sliding it into position, it is turned round for a ¼ revolution, when two lugs are provided and ⅙ when there are three. The dotted line shows one of the two slots to be made for the two lugs; the other is, of course, exactly opposite to it.*

gashes, or grooves, with a coarse file. It will be seen that, if a strip thus treated is fitted and wired closely to a body, carefully boraxed and fired, the solder will flush with great neatness and soundness. If more solder is needed it may be added, in strip or panel, taking care to apply it at a point where any surplus may be filed away easily and cleanly.

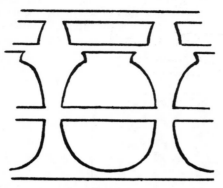

FIG. 149.

FIG. 150.—*Section of junction of body and top. The sheet metal parts in black lines. The top moulding and fitting shaded. The body moulding plain.*

The strip being carefully prepared, the leaf forms are marked on it. The beginner might well be advised not to cut the leaf forms out and leave them unsupported except at their bases, but to leave joining strips, Fig. 149. This will make it quite a simple matter to bend the strip and make it perfectly round by malleting on a mandrel. Without the strips the narrow leaves would be very difficult to manage. It will be well to solder the ends of the band together to ensure a good fit. Do this with the greatest care to avoid disturbing the solder floated over the inner surface. Paint the whole inner surface carefully with borax and water. Scrape bright after pickling. The strips, left for support, can easily be removed with a piercing saw at the last minute before the leaves are finally wired on.

For soldering of this kind it will be safer to use borax, rubbed on a slate, rather than powdered borax mixed with water. Obviously, the smoother kind will flow into the smaller spaces more easily than the somewhat gritty mixture.

The template for the top, a short truncated cone is set out by the usual method—see exercises 3 and 5—and if we are certain of its accuracy we may draw the pattern directly on the metal and pierce it before bending and soldering. To make quite sure it is better to bend, solder, mallet or hammer it round, and true it on the lathe. Being satisfied of its accuracy, set out and scribe the vertical lines of the pattern as described in the section on chased work then cut through the seam, flatten out the cone, complete the pattern and pierce it.

Once again the writer would urge his readers to learn to draw, not so much as an end in itself but as the one thing needed to make the workman a real craftsman. A true craftsman is one who never rests content until in his work he realizes the highest ideals he can form.

FIG. 151.—*A suggestion for piercing the slightly domed cover of the top.*

Piercing by a mechanically operated press. Hand saw piercing is too slow and costly for many purposes.

When such large numbers of things are wanted that the preliminary expense of making the tools is warranted, mechanical methods are used.

For simply shaped openings and patterns the tools are not unduly expensive. A "bed" of hardened and tempered steel in which one or more openings of the required shapes are cut is fixed in the press, this is stationary. A punch of soft steel is made fitting the openings exactly and fitted in the moving part. The metal to be pierced is held on the bed, the punch is forced down pushing the metal through the openings.

Elaborate work calls for more complicated and costly tools. Press tool making, as diesinking is regarded as a trade in itself.

The need for avoiding weaknesses, beds or tools with long thin points which would break easily, is a vital factor in designing for press pierced work.

CHAPTER 18

THEORY

APPRECIATION

THE following short notes on "Appreciation", "Criticism", "Taste" and "The Modern Style" have been added for the use of those who are unable to place themselves under a competent teacher of the whole art and craft of the silversmith.

From the earlier parts of this book readers will have found that the writer holds that the art and craft of the silversmith calls for appreciation and understanding of something more than the technical and materialistic elements.

A true craftsman, one whose work is his own conception and for the execution of which he is directly responsible, puts all his being, body, mind and spirit into his work.

Some may ask where the last member of this trinity comes in? The answer is, the value of all the things men and women make must be measured by the degree they succeed or fail in satisfying their whole being. Measuring is no easy or simple task. To attempt it we must use all our faculties. To get near its accomplishment takes a lifetime. Without these efforts we shall be at the mercy of every chance gust of opinion we meet. Much as we may learn from others it is our own judgments that count in reality. Not until we have worked upon and tested in the laboratories of our minds the ideas that crowd upon us from every direction, can we attain a reasonable and steady judgment.

Man's outstanding privilege is his ability to create. To do this, being what he is, he must have something to create with. "Out of nothing nothing can be made" said the ancients. To create anything worth while we must store our minds with worthy thoughts, sights and sounds. *Appreciation* of these is an essential. How are we to know them? Fortunately, there are so many of these that have been universally accepted and they are so varied that it is easy to choose without fear of wasting our admiration on the worthless or doubtful.

For all things that appeal to us through our eyes *Nature*, using the word in its fullest sense and meaning, is the inexhaustible storehouse. In these days of the seemingly illimitable power man has over material things it is not easy to realise the obvious fact that the substances a craftsman fashions are natural. Beyond that, the way in which a substance, even a synthetic one, behaves under the tool, implement, process or machine is also a part of nature. Silver is just as natural as air or water.

A silversmith must appreciate and admire his metal and work it with such sympathy that its beauty is heightened. Moreover, the uses to which we put silver are natural. From this it follows that the silversmith should think of his wares in use in every day life. Is it not obvious that the mirror-like surface and glitter of new commercial silver cannot be maintained in daily use? Do we not all feel that the softer look of well and lovingly cared for table ware has a charm that we seek in vain in new shop silver?

A craftsman cannot have too wide a vision. He should strive, when he finds what appeals to him as fine in form, texture or colour, to think how and why the attraction comes. Let him begin by comparing one thing with another, questioning himself unceasingly and trying to find reasons for his likings. In his youth the writer, being attracted by the then fashionable "Art Noveau", and finding it disliked and disparaged by one of the best and most enlightened teachers of his time, took courage to ask why it was so heartily condemned. The reply was ready and convincing, "its perpetrators have forgotten Shakespeare's 'o'erstep not the modesty of nature'."

Rightly viewed, nature is what Wordsworth said of her, "a Power that is the visible quality and shape and image of right reason"—"Holds up before the mind intoxicate with present objects, and the busy dance of things that pass away, a temperate show of objects that endure".

Appreciation of Nature and of the nature of things, especially of those we use in our work will help us to get and keep a well balanced mind. We shall be able to see the specious and insincere as they really are.

CRITICISM

Let each worker be his or her most severe critic, remembering that criticism is appraisement of value, not mere fault finding. We have already seen that we can learn to appreciate by forming the habit of comparing one thing with another. From this we shall, in due course, find that we have formed in our minds a vision of what our real selves most desire to do. Here it is necessary that we distinguish between fancy and imagination. Fancy is not to be disregarded, our own good sense will tell us when fancy is getting dangerously near the absurd. But fancy is on a far lower plane than imagination which, to quote Wordsworth again, "Is but another name for absolute power and clearest insight, amplitude of mind, and Reason in her most exalted mood".

We must be true to our beliefs. If we see a piece of silverware and find it attractive we must remember that unless it is fit for its purpose and is severely practical it must be rejected. A vessel, say a tea or coffee pot, with a dribbling spout, or with a handle wrongly insulated, so that one is liable to burn one's fingers in using it, no matter how novel or attractive it may be, is useless. Development of the power of calling up mental images so that all practical problems, those arising in the use, as well as in the making, are seen clearly, must be practised until we find that all these apparently matter-of-fact points are a stimulus, not a hindrance.

Personal predilections must not be allowed to harden into unreasoning prejudices neither must they be ignored. One person may be a romantic, while another may care only for restrained, clear-cut, classic ideals. Both may be equally true to themselves, but both should try to be so much in sympathy, as to be able to say in all sincerity that the other's work is "good of its kind".

The most gifted and accomplished craftsmen do not infallibly turn out works that can be unreservedly accepted. Neither should one think of the works of the past as immune from criticism. It is as foolish to accept works of the past as inevitably good as it is to condemn those of the present day solely because they are new.

Novelty and freshness are not always easily distinguished at first sight. The first is usually cheap and alluring to shallow minds. The last is the exact opposite. There is danger that we shall overlook it just as we are prone to overlook familiar things and fail to realise their worth. Ordinary flowers are often far more satisfying than are their newer and stranger varieties.

Of all tests of worth the best and most searching is Sincerity. Time after time it has happened that works designed and made for exhibition quickly become uninteresting, even repulsive. They fail because their makers, in their desire to outshine their competitors, have failed to be themselves. It is easy to say "know what you really want to do and do it", but actually to practise it is very hard.

TASTE

Some will be tempted to ask if there can be any accounting for tastes. The first answer is that one who has been familiar, from his earliest years, with fine things will be more likely to have good taste than will another who has never seen anything but the cheap and vulgar. Remember, exceptions are plentiful, the results not inevitable.

Each one must form his or her own taste. If we learn from someone, in whom we have confidence, that he or she admires a certain kind of work we must find out, as far as we can, why it is valued. Don't accept anyone's judgment until you have tested it for yourself.

Beware of catch words and phrases. To say a thing is "fit for its purpose" is far better than the newer "functional". Each generation will use different terms, just as each generation sees things from a different point of view. What matters is that the terms really mean something and that the views are broad and true.

To those who are unable to get good teaching, or are too old to become students in the usual way, the writer would suggest that each one should get good photographs of a few historic pieces that he or she feels can be accepted without reservation. Look at them until they begin to tell the secrets of their appeal. Then sort out the elements that belong to the work peculiar to the age that produced them from those that are universal and ageless. When these last are clear a standard against which we can measure our work and the work of our time will begin to form in our minds.

The question "can machine-made or mass produced work ever have the value of skilled hand craftsmanship?" is certain to arise. The answer is that the values of each must be assessed on the qualities peculiar to each. The accuracy and smoothness of the one, and the life and movement of the other, are both, in their own way, admirable. It is wrong to attempt to make die stamped work imitate hand work just as it is wrong for the crafts-man to emulate the smooth slickness of the power-press product. On the other hand there is no merit in doing laboriously by hand what a machine will do better. Both methods have their own idioms. It is for us to use them wisely.

THE MODERN STYLE

The absence of any reference to modernism in this book must not be taken as a condemnation, or even a disparagement, of endeavours to design and make silver wares that take their places fittingly in the present-day world.

Here are a few remarks which may help readers to form and clarify their thoughts.

We must always be moving forward; yet we must never forget that mere change is not necessarily progress. We can no more neglect fashion in design than we can in our dress; yet if we care more for being up to date than we do for being right, our work will soon "date" badly.

The best modern work has one mark which has always appeared in the work of great periods. It is entirely of its own age. We live in an age of ever-increasing mechanization: it is useless and futile to refuse to recognize it. Our engineers have shown us that absolute efficiency and fitness satisfy the eye. A well-designed motor-car, an aero-engine, or a locomotive, can give us pleasure something akin to that we get from the sight of living organisms.

Many things in our present-day life are less pleasing than those our fathers knew; but if these pleasant things do not fit into modern life we must leave them. If ideas are really vital they will spring into new life when a more congenial season comes.

In the best modern work we see evidences of a cool, clear, logical, intense spirit. Let us see to it that this is manifest in our own work. If it be lacking, our work will never be more than merely fashionable.

APPROXIMATE WEIGHT PER SQUARE INCH OF STANDARD SILVER
(Specific Gravity 10·31)

Thickness in Decimals of Inch	Birmingham Metal Gauge (Shakespeare Metal Gauge)	Weight in Decimals of Ounce Troy	Thickness in Decimals of Inch	Birmingham Metal Gauge (Shakespeare Metal Gauge)	Weight in Decimals of Ounce Troy
·0085	1	·04626	·032	11	·17416
·0095	2	·05170	·035	12	·19049
·0105	3	·05714	·038	13	··20682
·012	4	·06531	·043	14	·23403
·014	5	·07619	·048	15	·26124
·016	6	·08708	·051	16	·27757
·019	7	·10341	·055	17	·29934
·0215	8	·11701	·059	18	·32111
·024	9	·13062	·062	19	·33744
·028	10	·15239	:065	20	·35377

The weights of square sectioned wires may be estimated thus:

$$\left.\begin{array}{l} 1 \text{ cubic inch} \\ 4'' \times \tfrac{1}{2}'' \times \tfrac{1}{2}'' \\ 16'' \times \tfrac{1}{4}'' \times \tfrac{1}{4}'' \\ 64'' \times \tfrac{1}{8}'' \times \tfrac{1}{8}'' \end{array}\right\} = 5\tfrac{1}{2} \text{ oz. Troy nearly.}$$

TROY WEIGHT

IS THE WEIGHT USED IN THE SILVERSMITH'S TRADE

24 grains make one pennyweight.

20 pennyweights make one ounce.

12 ounces make one pound.

The legal weights below one ounce for Silversmiths are now the Decimal weights

The grains in Troy weight, Apothecaries' weight, and Avoirdupois are equal. To compare Troy weight with Avoirdupois reduce both to grains.

The ounce Troy and the ounce Apothecaries contain...   ...   . 480 grains.

The ounce Avoirdupois contains   ...   . 437½ grains.

The pound Troy contains   ...   . 5,760 grains.

The pound Avoirdupois contains   ...   . 7,000 grains.

To convert ounces Troy to grams, multiply by 31.104
To convert grams to ounces Troy, multiply by 0.03215
To convert inches to centimetres, multiply by 2.54
To convert centimetres to inches, multiply by 0.3937

Assay and Hallmarking

Makers of silverwares should send their work to one of the following Assay Offices: Goldsmiths' Hall, London E.C.2.; Birmingham, Sheffield or Edinburgh. There is an Assay Office in Dublin for the Irish Republic. It is illegal to sell as silver any object which weighs more than 7.78 grams and which is not hallmarked. If it is not hallmarked, it must be described as 'white metal', or the vendor is liable for prosecution under the Trades Descriptions Act.

TROY WEIGHT
SUB-DIVISIONS OF THE OUNCE WITH THEIR DECIMAL EQUIVALENTS

Dwt.	Decimals of an Ounce Troy	Dwt.	Decimals of an Ounce Troy	Grains	Nearest Decimals of an Ounce Troy	Grains	Nearest Decimals of an Ounce Troy
1	·050	11	·550	1	·002	13	·027
2	·100	12	·600	2	·004	14	·029
3	·150	13	·650	3	·006	15	·031
4	·200	14	·700	4	·008	16	·033
5	·250	15	·750	5	·010	17	·035
6	·300	16	·800	6	·012	18	·037
7	·350	17	·850	7	·014	19	·040
8	·400	18	·900	8	·016	20	·042
9	·450	19	·950	9	·019	21	·044
10	·500	20	1·000	10	·021	22	·046
				11	·023	23	·048
				12	·025	24	·050

SPECIFIC GRAVITIES AND MELTING POINTS OF METALS REFERRED TO IN THIS BOOK

	Specific Gravity	Melting Point Deg. Centigrade
Copper	8·93	—
in reducing atmosphere	—	1,083
in air	—	1,062
Lead	11·37	327
Fine Silver	10·5	—
in reducing atmosphere	—	962
in air	—	995
Standard Silver	10·31	900(approx.)
Tin	7·29	232
Zinc...	7·1	418

ALLOYS IN COMMON USE

Brass—copper 60% to 70%; zinc 30% to 40%.

Gilding Metal—copper 80% to 95%; zinc 5% to 20%.

Nickel-Silver—varies considerably, an average mixture—nickel 10%; copper 65%, zinc 25%.

APPROXIMATE WEIGHT OF STANDARD SILVER CIRCLES (0·925)

Weight of the Circle if in Gauges as under (Birmingham Metal Gauge)

Area of disc = square of diameter (i.e., diameter multiplied by itself) multiplied by 0·7854

GAUGE

Diameter of the Circle	6	7	8	9	10	11	12	13	14	15	16	17	18
in.	oz.	oz.	oz.	oz.	oz.	oz.	oz.	oz.	oz.	oz.	oz.	oz.	oz.
4	1·14	1·35	1·53	1·71	2·00	2·28	2·50	2·71	3·07	3·42	3·64	3·92	4·20
4½	1·44	1·72	1·94	2·16	2·53	2·89	3·16	3·43	3·88	4·33	4·60	4·96	5·32
5	1·78	2·12	2·40	2·67	3·12	3·57	3·90	4·23	4·79	5·35	5·68	6·13	6·57
5½	2·16	2·56	2·90	3·24	3·77	4·32	4·72	5·12	5·80	6·47	6·88	7·41	7·95
6	2·57	3·05	3·45	3·85	4·49	5·14	5·62	6·10	6·90	7·70	8·18	8·82	9·46
6½	3·01	3·58	4·05	4·52	5·27	6·03	6·59	7·16	8·10	9·04	9·60	10·35	11·10
7	3·49	4·15	4·69	5·24	6·11	6·99	7·65	8·30	9·39	10·48	11·14	12·01	12·88
7½	4·01	4·76	5·39	6·02	7·02	8·03	8·78	9·52	10·78	12·04	12·79	13·78	14·78
8	4·57	5·42	6·13	6·84	7·99	9·13	9·99	10·84	12·26	13·69	14·55	15·68	16·82
8½	5·15	6·12	6·92	7·73	9·01	10·31	11·27	12·23	13·84	15·44	16·43	17·70	18·99
9	5·78	6·86	7·76	8·66	10·10	11·56	12·64	13·72	15·52	17·33	18·42	19·85	21·29
9½	6·44	7·64	8·65	9·65	11·26	12·88	14·08	15·28	17·29	19·31	20·52	22·12	23·72
10	7·13	8·47	9·58	10·69	12·48	14·28	15·60	16·92	19·16	21·40	22·74	24·50	26·29
10½	7·86	9·34	10·56	11·79	13·76	15·73	17·20	18·67	21·12	23·59	25·07	27·02	28·98
11	8·63	10·25	11·59	12·94	15·10	17·27	18·88	20·49	23·18	25·89	27·51	29·65	31·81
11½	9·42	11·20	12·67	14·14	16·50	18·87	20·62	22·39	25·34	28·30	30·07	32·41	34·77
12	10·27	12·20	13·79	15·40	17·97	20·55	22·47	24·38	27·59	30·81	32·74	35·29	37·85

MODERN DESIGNS

by Anthony Elson DesRCA

The main text of this book deals admirably with the various skills needed to make handmade silverware. The following designs therefore have been prepared to assist the student when he comes to the problem of creating three-dimensional shapes. Only simple forms have been used; and the techniques involved in producing such items as the candlesticks, vases or beakers, should be within the capability of the First Year student. The more experienced silversmith should have no difficulty in making the tea and coffee sets.

Most of the drawings have areas marked with shading. This indicates which part of the design would be most suitable for decoration. There are many different ways of producing a decorative effect on silver, but the techniques described below are probably the most useful.

The student, under the guidance of his tutor, should attempt as many of these techniques as is possible. Each one requires a whole range of special knowledge and skill. It is not the purpose of this chapter to go into any detail on any of these methods, but only to introduce the silversmith to the possibilities and then leave him to tackle the problem in his own individual manner.

Texture
This can be achieved with a hammer, the head of which has been roughened, or with an electric pendant drill using a variety of drill bits to produce various degrees of marking. This technique is effective if used with imagination. There is no visual pleasure obtainable however, from large areas of uniformly roughened surfaces.

Chasing

A high degree of skill is, of course, required in this technique, but simple geometrical patterns — or perhaps free-flowing lines, flat chased — should be attempted.

Engraving

Great effects can be achieved by making a series of small deep cuts into the metal. These bright cuts can be grouped and arranged in many interesting ways.

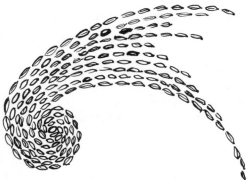

Pattern-making for casting

Spouts, sockets, finials and handles all can be sand-cast; the master pattern can be made in wax, wood, plastic or some other material which is suitable for carving or moulding. If the lost wax (*cire perdue*) method of casting is used, then the master pattern must be made of metal. Much detail may be worked into the metal, as this form of casting can reproduce detail with great clarity. Strips, approximately 6 inches in length, incorporating a complex motif, may be cast. These are then joined together and turned into rings which are suitable for the base of a coffee or tea pot.

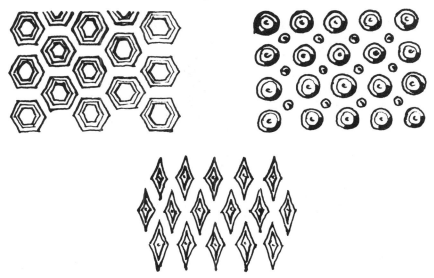

Photo-etching
Pictures and designs can be projected on to flat surfaces of silver and these resulting images can then be etched into the metal. Before this can take place, however, the design must be carefully drawn in black on white paper. This black and white detail is what is projected on to the sensitised silver. The student must bear in mind the restrictions which flat surfaces will impose upon his design; although he will later be able to turn the original sheet into a basic cone or cylinder.

Laminating metals
In this process, several alternate sheets of silver, brass, copper or gold are soldered together one on top of each other, and then put through the rolling mill to form a larger, thinner sheet which has been rolled to a workable thickness. This laminated sheet can then be formed into a simple shape, such as a bowl or perhaps a tube or ring. During this part of the process, the outer layer will be worn away, thus exposing the different underlying metals. The interesting colour effect which this produces, can be increased by oxydising the different metals.

Electro-forming

The student should explore the possibility of reproducing some of his master patterns by electro-forming. This method is capable of depositing fine silver into a mould taken from shapes ranging from flat panels to hemispheres. When the silver which has been formed in the mould, is removed, the surface detail should be so precise and clear that no further finishing, other than gentle polishing, is needed.

Reticulation

One other common method of texturing is to burn the surface of the metal, thus producing a crinkled effect. Paste your rouge on to the back of the sheet before commencing, because this retards the melting point of the back. It will be found that the flame produced by bottled town gas will give a better result than that from the rather hotter North Sea gas.

The 24 pieces of domestic silverware illustrated on the following pages have been specially designed by Anthony Elson DesRCA for this new edition of A Silversmith's Manual. Both Imperial and metric measurements for the full-size designs are given in the relevant captions.

Left: Tall candlestick; 7.25 in (18.5 cm) high, base diameter 3 in (7.5 cm).

Centre: Stumpy candlestick; 3.45 in (8.75 cm), base diameter 4 in (100 cm). Right: Small candlestick; 3 in (7.75 cm) high, base diameter 3.25 in (8.25 cm).

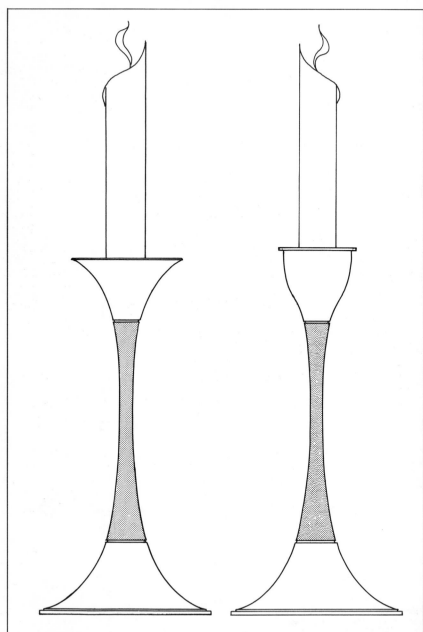

Left: Candlestick; 8.25 in (21 cm) high, base diameter 3.75 in (9.5 cm).
Right: Candlestick; 8 in (20 cm) high, base diameter 3.75 in (9.5 cm).

Left: Vase; 6.25 in (16 cm) high, base diameter 2.2 in (5.5 cm).
Right: Vase; 7 in (17.5 cm) high, base diameter 2.2 in (5.5 cm).

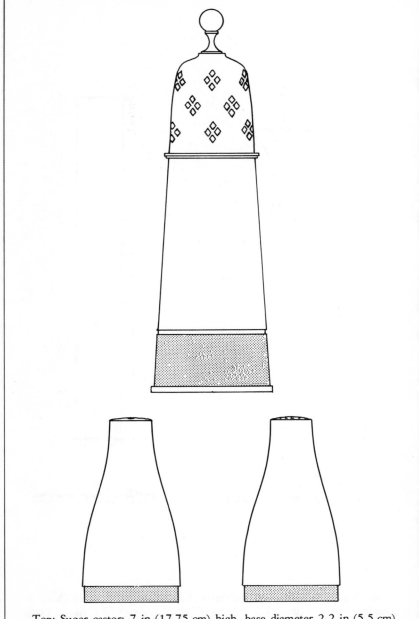

Top: Sugar caster; 7 in (17.75 cm) high, base diameter 2.2 in (5.5 cm).
Above: Salt and pepper set; 3.35 in (8.5 cm) high, diameter 1.8 in (4.5 cm).

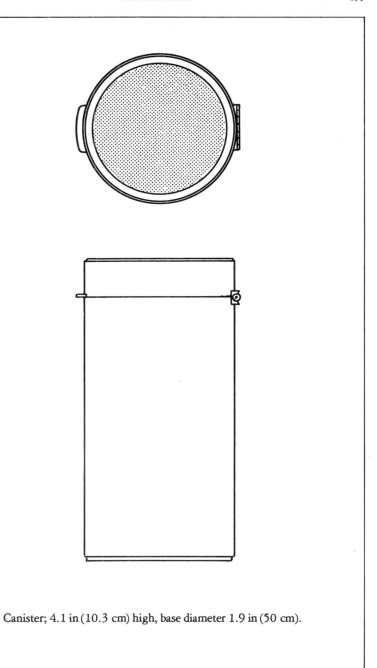

Canister; 4.1 in (10.3 cm) high, base diameter 1.9 in (50 cm).

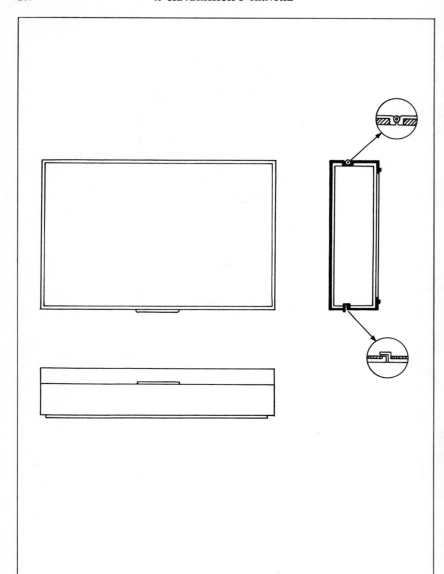

Rectangular box; top measures 4.8 in (12.25 cm) x 3.25 (8.25 cm), height 1 in (2.5 cm).

Tankard; 3.64 in (9.25 cm) high, diameter 3.2 in (8 cm).

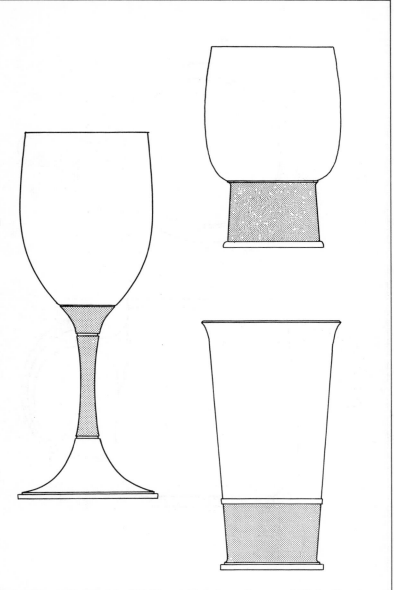

Left: Wine goblet; 7.4 in (18.75 cm) high, base diameter 2.75 in (7 cm).
Above right: Squat beaker; 4.5 in (11.5 cm) high, lip diameter 2.7 in
(6.75 cm). Below right: Long beaker; 5.5 in (14 cm) high, lip diameter 3 in
(7.75 cm).

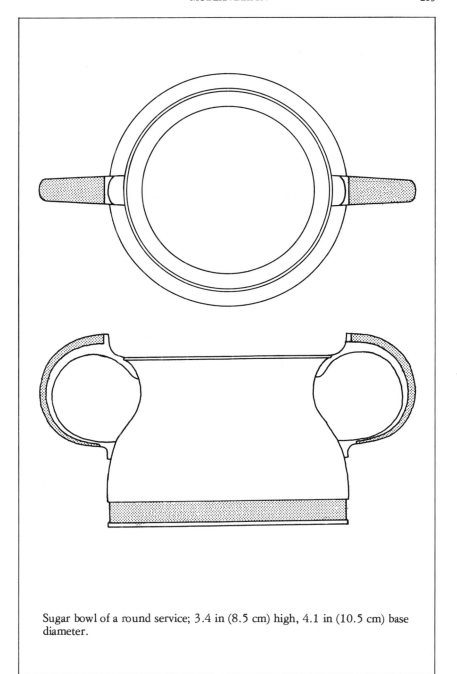

Sugar bowl of a round service; 3.4 in (8.5 cm) high, 4.1 in (10.5 cm) base diameter.

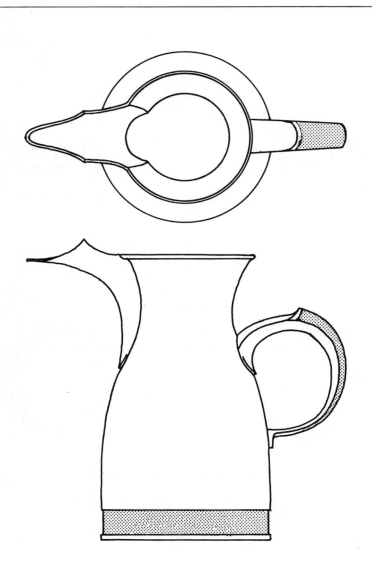

Milk jug of a round service; 4.5 in (11.5 cm) high, base diameter 2.6 in (6.5 cm).

Teapot of a round service; 6 in (15.5 cm) high to tip of finial, base diameter 5.3 in (13.5 cm).

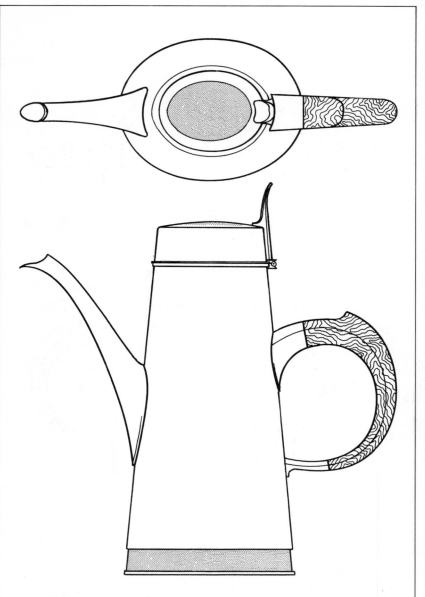

Coffee pot of a round service; 10 in (25.5 cm) high to tip of finial, base diameter 4.25 in (10.75 cm).

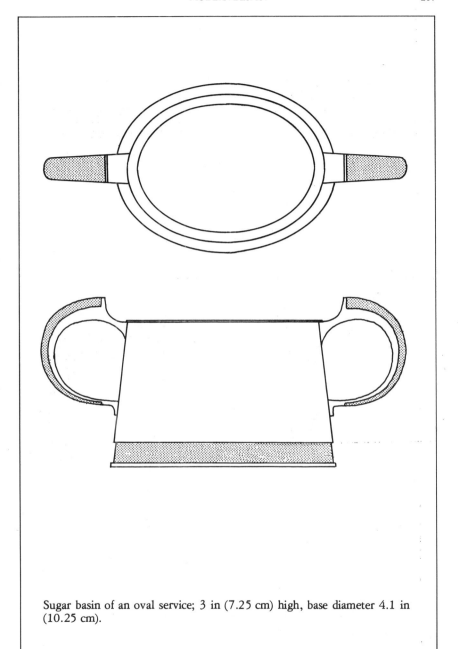

Sugar basin of an oval service; 3 in (7.25 cm) high, base diameter 4.1 in (10.25 cm).

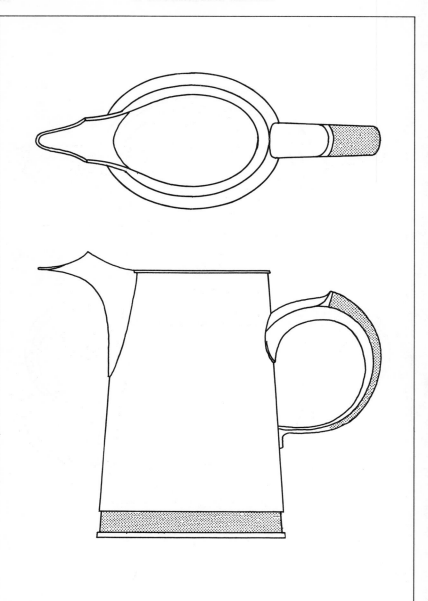

Milk jug of an oval service; 5 in (12.75 cm) high, base diameter 3.25 in (8.25 cm).

Teapot of an oval service; 6.9 in (17.5 cm) high to tip of finial, base diameter 4.6 in (11.75 cm).

Coffee pot of an oval service; 10.5 in (26.5 cm) high to tip of finial, base diameter 4.4 in (11.25 cm).

INDEX